From the Whit

My good friend Peggy Stanton brings a reporter's eye and a believer's heart to this engaging memoir. From the corridors of power in Washington, D.C., to the humble hilltops of Medjugorje, she allows us to tag along for an insider's look at a unique and uplifting life.

— **His Eminence Timothy Cardinal Dolan**
Archbishop of New York

Great memoirs are engaging, yet provocative, introspective, yet inspirational. *From the White House to the White Cross* accomplishes this and more. Fascinating tales of political insiders and celebrities are but a part of the riveting and deeply personal account of spiritual transformation, and one woman's determination to stand up and spread the Good News.

— **Tom Monaghan**
Founder, Domino's Pizza
Founder, Ave Maria University and Ave Maria School of Law

Peggy Stanton is a gifted writer who has given us an engaging account of her life as a pioneering network news correspondent in Washington, D.C. where she meets and marries Ohio Congressman Bill Stanton. She draws on her diaries to recount her interactions with D.C. power brokers and newsmakers. She movingly shares with us that her greatest blessing was how Our Lady drew her closer to Christ. This book is an inspiring testimony of how faith in God leads us along paths where joy overcomes sorrow.

— **Rev. Gerald E. Murray**
Pastor, Holy Family Church, New York, NY

Peggy Stanton has the eye of a journalist and the heart of an apostle. As my colleague at Ave Maria Radio for many years, she has often delighted me with stories from her years as a pioneering broadcast journalist at ABC-TV, a congressional wife and president of the Republican Congressional Wives Club, a Dame of the Knights of Malta with many pilgrimages to Lourdes, a champion for the apparitions of our Lady at Medjugorje, a creative artist and a loving and diligent mother and grandmother.

But I wasn't prepared for the dizzying, kaleidoscopic array of stories in *From the White House to the White Cross*. We see professional success, marriage to an extraordinary and gallant public servant, the whirl of political campaigning, international travel.

But, as often happens, comes the crisis of emptiness. She had been faithfully *in* the pew but she hadn't become *of* the pew. God calls her to an ongoing conversion that doesn't come easily. Even in Medjugorje, she finds herself in the intense grip of a drive to flee this place. How this interior fight shapes her is one of the most compelling in the memoir and leads to her apostolic work in healing, peace programs and relief assistance.

In Peggy's life we see God gradually unfolding a plan against a backdrop of iconic public events like the assassination of Robert F. Kennedy, Watergate, 9-11, the first Gulf and the Balkan Wars. Encounters with some of modern history's best known figures like Fidel Castro, Robert and Ethel Kennedy, Salvador Dali, Gerald and Betty Ford, and George H.W. Bush enrich the narrative.

But through all the towering events and renowned characters, the Holy Spirit is telling a more profound story of healing and supernatural grace that makes all the pretensions of this world and its actors look small and deficient. This memoir bears witness to a Kingdom not built through the ambitions and exertions of human beings but by the love of God. For that we owe Peggy a deep debt of gratitude.

— **Al Kresta**
President/CEO, Ave Maria Communications
Host, "Kresta in the Afternoon"

This is an amazing book about an accomplished pioneer news reporter (first woman Washington correspondent for ABC News) who experiences conversion in Medjugorje and then allows her resulting trust in God to guide her through difficult decisions that have worldwide ramifications. As a Dame of Malta, Peggy now strives to follow the guiding principles of the Order: promote God's glory and the world's peace, and serve the sick and the poor.

— **Peter J. Kelly, MD, GCM**
President, Order of Malta American Association

I dare say few books have been written that include a greater cast of characters. *From the White House to the White Cross* has them all. Peggy Stanton shares stories of presidents, soldiers, kings and queens, canonized saints, and Moses (aka Charlton Heston). And, if that's not enough, Julie Andrews makes a cameo. Remarkably, every story is personal. Peggy is not writing about people she's only read or heard about. She's telling about the time she danced with President Ford, how she grieved at Bobby Kennedy's funeral, and her visit to war-torn Mostar during the Balkan War. She's a wonderful storyteller who draws her readers into each story and gives us an inside glimpse of a world most of us will never know.

While there are many powerful and interesting characters in *From the White House to the White Cross*, the most prominent and impactful are Our Blessed Mother and her Son, Jesus. Describing herself as a Catholic "in the pew but not of it," Peggy says her life radically changed when she visited Medjugorje and encountered Our Lady and the faith of a pilgrim people. From these encounters, and the changes that came from them, Peggy shows what a life surrendered to God and His Will looks like.

No doubt readers will be inspired and challenged by Peggy's remarkable life. I know I was.

— **Father Dave Pivonka, TOR**
President, Franciscan University of Steubenville

From the White House to the White Cross is a riveting read that chronicles the perennial drama of finding purpose in life. Peggy Stanton takes readers on a fascinating journey from elite gatherings in Washington D.C. to the small mountain village of Medjugorje, from a life of glittering parties to the life of a restless heart, searching for the peace and purpose that only God can give and discovering the Blessed Virgin Mary as the best guide to her Son. It's an inspiring read for pilgrims and searchers of all ages.

— **Deana Basile Kelly, Ph.D.**
Ave Maria University

From the
White House
to the **White Cross**

Confessions of a
TV News Correspondent

Peggy Stanton

Available from:
Marian Helpers Center
Stockbridge, MA 01263

Prayerline: 1-800-804-3823
Orderline: 1-800-462-7426
Websites:
ShopMercy.org
Marian.org

Library of Congress Control Number: 2022912995
ISBN: 978-1-59614-569-6

Imprimi Potest:
Very Rev. Chris Alar, MIC
Provincial Superior
The Blessed Virgin Mary, Mother of Mercy Province
August 22, 2022
The Queenship of the Blessed Virgin Mary

Nihil Obstat:
Robert A. Stackpole, STD
Censor Deputatus
August 22, 2022

Scripture quotations are from the *New Revised Standard Version Bible: Catholic Edition*, copyright © 1989, 1993 the Division of Christian Education of the National Council of the Churches of Christ in the United States of America. Used by permission. All rights reserved.

This book is a memoir. It draws upon the author's journals as well as her present recollections of experiences over time. The opinions expressed within are entirely the author's own.

DEDICATED TO

My four grandchildren,
Jack, Charlie, Megan, and Peter,
who were the motivation for writing this book
and my beloved daughter Kelly,
without whom it would never have happened.

Table of Contents

PREFACE

This is the story of a conversion. But it is not the story of moving from atheism to Christianity as so many conversion stories are. It is the story of a cultural Catholic becoming a committed Catholic. St. Ambrose said there are two kinds of baptism: baptism with water and baptism by tears of repentance. This is the story of a Pharisee becoming a publican.

Like many Catholics brought up and bred by devout parents, I practiced my faith motivated more by habit and duty than by heart, more concerned with power and politics than piety. A journey to a strange land where I did not want to go put me on a path that encompassed adventure, drama, sadness, and joy, and changed my life forever.

Storytelling is so deeply embedded in my DNA that I became a compulsive journal keeper when I traveled with my late husband, Congressman Bill Stanton, on his many professional trips overseas, be it as a Member of Congress or counselor to the president of the World Bank. The experiences were too rich to leave on the streets of Paris, Rome, or Havana, as was the history being made in Washington, D.C. Eventually, my drawers were filled with journals, all handwritten on planes en route home. Over the years, some came out of the drawers and found their way into a newspaper, a magazine, or even the *Congressional Record*. Many are still in drawers.

The White House experiences come from scripts I had written for broadcast while covering the White House, as well as a journal I kept to recount human interest stories occurring in that historic mansion that were not suitable for brief news reports.

They all lead to a pilgrimage where the adventures *really* begin, focusing the lens on the Master at work as He attempts to chisel a poor piece of clay into what He intended her to be. The word "attempts" is not meant to describe the limitations of the Sculptor, but rather the stubborn resistance of the clay.

My hope is that, as you read my story, you will find familiarity with your own journey with the Master, perhaps realizing moments when He was with you even when you didn't recognize Him.

PART ONE

I fled Him, down the nights and down the days;
I fled Him, down the arches of the years;
I fled Him, down the labyrinthine ways
Of my own mind; and in the mist of tears
I hid from Him, and under running laughter.
Up vistaed hopes I sped . . .

— Francis Thompson, "The Hound of Heaven" (1909)

1

A NOSE FOR NEWS

I was born nosy. And then I found out they paid you for it.

All I ever wanted to be in life was a storyteller. Whether I was working on a television news story, a feature story, a column, a painting, or an illustration, it was all about *The Story*.

As a child cartoonist, my first heroine combined words and pictures. Her name was Linda Lake. I think she was a movie star, but I'm not sure. I drew her with long blond hair and lots of eyelashes, neither of which I had.

Without a doubt, my professor father, C. Brooks Smeeton (or "C. Brooks" to his students, "Pop" to his children), was my illustrator inspiration. Pop balanced a big brain with an equally large sense of humor, which may have been a key factor in his twice being voted most popular professor on the Indiana University campus. Pop drew cartoons about his children and pasted them on our bedroom doors for contemplation.

Pop's sense of fun was inherited from his father. My English grandfather, Cecil Brooks Smeeton I, known to us grandchildren as "Popsie," was born across the sea in Shakespeare country, Stratford-upon-Avon. I like to think the ink in my and my daughter's veins flows indirectly from the Bard.

Popsie was a lawyer and an accountant, not a writer. Though slight in build and small in stature, he was a larger-than-life figure to children. Referred to as the "Pied Piper" by his Evanston, Illinois neighbors, he regularly drew a throng of children to him in the evening as he walked home from the train station with his pockets full of candy.

He sang funny little ditties. "My gal's a high-born lady … down the line we shoot and shine … that high-born gal of mine."

He warned us to behave or "I'll jump down your throat and teeter-totter on your wishbone."

Even his little black Scottie dog, Mac, cherished Popsie's company, parking himself in front of the big clock in my grandparents' home precisely at 5 p.m., anxiously awaiting Popsie's arrival.

One day, Mac waited in vain.

Popsie had always said he wanted to "die with his boots on." God granted his wish. En route home from his downtown Chicago office, Popsie collapsed while waiting for the L train and died of a heart attack.

Grandma, who was as large as Popsie was small, found his sudden demise hard to comprehend. Succumbing to a stroke shortly thereafter, she asked my Uncle Irv where her husband was. "Dad died, Mother," my uncle responded.

"Hmph," huffed Grandma. "Well, he sure is a lively dead one!" — a comment that lived on in the annals of Smeeton lore, long after Grandma herself had died.

I come from comedic stock. My father's droll English wit played against my mother's whimsical, somewhat flirtatious Irish humor. Thomas Rooney, or TR, the oldest of our quartet, was corny. John Brooks, or JBS, was sardonic. I was sarcastic in defense against my two domineering brothers, who preferred my absence to my presence. Our baby sister, Mary Anne, whose brain was severely damaged by a lack of oxygen when the umbilical cord caught around her neck during her birth, quietly observed a house that was loud with laughter, sometimes at each other's expense.

TR and JBS were inventive. Our garage was turned into a Halloween spook house; a basement into a political convention; a backyard into the neighborhood Olympics. When JBS wasn't broadcasting sports events from his bedroom, he was wearing a blanket and playing priest, preaching sermons to his sibling parishioners. Neither of these preoccupations seemed likely to prepare him for his eventual career as a professional golfer.

One summer, TR and JBS thrilled their playmates with a mysterious figure wrapped in a white sheet who ran through the streets at twilight. Soon, all the neighborhood kids were running after him, yelling, "It's the Cat Man! It's the Cat Man!" This conspiracy may have been inspiration for TR's work as a real-life "spook" in the Central Intelligence Agency. In order to allay suspicion as to the identity of this frightening creature, TR and JBS took turns playing the Cat Man so that there was always a Smeeton boy leading the posse.

My 5-foot-2, eyes-of-piercing-blue mother was struggling with four children encumbered with constant injuries and diverse diseases, such as pneumonia, scarlet fever, and meningitis, when Pop proposed leaving the lucrative field of advertising for the impoverished life of a university professor.

"We will probably halve our income at the beginning," he warned her. "Maybe someday we will get back to where we are now." But no guarantees. My mother, who had grown up with considerable material comfort that had provided her with a six-week "grand tour" of Europe, a luxury afforded few single girls in the early 1900s, responded, "If that's what you really want to do, do it."

I learned this story, not from my mother or father, but from the podium at a banquet in Milwaukee, honoring C. Brooks as "Man of the Year." The lesson remained embedded in my values file: The most important thing when considering a career was not the paycheck, but affection for the work. When you love your work, it ceases to be work. And Pop *loved* teaching. He also loved telling stories on himself.

If a student slumbered during class, Pop would ask the student next to him to tap the sleeper on the shoulder and ask him if he had left a call for 10 o'clock.

One time, the joke backfired on C. Brooks. "Wake him up, yourself," the student responded to C. Brooks' request. "You put him to sleep." Pop laughed as hard as the students. "Class dismissed," he announced.

"There was no point in trying to teach after that," he concluded.

He was a young teacher at Notre Dame during the university football team's famed undefeated era. Occasionally he was asked to substitute for the tall, gray-haired, mustachioed, and intimidating head of the business school, Dean McCarthy. The class was filled with the celebrated football players. My father, who was a slender, unimposing 5-foot-10, looked like red meat in front of lions. And did they roar! "They didn't just talk to the guy next to them," C. Brooks recalled. "They yelled to a guy across the room." That night, Pop strategized as to how to capture the players' attention without "getting angry."

The next morning, he instructed the class to take out a blank sheet of paper. "We're having a test."

"Wh-a-a-at? You didn't tell us we were going to have a test!"

"This is an unannounced test." Whereupon, Pop gave the students a five-part essay question.

Just as their heads bent over their papers, struggling with their answers, C. Brooks began marching up and down the aisles, loudly singing the Notre Dame fight song,

"Cheer! Cheer! For old Notre Dame…"

Stunned eyes were wide with incredulity. Who was this nutty professor?

Pop stopped, looked them all in the eye, and asked, "Little hard to concentrate, isn't it, with all that noise?"

"Never had another problem again," he concluded a touch smugly.

Pop believed that God put each one of us on earth to accomplish a specific purpose, and that He paired that job with the desire to accomplish it. Pop also believed that if we did not perform that task, it would be left undone. On the top of his bureau drawers rested the book *Imitation of Christ*.

If Pop was the teacher, Mother was the preacher. She organized apostolates and study groups, as well as writing spiritual poetry and letters to the editor. A big believer in Fr. Patrick Peyton's motto, "The family that prays together, stays together," she gathered us all around her after dinner to recite the Rosary. To this day, my brothers and I, though separated by geography, thread the beads daily.

One morning, while hanging clothes to dry in the back-yard, Mother was felled by a mosquito who gifted her with encephalitis and chronic illness. Alternately known to her children as "Glossy Flossie" and to her grandchildren as "Mimi," Mom handled reduced mobility by orating from the couch. While never raising her voice, Glossy Flossie was clearly the CEO of the "Smeetonian Institute."

Pop, whose ability, popularity with students, and passion for his work brought him offers from Indiana University, Notre Dame University, and Marquette University, among others, was more than happy to operate as the CFO and turn domestic administration over to "Glossy Flossie."

Pop did attempt discipline — once. In honor of the Biblical admonition, "Spare the rod and spoil the child," he threatened his rambunctious children by substituting his belt for the rod. As we all ran screaming around the dining room table, Pop moved in deliberate slow motion behind us, never *quite* able to catch us.

Pop's fondness for his work influenced my thinking that the most important element in a career choice was joy performing the job. Not until my junior year at Marquette University did I discern what my own profession was going to be. I knew the ingredients I wanted the job to contain: writing, adventure, people, history, purpose. I just didn't know what job contained all of those components.

One evening I was watching "NBC News," and a woman named Nancy Dickerson delivered a news story from the field. "That's it!" I exclaimed. "That's exactly what I want to do!" From that moment through graduation, my eyes focused laser-like on life as a network news correspondent, covering stories in Washington, D.C.

The challenge was how to break into a field populated almost solely by males. In some ways, that may have been part of the attraction. From my grade school years, I had been fascinated by heroines in boots and wide belts forging a future on the Western frontier. Did this unconsciously fuel my desire to pioneer in the widening world of broadcast journalism? Perhaps, but I never thought of myself in those grandiose terms. I just wanted to report stories about current events.

Newsrooms were definitely male bastions in the mid-1960s. If a broadcast facility had one female and one black employee, we used to joke, they had made their quota. This generated in me a "*carpe diem*" mindset that lingers to this day. You dare not pass up a present opportunity in hopes of a better opportunity in the future.

So, though I had dreamed of a gap summer after graduation — months of carefree existence and travel before entering "real life" — I denied myself that dream when two broadcast opportunities arrived shortly after I received my diploma.

The first was to serve as the heir apparent for the hostess job of a long-running daily radio show at the leading radio/TV station, WTMJ. WTMJ was operated by the top newspaper in that city, *The Milwaukee Journal*. The current host was growing into retirement and, upon her leaving the stage, I was to emerge from behind the curtain to take her place.

The second was as a "girl Friday" in the newsroom of a CBS affiliate station, WISN-TV. No airtime promised or indicated as at WTMJ, just writing news scripts and filing; I would literally be a "gofer" at the beck and call of the newsmen and on-air personalities.

"Which job leads you closer to the work you actually want to do?" wise heads asked me as I was pondering my decision. If I wanted to be an on-air personality, perhaps WTMJ was the choice. If my goal was to cover news, then being in the newsroom, however lowly the job, was the answer.

"Just get your foot in the door, even if it is only sweeping the floor."

It was prescient advice. I took the newsroom job where I was the only woman, and within months I was on the air simply because my foot was in the door.

Mine was the only foot in the newsroom one morning when all the newsmen were out in the field covering other stories. Suddenly, breaking news came over the news wire that there had just been a double murder downtown. Murder in local news, especially in the morning, leads the evening newscasts. With no one but the "gofer" to tell the tale, I grabbed the lone cameraman and headed for the scene of the crime. When I returned with a batch of filmed witness interviews, the joke in the newsroom was that I had "interviewed everything but the barstool."

By the end of two years, the job broadened to on-air reporter, assignment editor, and commentator in a two-minute analysis of the day's events with the news editor, each of us taking a different perspective on the day's events. It also provided my first trip to Europe, covering the making of three 20th Century Fox movies, one of which was the all-time classic, "The Sound of Music."

2

THE HILLS ARE ALIVE

June 1964 . . . .

"Oh, we are going to die!" announces our guide, her heavy Italian accent adding extra gravity to our peril.

We are some 3,000 feet high in the Carrara mountain range of Italy in a small Volkswagen bus transporting us to observe a two-ton piece of marble being shaved off a mountain side. The bus, however, is now poised immobile on the edge of a cliff.

We journalists from all across the United States are guests of 20th Century Fox Film Corporation. Fox is hoping that the stories we will write and/or televise about their three "roadshow" movies, all in production simultaneously, will dispose of rumors that the company is no longer a thriving movie enterprise, despite its near-bankruptcy due to cost overrun from the film "Cleopatra."

The movies we will report about are "The Sound of Music," filming in Salzburg, Austria; "The Agony and the Ecstasy," filming in Italy; and "Those Magnificent Men in Their Flying Machines," in production in London. We will meet and interview the stars, the producers, and the directors of the various films and visit the movie sets for a rare inside view of filmdom in action.

I am barely out of college, a TV news reporter working for WISN-TV. It is my first job after college graduation. I am still learning the journalism trade, still guessing as to the proper location of the who, what, where, how, and why of a story.

When I am sent on assignment, I am always accompanied by a cameraman who understands technology, which I do not. On this journey, however, I am on my own. My cameraman has not been invited. So I borrow a tape recorder and buy a camera, neither of which I know how to operate.

My fellow sojourners are sophisticated scribes, keenly attuned to the world of entertainment. I am a reporter educated in politics and government, reared by a mother who strictly follows the Catholic Church's Legion of Decency film ratings. She deems Hollywood "Hell's Toolshed," which has had the effect of denying my presence at most box office hits.

In short, my first trip to Europe is a fabulous adventure that I am ill-equipped to cover.

Our initial stop on the itinerary is Salzburg and the set of "The Sound of Music." We are anxiously anticipating London and Rome, where we will hobnob with megastars Rex Harrison and Charlton Heston while touring two of the world's megacities. The small Austrian mountain town of Salzburg does not sound nearly as exciting.

So we are unprepared to fall in love with Mozart's hometown in the land of stringed music and lederhosen, as well as with "Sound of Music" star Julie Andrews, which we all do. The word most often used to describe her incandescent quality is "glowing." There is nothing of the diva about this unassuming, somewhat shy young actress. Quite the opposite. There is an aura of genuine humility. With her cropped almond-colored hair, she is naturally lovely. She is also open and candid.

At 28 years old, Julie Andrews is just three years older than me. She is not well known to moviegoers, as she usually performs in the theater. On stage in London and Broadway, she starred as Eliza Doolittle in "My Fair Lady" opposite Rex Harrison. When, however, it is decided to make a film of the play, Harrison continues in the role of Professor Henry Higgins, but Julie loses her role to the more established movie star Audrey Hepburn. The loss is reported to be a great disappointment to Julie.

She is, however, very earnest in her efforts to perfect her performance in "The Sound of Music," a quality especially evident as we watch her rehearse a difficult moment in the movie.

Our first morning on the set, we stand on the side of a dirt road to observe the careful preparation for filming Maria the postulant exiting the convent to enter the household of Baron von Trapp, where she will become governess to his seven children. Maria is frightened, and to bolster her morale, she dances and sings her way to the Baron's castle.

It is an exercise in multitasking. The actress must dance down the road, carrying a suitcase in one hand and a guitar in the other, while synchronizing her lips perfectly to the words of the song "I Have Confidence," which she has prerecorded.

In order to visualize how she will appear on screen performing this feat, Julie sits astride a camera dolly with film director Robert Wise, observing her choreographer, Mark Breaux, executing the dance exactly as she must. So precise is his rehearsal that he, too, lip-syncs the words of the song. Then it is Julie's turn to attempt the dance. For a number of trial runs, she is dressed in casual attire, black slacks and a white blouse.

As the morning fades into afternoon, Julie dons her Austrian costume, dancing and lip-syncing her way down the dirt road again and again. Director Wise tells me there may be as many as 20 rehearsals out of costume and just as many in costume. Julie later confides that her day begins at 6:30 a.m. and ends at 7 p.m. Discovering how much effort and tedium goes into what I had thought of as a glamorous profession is an eye-opening revelation.

The tedium does not end with film takes. Julie Andrews must endure endless interviews with us junketeers, to which she graciously submits. We are lined up to question her one by one under everyone else's watchful eye.

I, being the neophyte of the troop, am last to the question box. Julie has been queried about every conceivable aspect of her profession, from costume to cosmetics. What, I wonder, is there left to probe?

"Is there anything you haven't been asked, that you would *like* to be asked?" I whisper.

"We could talk about my baby," Julie responds wistfully.

I later learned that, while many in the cast enjoyed late-night sing-a-longs at the hotel with Christopher Plummer playing the piano, Julie was upstairs in her room, being a mom to her 18-month-old daughter, Emma.

Had Julie Andrews succeeded in playing Eliza Doo-little on screen, she would not have been available to accept the role of Maria von Trapp. "The Sound of Music" became the number one box office hit of all time and held that title for five years. The film grossed $286 million. "My Fair Lady" took in only $72 million at twice as much production budget. In later years, Julie Andrews admitted that "The Sound of Music" made her movie career.

Rome, June 1964

From Austria, we fly to northern Italy to watch the filming of "The Agony and the Ecstasy," the story of the great Renaissance artist Michelangelo and his painting of the Sistine chapel under the impatient eye of Pope Julius II. The movie stars Charlton Heston as Michelangelo and Rex Harrison as Pope Julius.

Our schedule for Wednesday, June 10, says that we will look at the quarries from which Michelangelo extracted marble for his statues. Following the examination of the quarries, the itinerary says, we will have lunch and cocktails with 20th Century Fox president Darryl Zanuck and movie star Charlton Heston.

Assuming the luncheon with these world famous figures will be in a high-end Italian bistro, the ladies of the press are attired in their snappiest frocks and high heels. One lady sports a black straw bonnet.

What the schedule does not say is that the cocktails and luncheon will be 3,700 feet in the air. Perhaps the reason no one mentions that the quarries are at the top of the Carrara mountain range, and that we are going to ride the range in flatbed trucks and minivans, is because someone rightly suspected we are cowards.

A few journalistic hairs go gray upon first seeing the narrow roads we will travel, and many more strands change colors when the reporters learn that the Italian drivers have never before traversed these narrow roads! As a matter of fact, tourists are not allowed to go up the Carrara mountains. 20th Century Fox being 20th Century Fox, the company has gotten special permission to risk our lives.

As our Volkswagen minibus ascends the hills, it encounters an impasse. The driver, unperturbed, backs up to within a hair's breadth of a 3,000-foot cascade down the mountain. When our Italian guide screams at our impending doom, the driver leaps out of the vehicle, leaving us and our only transport dangling close to the cliff.

We have no choice but to exit the bus and resort to whatever mobility our high-heeled feet can manage. Desperation provides agility we did not know we possessed.

Eventually, I notice a man climbing behind me. He's swathed in Renaissance garb, and his head is turbaned in cotton. A closer look reveals it is the star of the film, Charlton Heston. He is tall, with a lean, muscular build and angular, bronzed features. Moviedom's Moses and Ben-Hur humbly assists columnist and TV star Dorothy Kilgallen (and her polka dot organza gown) up and over the rocks.

At the top of the mountain, we are greeted by Darryl Zanuck, chomping on an ever-present fat cigar. He expresses great relief that we are actually there to be greeted. He had visions, he says, of 50 ambulances racing up the mountains to recover the bodies. One wonders why that possibility did not concern him *before* he invited us on this risky adventure.

Unexpectedly, I find Charlton Heston standing next to me, gazing at the magnificent view of the mountains. This is no time to waste admiring the scenery or the handsome actor, I think. "*Carpe diem* — seize the moment." So, intimidated though I am by this film idol, I ask for an interview, employing the tape recorder I have borrowed from the radio side of WISN-TV, despite the fact that it will be my first time using the machine.

Heston agrees to the interview. I turn on the recorder and begin babbling questions of no consequence. "I think something is missing," Heston interrupts. Indeed. The tape has leapt from its spool and is flying down the mountain. It is all I can do to rescue it and myself from a stony fate. The interview has already met its demise.

Undaunted by such an embarrassing technological defeat, I boldly attempt photography with my newly purchased camera. Darryl Zanuck sees me aiming the camera and assumes I want to photograph him (which I do not). He obligingly strikes a pose. I press the button. No click. I press again. Still nothing. Mr. Zanuck keeps on posing. "Just one more," I pretend. Zanuck thinks this is going to be the greatest picture since "Gone with the Wind."

I know I have no photograph. Zanuck does not (hopefully). I thank the movie mogul for his patience. Out of sight, I discover the problem. There is no film in the camera.

The cocktail party for which we have worn our most dazzling dresses turns out to be food under a tent, cocktails in paper cups served in our laps, and seats on the mountainside. The bejeweled and bedecked ladies may not have agreed that the best accommodations in life are free, but the ambience is definitely breathtaking.

Come the end of the day, however, we have to face another harrowing ride over skinny roads back down the mountain.

No one has grown any braver with experience. One man holds so tightly to another reporter's arm that there are five soaking wet fingerprints on the supporting player's shirt sleeve at ride's end.

We women are supposed to ride in Volkswagen buses, but some of us opt to rough it and ride in the open, flatbed trucks with the men, not because we are courageous, but because if we are going to die, we might as well enjoy the view on the way down.

From Carrara, we travel by train to Rome, where my misadventures continue. After such a challenging day, Hollywood's pilgrims relax and enjoy bountiful refreshments en route to the

Eternal City. Being the daughter of parents who are abstemious as well as absent from movie theaters, I am also innocent of the power of *vino*. So, when the train pulls into the Rome station, I am blissfully unaware that this is our point of debarkation.

Upon discovering that I am still on the train but my fellow travelers are not, I am mortified — and without lira. In desperation, I hitch a ride with an Italian truck driver. By God's mercy, he does not live up to the licentious reputation of some Italian men that I have been warned about and actually delivers me safely to the Cavalieri Hilton hotel.

I am now wondering what further humiliation awaits this green reporter. Charlton Heston gleefully steps into the role. The movie actor finds the story of our mountain interview so amusing, he relates the tale to a press conference in Rome.

I am embarrassed and furious. "I'll show him," I declare to myself. The next morning, Heston is to be our guide through the Sistine Chapel, so tonight, I stay up until the wee hours trying to understand and repair my fallen tape recorder.

Having triumphantly and finally accomplished the feat, I am dismayed to discover that no cameras or tape recorders of any kind are allowed in the chapel as the result of a bomb threat two years ago. Several minutes of urgent arguments, persuasion, and consultation finally gain admission for the recorder.

Our movie Michelangelo is to describe the ordeal of painting "The Last Judgment," which the great genius executed at the age of 57, 20 years after painting the Sistine Chapel ceiling. Apparently the clout 20th Century Fox exerted in commandeering the Carrara mountain range failed to result in similar privileges from Vatican Museum officials. We do not have the chapel to ourselves. It is filled with thousands of tourists whose personal commentaries are loudly competing with Heston's art history lesson. Recording him is complicated by the fact that I am shorter than most of the people hemming me in.

It is looking like another Heston hanging when a guardian angel named Mark Evans comes to my acoustic rescue. Mark is an executive with WTTG-TV in Washington, D.C., and is immediately aware of my problem. A very tall man, about the same height as Charlton Heston, he volunteers to hold the recorder high above the crowd, close to Heston. So, despite the surrounding sounds, all of the actor's commentary is captured and easily discernible on the tape.

As the tour concludes, we visit the Vatican Museum gift shop, where what to my wondering eyes should appear but an extensive slide presentation of the Sistine Chapel. When I return to Milwaukee, the trip becomes a half-hour documentary called "Diary of a Movie Junket." An extensive portion of the show is a tour of the Sistine Chapel using the museum slides with Charlton Heston as my narrator.

The program wins an award for which I am reluctantly grateful to Heston. Had he not irritated me by recounting our Carrara mountain misfire, I might not have been motivated to forsake a night's sleep to repair the recorder that captured his Sistine Chapel performance. And Mark Evans, the broadcast executive who held my recorder, might not have become my boss in Washington, D.C.

3

CLIMB EVERY MOUNTAIN

At the age of 25, I am established in a major television market, Milwaukee, Wisconsin, but I have not attained the goal on which I have set my sights as a junior in college — network news correspondent covering national and international news. Those opportunities are only in Washington, D.C., or New York City.

Prevailing employment wisdom dictates one never looks for employment *while unemployed*. You are always more attractive jobbed than jobless. And you certainly never leave a secure position in a market almost closed to your gender with no future possibilities on the horizon.

I know, however, if I do not make the move at 25, I will grow too comfortable in familiar territory, surrounded by family and friends, and I will most probably not do it at all. It is now or never.

So, despite everyone's advice and my boss pleading with me to stay, I pack up "Harry," my little red Volkswagen, with just $1,000 in savings, and drive myself to Washington.

NBC, ABC, and CBS are not waiting for me on the National Mall.

I am able to secure auditions with NBC and CBS. Those always conclude with "nice job, but no openings (for women) at the moment." NBC has Nancy Dickerson. CBS has Marya McLaughlin. ABC has no women in Washington.

Wisconsinites familiar with my work at WISN-TV wrote generous letters of recommendations that, oddly enough, prove to be a hindrance rather than a help. "Overqualified" is the reaction of employers outside of broadcasting. Not very encouraging. Two years ago, as a college graduate, I was underqualified with no job experience. Now with good job experience I am "overqualified."

Every morning, I get up, dress up, and walk to Mass at St. Matthew's Cathedral on Rhode Island Avenue with resume in hand, treating job hunting as a job.

Friends from Wisconsin who have preceded me to Washington give me temporary lodging on the third floor of a townhouse on R Street just off a main artery, Connecticut Avenue. It is owned by a dentist who drills his patients on the first floor. From our "penthouse" quarters, we can stare down the spiraling staircase to survey and comment on his next victims.

Unfortunately, the stay is short, as the room is on loan from my friends' permanent roommate, who returns from Europe all too soon. As my funds dwindle to near nonexistence, I resort to searching for any job in any field that will keep me fed and housed.

I am strangely at peace, knowing that from the outset it has all been an elephantine gamble. Better to have tried and failed than never to have tried at all. If my return to broadcasting was not to be, at least I was living where history is being made. I can still smell the coffee, even as I miss the caffeine.

The Iranian embassy briefly hires me as a press attaché. But before my first day, I am unhired. "Overqualified." They conjecture that, if and when a broadcasting job presents itself, I will quit the embassy for greener pastures. Of course they are right, so I cannot argue.

Enter Auntie Mame, alias Esther "Pat" Sullivan. She is the statuesque assistant to the vice president of NBC in Washington. The epitome of the glamorous, professional woman, Pat never walks into a room. She sweeps in, dark auburn hair swinging side to side. Once engaged to Senator Joe McCarthy, she is now the widow of John Sullivan, who had been the number three man at the FBI. He died of a heart attack the night they were to attend JFK's inaugural gala.

Pat Sullivan is my first introduction to multitasking. One day, I watch with fascination as Pat, hat on head, cigarette dangling from the corner of her mouth, is simultaneously typing on her typewriter while animatedly conversing on the phone, which is jammed between her ear and shoulder.

Pat decides I should audition for the "Today Show." The female hosts on NBC's popular morning show were usually Hollywood actresses, easy on the eyes but not newswomen.

Despite my doubts of being ready for such a lofty job at age 25, she sets up an appointment with New York executives.

My audition goes well, and the NBC executives are complimentary. But they have a girl, they say, who has been on staff for 10 years and they have promised her the next try at the host job. "If she doesn't work out, we will call you."

"What's her name?" I ask.

"Barbara Walters" is the response.

I was aware of Barbara Walters before that audition. Occasionally when I was in college, I would see this very intelligent woman sub for the regular host. "Why don't they use her?" I wondered. "She does a much better interview than the actresses."

"You will never call me," I think, but keep it to myself. "She is going to make it."

Barbara not only makes it; she becomes legendary. When we later meet in Washington, Barbara jokes, "Don't you come to New York — I'm serious!"

"Don't worry," I think and again keep it to myself. "I came and you won."

Finally, I accept a job as far removed from the excitement and adventure of broadcast journalism as one can go. The title is "Promotions Manager for the National Institute of Dry Cleaning." Mundane as the position sounds, it provides me with a private secretary, a private office, and my name on the door, none of which was ever proffered in broadcasting newsrooms, where it was first come, first desk.

The job also gives me the opportunity to engage my love of illustrating. I launch a nationwide dry-cleaning promotion campaign with a banner and a miniature comic book called "Elegance is Clean Living" for dry cleaners to buy and give out to their customers. It becomes a best seller.

Nevertheless, after six months, when Wisconsin congressman Glenn Davis offers me a job as his press secretary, I take it, but find it disappointingly confining as it affords little opportunity to leave my desk and watch the history that is being made so near and yet so far away.

So I am elated when the auditions that had taken place at NBC bear fruit within the year. Metromedia, a regional radio broadcast network, begins hiring correspondents for its Washington bureau, and NBC recommends me.

The bureau is very small. Jim Randolph, a kindly, short, gray-haired man, is the boss. Dan Blackburn — slick black hair, eager, and intense — and I are the correspondents. Our broadcast territory envelops the East Coast, including New York.

The challenge of a minute bureau covering such important news across a vast territory demands all of our wits and energy. It also provides fascinating assignments, an entrée to interesting characters, and innumerable opportunities to grow. One day, I am required to sprint between the House and Senate to conduct seven different interviews with seven different senators and congressmen in two hours. In heels!

4

A MAN TO "DO"
THE RIVER WITH

Metromedia assigns me to cover Capitol Hill and the White House, with the latter gradually taking most of my time. My task at the White House is to monitor every move of the president of the United States, Lyndon Baines Johnson, reporting his most significant actions to our eastern regional network stations in one-minute radio broadcasts. The fact that I am observing the day-to-day moves of the most powerful man in the world prompts me to keep a journal of White House daily doings that are not worthy of a newscast, but are revealing of the personalities making the news.

October 5, 1965

Over the airwaves, on the wires, via the rumor factory, reporters covering President Lyndon Johnson are alerted to be at the White House *now*. "Now" usually signals a major announcement.

White House press secretary Bill Moyers will not confirm our assumptions, but he won't deny them, either. During his briefing, we are called into the president's office to see Sargent Shriver, his new deputy director at the War on Poverty. Shriver, the least heralded (though handsomest) man of the Kennedy clan, has the rare combination of brains, dashing charm, and spirituality. A daily communicant, he is a Kennedy administration holdover, married to Eunice Kennedy, and director of both the first Peace Corps and the War on Poverty. But he is not major news today.

About a half-hour later, we are in the Oval Office again to see five 4-H Club members give the president a bell. Johnson says he is going to use it to summon the press. Amusing, but hardly a headline.

Fifteen minutes later, we are hailed once more, this time to see the two people who are cochairing the White House Conference on Civil Rights. In the course of all the toing and froing, my voice, afflicted with laryngitis, fades to nonexistence. One of the press secretaries keeps stuffing me with coricidin and telling me there is "something big coming."

As evening approaches, my afflicted tonsils and I give up on "something big" and go home — just in time to miss "something big" when it finally arrives. The president announces he will be entering the hospital for major surgery to remove his gall bladder. When the most powerful leader in the world says he is going under the knife, it *is* big news indeed.

And I had to *listen* to the report instead of *giving* it.

Pre-operation week

All day, every day, since the major surgery announcement, President Johnson has engaged in a veritable hurricane of activity as if to distract himself and the public from the upcoming operation. Yesterday he seemed a bit mechanical. But he attempted to offer us some human-interest material, even inviting his dog "Him" to a ceremony in the Cabinet Room.

Operation morning, October 8, 1965

It's 7 a.m. in Bethesda Naval Hospital and I am on Operation Vigil (or the "body watch," as United Press International [UPI] correspondent Helen Thomas dubbed it). Just a few feet away from me are the A-Team of news — ABC, NBC, CBS — whose territory is the entire country.

My laryngitis has reduced my voice to a whisper. In order to perform my job, I am medically required to remain mute, except for one-minute radio reports, enabling my voice to assemble enough timber to speak for a 60-second broadcast.

The austere prescription actually works.

Pre-operation report

President Johnson went to the operating room about a half-hour before his 7:30 surgery. He goes on the operating table 15-20 pounds trimmer. His doctors report him in excellent condition. The removal of Mr. Johnson's gall bladder is called "preventive maintenance." It is major surgery, but not generally dangerous. Rather, it is uncomfortable. It is expected to last two hours. The president, if all goes well, is expected to be up for a short time this afternoon. But he will not feel fully recovered for possibly six weeks. Peggy Smeeton, Metromedia News, reporting from Bethesda Naval Hospital.

Mid-operation report

As word is awaited concerning the president's operation, reporters here at Bethesda Naval Hospital are reflecting on Mr. Johnson's studied lack of concern and hectic pace the last few days. The president whirled through expected and unexpected events like a driven man. He was generally cheerful, though not exuberant. On one of his surprise strolls around the White House yesterday, he chided reporters for trying to interpret his every attempt to exercise. Another time, he seemed to almost brush off good wishes, like a man who thought his operation was too insignificant to worry about. It is doubtful Mr. Johnson really feels this way, but it is clear all his efforts have gone toward reassuring the American people that his illness is minor; that the affairs of government will only be momentarily interrupted. This is Peggy Smeeton reporting for Metromedia News at Bethesda Naval Hospital.

Operation over — outcome good

White House press secretary Bill Moyers has just announced to reporters that President Johnson's

operation has been completed and that it was entirely
successful. Dr. James Cain of the Mayo Clinic, long-
time Johnson physician, said, "Everything went
beautifully. The gallbladder was removed. It contained
a stone. Another stone in the ureter was also removed."
Bill Moyers said the president is resting comfortably in
the operating suite. This is Peggy Smeeton, reporting
for Metromedia News from Bethesda Naval Hospital.

Having successfully followed the president's status
throughout his surgery, I go home and sleep for three hours,
then return to the hospital for the 7 p.m.-3 a.m. shift.

All is quiet until White House press secretary Bill Moyers
strolls to the press room unexpectedly. We immediately assume
there has been an unexpected turn for the worse. It's the
nature of the news beast.

But no. He has just dropped by for informal, off-the-cuff
remarks, relating that all is well.

White House press secretary Bill Moyers interrupted the
calm in the Bethesda Hospital press center to hold an
informal 15-minute news briefing. He told reporters
the president had gone to sleep about 9:45 p.m.; that he
expected to have a smooth night. The doctors report his
progress is par for the course. Mr. Johnson took a second
short trip from his bed about 6:30. He was aided by a
nurse and doctor. Moyers said the president is being
fed intravenously. He is under sedation, but much less
than expected. He is more comfortable now than ear-
lier. According to Moyers, President Johnson conversed
a good deal during the day. His only company were
his two daughters, Mrs. Johnson, and his pastor. Mrs.
Johnson and [daughter] Lynda Bird are spending the
night here at the hospital. Peggy Smeeton, reporting
for Metromedia News from Bethesda Naval Hospital.

About midnight, Moyers' assistant, Hal Pachios, drops
by for a chat and proceeds to deliver a revealing profile of LBJ.

He describes the president as "larger than life ... consumed by everything. His mind never stops ... unpredictable ... has no trouble making up his mind for the moment ... but 10 minutes later, he may want something else."

Hal says the president is a "voracious lover. ... He almost devours people; loves having people around him. Nothing escapes his notice. ... He can be talking about the most profound subject and notice the smallest things. ... 'Hasn't this rug *ever* been cleaned?'" Or the other day, he issued Hal a fashion rebuke: "*Where* did you get that tie?"

Portrait of the president concluded and subject sleeping, Hal, Chuck Langston, and I repair to the cafeteria for chocolate milk and apple pie, then head out to Hal's car to pick up his shaving kit. When Hal tries to reenter the hospital, the security guard carefully examines his kit and makes the president's press aide show his credentials *twice!*

Nary a word or an inspection of the humble reporters.

The hospital vigil continues for several days, with we the press informing the world of every minute detail concerning the recovery of the most dominant man on the planet.

Resting in his third-floor VIP suite, tonight President Johnson is surrounded by the members of his immediate family. Mrs. Johnson and youngest daughter Luci spent last night in adjoining rooms. This evening, Lynda Bird flew in from the University of Texas, and she will remain at the hospital tonight. It is not known whether Luci will spend a second night here. She stayed with her mother during the morning, left the hospital for college classes around 1:15 p.m., attended a late Mass, and returned to the White House. White House aides report the Johnson women very calm. The first lady herself described her preoperative state of mind as "concerned, but not anxious." This is Peggy Smeeton at Bethesda Naval Hospital reporting for Metromedia News.

Hubert, the "Happy Warrior"

Vice President Hubert Humphrey is making a speech. He is my assignment, and I arrive too late to record him because the daybook listed the speech time an hour-and-a-half later than it actually began.

I am headed back to the bureau with an empty tape. As I stand waiting for a cab, Vice President Humphrey emerges and heads for his limousine. He sees me and comes over to say hi.

"I didn't get your speech," I complain.

"But," Humphrey says, "I saw you come in with your machine."

"I know, but you had already started speaking when I got there."

"Where are you going?" he asks. "I'm going to the Capitol. I'll give you a ride."

"Will you do an interview on your speech?"

"You don't want that, do you really?"

"Yes, I do."

"OK," says the vice president, "get in."

Once we are in the limousine, HHH queries the Secret Service as to whether he ought to get a haircut. He decides he should.

"OK," he says, turning to me. "Open that squawk box."

And we conduct an interview all the way to the Capitol. As the vice president suspects, I'm really interested in his thoughts on the latest developments in Vietnam. Happily, I have learned a thing or two about tape recorders since Charlton Heston.

December 28, 1965

It is nighttime in a nearly empty White House, which has been deserted by the principal occupants for a Christmas respite in Texas. We are viewing the Christmas decorations as guests of my housemate, Patsy Derby, a Johnson relative as well as an employee in the East Wing.

In the dark silence, there is a spectral quality to this historic residence, especially when one is accustomed to covering the daily dynamics that so dominate it when the living commander in chief is in residence. Thus I am slightly unnerved when, as we walk down the unlit, hallowed halls, out of the shadows emerges the large, somber face of Abraham Lincoln. How different the vacant State Dining Room looks from the grandeur and glamour of VIP banquets. We seat ourselves at the main table just to be able to say that we have.

The White House Christmas Tree is voluminous, reaching close to the ceiling of the Blue Room and nearly engulfing it. It is decorated with everything from stringed popcorn to gingerbread men and houses.

In the East Room, Patsy's beau, Buzz Cheney, sits down at the piano and plays Harry Truman's favorite number, the "Missouri Waltz." I dance to it on the empty floor.

We giggle, speculating that a long-time guard hearing Buzz playing might be thinking he had lost a few years and that Harry S. is back in the Big House.

There is something quite special, romantic, and oddly memorable about the evening: three 20-somethings freely roaming the most protected and famous house in America like little mice scampering in the attic after midnight.

January 12, 1966 . . . .

The main event today: the president's State of the Union address. All day long, we are anticipating the text. At first, it is promised at 3 p.m., then 6 p.m., 7 p.m., 8 p.m. Latest alert: probably not till 9 p.m.

Actually, as it turns out, the first section rolls off the presses at about 6:30 p.m., the second at 7:15 p.m. We find nothing revealing in the contents.

This morning at the press conference, Bill Moyers told us, "Off the record, it's still being written." He acknowledges it will be about 5,000 words. A reporter asks, "Does that mean it's 10,000 now?"

"No," answers Bill, "That means it's 250 words now and we're wondering where to go from here."

January 31, 1966 ·

Washington, D.C., manages world crises and wars, but does not tolerate winter wonderlands well. Faced with eight inches of snow, the nation's capital is paralyzed, which gives a festival atmosphere to the first "snow day" in this overworked government town. With the city trapped in a world of white that clogs streets and immobilizes automobiles, the normal business of D.C. gives way to building snowmen and sipping hot chocolate.

This morning, however, there is no holiday at the White House. The president of the United States calls the news media in early, to make an important announcement. And if it is the announcement everyone has been expecting, there is no playing hooky.

Cars are buried, including my little red Volkswagen. Cabs are not available. So it is a case of walking and hitching a ride from drivers fortunate enough to live on streets that are shoveled. Patsy Derby and I set out from 2461 P Street in Georgetown for 1600 Pennsylvania Avenue in downtown Washington.

Our skinny white-brick townhouse with the salmon-pink door overlooks Rock Creek Parkway, a curving path to our destination. On a normal weekday, the parkway (which winds all the way to Maryland) would be trunk to bumper with government commuters. This morning, it belongs to booted feet trudging through the snowdrifts.

One cannot help but delight in the beauty of the capital and its monuments wrapped in white pearl — Abraham Lincoln solemnly staring out over ice-laced tree limbs matching his marbled arms.

Two walks and two hitchhikes later, we arrive at the White House. All the newsmen are in construction boots and lumberjack shirts. Surprisingly, only about 17 reporters have trudged to the post.

The president seems in fairly good humor for a man with such grim tidings to relate: *The bombing lull over North Vietnam is over.*

McGeorge Bundy, another JFK holdover, gives us a briefing on Vietnam. He, too, is in puzzlingly good humor, smiling broadly. His teeth are on high a good deal of the time. Someone comments that Bundy gets more good-natured each day he is closer to departure. Bundy glances around the room. "It's interesting to see who made it today." In the physically fit Kennedy administration, this may have merited a medal or at least a granola bar.

At one point, utilizing a long string of words, Bundy dodges a question. At the end of the string, he grins: "I am getting so I can give longer and longer non-answers."

February 1, 1966

WGN, a premiere broadcasting station in Chicago, has offered me a job for almost $11,000 a year (nearly $98,000 in 2022). Harry Reasoner of ABC and Bob Pierpoint of CBS take me to lunch, Harry carrying my tape recorder, Bob my briefcase, and both sporting Siberian-style boots.

They convince me that if my goal is to become a network correspondent (which it is), wisdom dictates, despite the salary, that I stay in Washington. In scarcely a few months, it will become apparent how prescient that advice was, and how different my future life would have been had I not taken it.

Capitol Hill

I am waiting for a taxi in front of the House of Representatives. A long, sleek, black Lincoln Continental pulls up in front of me and pauses. The driver is a dark-haired man with thick black brows hovering over large, hazel eyes. I recognize him as one of the newly-elected Republican congressmen, one of the few to survive the Democratic LBJ landslide. But I don't know his name.

"Would you like a ride?" he inquires.

"Oh, no, thank you," I respond, automatically assuming a man that good looking and obviously older than I, is, of course, married. Too bad, he certainly is handsome.

February 4, 1966 ....

President Johnson holds an informal press conference in the Oval Office with the commander in chief's usual air of mystery surrounding the event. He so loves intrigue and hates leaks that one wonders if his bloodline includes Agatha Christie. He *hates* leaks. No one is to make big announcements except LBJ.

There is an early morning swearing-in ceremony that again reveals the renewed humor of the recent surgery patient.

When the ceremony concludes, the president disappears, then suddenly reappears. He looks puzzled. He walks over to the podium and bends down, his fingers grazing the floor. He rises with his tie clasp in hand, commenting, "You just have to watch yourself at all times with Fay Wells around." This for the benefit of white-haired Fay, who is standing next to him and gives an obliging giggle.

"Something big" has drawn a big crowd. Pending "bigs" at the White House spread like wildfire in Washington, and reporters from all beats scurry to 1600. "Something big" refers to a statement by Bill Moyers that we have a firm lid until 10 minutes to 2.

A firm "lid" means the president, in effect, promises not to make any news before 10 to 2. No guarantees after that. Such warnings usually indicate that indeed "something big" is coming. The actual occurrence of the "big" could be 10 minutes or 10 hours later, but definitely not *before* the stated time.

About 50 minutes past 10 to 2, we are called into the press office and, from there, moved into the Oval Office. We gather informally around the president, who is seated, very much in command, at his desk. He is quite patient as we assemble ourselves.

He builds the usual suspense, spending almost 10 minutes speaking about food and India before he gets to the main attraction. "I have another little announcement to make. You might be interested." That "little announcement" is that he will be meeting with South Vietnamese officials in a conference in Oahu, Hawaii *tomorrow*!

During a reception later in the East Room, the president gives me an elbow pump and asks, "Are you coming with us tomorrow?" Knowing that Metromedia's budget does not include last-minute flights to the Pacific, even with the president of the United States, but not wanting to admit that, I merely answer, "I hope so, sir."

Of course, I am right in my assumption that Metromedia will not send their White House correspondent to blue Hawaii. I get my news of the Honolulu conference like every other American: from newspapers and other people's newscasts, not my own.

There is some cynical conjecture that the hastily-arranged conference was devised to deflect attention from the Senate Foreign Relations Committee hearings on Vietnam being conducted by Senator William Fulbright, an opponent of the war, who has assembled a full cast of witnesses with his same mindset. Little of major import is credited to the conference, so I haven't missed much except a sun freckle or two.

Little do I know that, 10 months from this date, I will collect more than a freckle from the Hawaiian sun on a trip that I cannot now imagine.

Cloakroom, The House of Representatives . . . . . .

"Why won't you go out with Bill Stanton?" The question comes at me from Congressman Bill Ayres, a representative of Akron, Ohio, a jolly man with the air more reminiscent of a carnival barker than a Member of Congress.

We are standing in the House cloakroom, which is just off the floor of the House of Representatives and a good place for reporters to buttonhole a member for a quick interview.

"Who's he?" I ask.

Congressman Ayres points to another congressman standing across the cloakroom, the same man, I note, who had recently offered me the ride I had turned down.

"He's married, isn't he?"

"No, he's not married."

"He's never been married?"

"He's *never* been married," Ayres responds.

"Ohhhh. ..."

Small, navy blue books contain biographies of the members. I look up J. (John) William Stanton. He graduated from Culver Military Academy, where he held almost every notable position to be had, from captain of the football and baseball teams, to president of numerous clubs and classes, to regimental commander in his senior year. He turned down an appointment to West Point and went to World War II at the age of 18, emerging at 21, the youngest captain in the Pacific, with multiple medals including the Purple Heart and the Bronze Star. He graduated from Georgetown University as the president of the senior class and returned to the Midwest to run a Lincoln-Mercury agency; at 24, he was the youngest franchised dealer in Ford Motor Company history. He served as county commissioner for eight years, the position that led him to run for Congress.

Not long after the exchange with Congressman Ayres, the still-bachelor congressman from the 11th district of Ohio, just east of Cleveland, asks the bachelorette from Wisconsin for a date.

This time she accepts.

Friday, February 11, 1966 ....

President Johnson again chooses late Friday to make news. He calls us into his office for another 5 p.m. press conference. Again, we gather around his desk in the Oval Office.

LBJ sits for part of the session, and stands or walks at other times. At one point, he parks in front of me, looking down at my scribbled notes. I am desperately hoping he has not perfected reading upside down, because I am very unsure my hasty scribblings are capturing his quotes correctly.

He needles the press gently, but is not openly irritated. He's often patronizing. When asked about polls that show his popularity is at its lowest, he shows disdain. "I haven't noticed much change. I hope it can continue."

When asked about Indian Prime Minister Indira Gandhi's impending visit, he swivels around in his chair and casually picks up a typewritten page. "Yes," he says, "I just had a letter from her last night."

"I don't want to be in a position of reading someone's confidential mail publicly, so you can say, 'It is believed she will be here the latter half of March.'" Then he reads aloud a couple of portions of the letter with the casual air of the absent-minded professor. "Let's see. No, she doesn't say exactly *when* she's coming."

The press conference concludes. Stories are filed. A group of us are waiting for cabs. Suddenly, out of nowhere, there is the president of the United States, squatting on his haunches in the middle of the front lobby next to a dark-haired little girl with curls named Courtenay Valenti, daughter of Jack Valenti, special assistant to the president.

The president coaxes Courtenay, "Who do you love?"

No answer, but much big-eyed staring at the gathering crowd.

"Who do you love?" Johnson persists.

Finally, Courtenay takes the cue. "Prez," she answers.

LBJ picks Courtenay up, puts her down, begs several kisses, and says she has called him on the phone and given him a valentine. The valentine reads, "We can make music together, dear." There is an illegible scrawl on the back.

Also along are two of presidential pet beagle Him's puppies. "That one's name is Freckles," says Mr. Johnson. Somehow the leashes get wrapped around my ankles, but the commander in chief manages to untangle them before I am on the floor with the puppies.

He asks me to ask Courtenay, who is once again in a presidential holding pattern, "Whose little angel are you?" So I obediently make the query.

"Prez's little angel." Courtenay has quickened to the cues.

"Prez" gives me a "how about that?" glance. Then I ask, "Is the 'Prez' an angel?" To which there is no reply. The "Prez" ignores the query.

"She called me on the phone," LBJ says.

I ask her, "What did you say?"

"Hello, Prez," she answers. The president throws me another "how about that?" look. At age 3, Courtney clearly has political potential and presents "Prez" a welcome distraction from questions of war and peace, as well as a reason to care how he handles those questions.

First date . . . .

Georgetown, 3522 P Street, an old three-story town-house that leans to the right, where my roommate, Carol Owens and I have moved from 2461 P Street and where Congressman Bill Stanton picks me up for our first date.

I climb into the passenger seat of his long Lincoln, pushing aside a thick black book to sit down. "Why is this here?" I want to know.

"It's a missal," Bill replies, "I go to Mass in the morning."

I try to mask my amazement. My father is also a daily communicant, but I never anticipate a *date* being one. Especially a congressman.

Conversation comes easily over beef stroganoff in a front booth of Billy Martin's Carriage House, the restaurant rumored to be the site of Jacqueline Kennedy's first public appearance after JFK's assassination. I discover a man who does not fit the media mold of the extroverted, backslapping, self-absorbed politician. The congressman listens more than he speaks. He says nothing about his achievements. It seems he has come to Washington to actually serve rather than be served. He has a sense of humor; his entry into politics resulted from a dare. As a young auto dealer, he expressed frustration to his father about the lack of action by Lake County Commissioners, which cost the county thousands of jobs.

"If you don't like what they're doing," his father challenged him, "Why don't you run for the job yourself?"

"Maybe I will," Bill responded.

"No, you won't," Frank Stanton taunted. "They meet every two weeks and you're never around."

Bill took the bait. "I'll bet you $1,000 I will run and I'll win."

He ran. He won, collected his $1,000, "and never missed a meeting." After eight years as county commissioner, he decided to try for a seat in Congress. Despite running as a Republican in a Democratic district, he survived the LBJ landslide, one of the few GOP candidates to emerge a victor.

Coupled with Mass attendance, it becomes evident that a man this interesting could ruin my career. So the next time Bill asks for a date, I am busy. And the next time. And the next time.

Eventually the invitations cease coming.

February 28, 1966

President Johnson attends the funeral of the son of the dean of White House correspondents, Merriman Smith, who has been killed in Vietnam. It is the first funeral of a soldier killed in the war that President Johnson has attended. His face is wreathed in sadness.

Merriman Smith, tough old Merriman with his patent-leather black hair and black mustache, looks ravaged with grief as he comes down the aisle. The chapel is filled with dignitaries and members of the press corps. Their faces reflect the stark reality of a war that has come home.

Gray day, pouring rain, horse-drawn carriage, taps, Marine band, rifle volley — so painfully reminiscent of JFK's funeral.

Vice President Hubert Humphrey arrives late and slips into a middle pew. Passing his limousine after the funeral, I see him weeping, his handkerchief covering his face.

March 3, 1966

A very different mood at the annual congressional reception at the White House. Together with Bob Pierpoint of CBS and Andy Glass, *New York Herald Tribune* scribe, I start the evening chatting with Senate Majority Leader Mike Mansfield.

Senate Minority Leader Ev Dirksen, his wavy gray locks askew, is conducting the Marine Band and singing "Danny Boy." He says the name "Smeeton" reminds him of the Smithsonian Institute.

Strange you should say that, I tell him. "Our home, when I was growing up, used to be referred to as the 'Smeetonian Institute.'"

"Good," he responds. "That's the way I'll remember it."

Oh, great. I am not looking forward to the day when I am referred to at a Capitol Hill press conference as "Miss Smeetonian."

The president is encircled by news hens, and he is clearly enjoying the company. He is relaxed, and talks freely and at great length about the Vietnam debate, which is getting nationwide attention via Senator Fulbright's televised Senate Foreign Relations hearings.

He says he thinks Defense Secretary Robert McNamara's exposition yesterday was "very good." He comments on Secretary of State Dean Rusk's television appearance, when Rusk asked the senators if it ever occurred to them that *they* might be wrong. Johnson dwells on the fact that his men are having a rough time.

"I don't mind for myself. I've had my political career. I've been in Congress, been in the Senate. I've been vice president and president, but these fellas ... ."

The implication is that the careers of men like McNamara and Rusk still have miles to go. He then tells us a story that he labels "off the record" because it involves the despair felt by a government official who has been under attack.

"That's a great story, Mr. President. Why not put it on the record?"

"No," he answers firmly, shaking his head.

He continues his thoughts about Vietnam and our commitment to help through the Southeast Asia Treaty Organization (SEATO) treaty. He says he didn't make the agreement, but "if I am driving down the street in a 25-mile-[per-hour] zone, I don't drive 50 miles an hour. I may not like it, but it is the law." He goes on to evoke an analogy to Hitler. He talks about the U.S. drawing a line, telling an aggressor they can go no further.

I notice a nervous twitch on the right side of his face, particularly evident when Andy Glass asks him a question he obviously does not want to answer. And does not.

Finally, Lady Bird, who has been standing off to the side, rescues Lyndon by asking him to dance with her. Later on, he is oozing the Johnsonian charm on his most vocal critic, Senator Fulbright. The senator has his hands shoved in his vest pocket, as if listening with a mentally cocked eyebrow. Mrs. Fulbright is being gracious and responsive.

Eventually the president is pulled away. Andy introduces me to Senator Fulbright. Almost speaking before thinking, I say, "Senator, you had the most marvelous expression on your face."

"What was it?"

"Don't try to snow me. I've been around."

He gave me a long, slow, wide grin. "You shouldn't come to places like this and read people's minds."

Vice President Humphrey asks me to dance, a request I hate because I don't know how to dance, and, of course, I tread on his toe.

"Was that your toe?" I ask by way of apology.

'No," he responds. "It was somebody else's."

That's statesmanship.

"Are you as much of a Hawk as you sounded when you returned from the trip?"

"Hawk? I'm no Hawk! I'm an eagle."

I ask if I may express an opinion. Permission granted.

"I think the administration should be more candid about the war."

"I think maybe you're right."

"Don't you think the American people can take it?"

"Yes," he says very positively. "I think they can."

At this point, understandably, he has had enough of me. He steers me over to a congressman to dance with the congressman's wife. "He's pawning me off on you," I warn the congressman.

"No, I'm not pawning you off! We're just going to mix up the dancing."

Young congressman Bill Green, age 27, who has inherited his father's congressional seat, tells us a story about his father and his two younger brothers, Michael and Patrick, age 13 and 9, visiting the White House during the Kennedy administration.

Former congressman Green is taking them to meet President Kennedy. He tells them not to "just stand there. Have a question for the president."

Michael decides he will ask the president how his father is.

Congressman Green then asks Patrick what his question is. Patrick says he is going to ask the president how his father is. Michael reminds Patrick that is *his* question.

So Patrick goes to the White House without a question. When they arrive and are greeted by JFK, Michael dutifully asks the president how his father is. President Kennedy says, "Fine. Nice of you to ask."

Now it is Patrick's turn. He walks around, carefully looks the place over, and finally comes out with, "Mr. President, how do you like it here?" JFK answers Patrick's question with a roar of laughter.

March 4, 1966

Today, we get almost certain confirmation that the press briefings are bugged by LBJ.

Associate Press Secretary Bob Fleming conducts the press briefing, giving us a long spiel about President Johnson's plans to go to Texas, where he will land at Randolph Field in San Antonio. He says the press will stay in San Antonio rather than Austin, etc., etc.

The phone rings. Fleming picks it up. "Yes, sir." Bob turns his back toward us. Only little mumblings and occasional "yes" and "no, sirs," can be heard. He hangs up. The phone rings again. Bob picks it up again. "Yes, sir. No, sir. Yes, sir."

Fleming hangs up and smirks, "Didn't change anything." The group briefing moves on to other topics. The phone rings again. Fleming picks it up. "Yes, sir." He again gives us his back. More mumblings and occasional "yes, sirs" and "no, sirs" can be heard. He hangs up and turns back to us.

A reporter raises another trip question. Fleming smiles. "I am far less certain we're going on that trip than I was two phone calls ago."

Georgetown, 3522 P Street ....

I find a postcard from Hong Kong in my mailbox. It reads "Thought of you today." Signed, "Bill Stanton."

Indira Gandhi visits the U.S., March 28 to April 1, 1966 ....

The long-anticipated visit of Indian Prime Minister Indira Gandhi finally materializes, and she is honored with a state dinner at the White House. Correspondents are mere observers of the *après* dinner dancing and socializing. Nevertheless, we women are required to dress as if we are guests, in long gowns.

I am standing next to the grand piano with a reporter from *U.S. News & World Report* who is wearing a crinoline undergarment to put flounce into her voluminous skirt. Suddenly "is" becomes "was."

"I'm losing my crinoline," she hisses in anguish. "What am I going to do?"

"You've only got one choice," I whisper back. "Step out of it and kick it under the piano so no one will know whose it is." Which is what she does, and flees the scene of the crime. When I realize that leaves me with a large undergarment at my feet, I, too, take flight.

From my "safe zone," I observe the first lady walking over to the piano with Chief Justice Abe Fortas. Lady Bird picks up the crinoline. She and the chief justice examine it carefully. Then Lady Bird places the slip on *top* of the piano cover, no doubt to facilitate the embarrassed owner discreetly reclaiming it.

But there it remains the rest of the evening. My friend from *U.S. News & World Report* is never to be seen again tonight.

As I am dancing with one of the Marine social aides, the president takes over, instructing the aide, "If she looks bored, cut in on us." I conjecture that is code for, "If *I* look bored, cut in on us."

One might think it is an honor to be asked to waltz with the president of the United States, and indeed it might be, if one knew how to waltz, which I do not. I am of the rock-and-roll college generation. Our motto is, "Never let your mind know what your feet are doing."

"Just dance on your tiptoes, and follow me" are my instructions from the commander in chief. Mr. Johnson soon discovers it is easier to lead the free world. As we stumble to the Marine band orchestra music, I attempt to distract from my lack of grace with conversation. He notes that violinist Isaac Stern, the evening's entertainment, glistened with perspiration throughout his performance. I mentally sympathize with Mr. Stern and hope I am not doing the same.

The president is impressed with Indira Gandhi. He says he can relate to her because she faces some of the same problems he had to deal with when he took over America after JFK's assassination, among them a troubled country and elections ahead. "I sort of felt like her brother. I told her I would help her all that I could."

April 1966: A "wilderness experience" . . . .

"You are headed for wide open spaces. It is two hours to everything! Relax, take a tranquilizer, enjoy the landscape. It's bigger than all outdoors. It *is* outdoors! Get with the wilderness spirit!"

So reads our itinerary handout from Lady Bird Johnson's press secretary, Liz Carpenter. Liz is a short, stocky, tough, white-haired Texan, full of "fun-sense," a former journalist with a keen wit and ingenuity.

We are on our way to Big Bend Country in far West Texas, the largest desert in the U.S., topping the size of Rhode Island. Texan Lady Bird Johnson has never been to Big Bend National Park, but has always yearned to visit. So she gives the trip a purpose and takes more than 70 members of the press and White House staff with her. Many of us are unaccustomed to "wilderness experiences," as Liz Carpenter dubs our adventures, or camping in territory that plays host to 5,000 "living things."

Dr. James Young, a White House physician and our traveling medicine man, warns us about some of the "living things" we may want to avoid, including bobcats, coyotes, and snakes.

Sometimes, the smaller those things are, the nastier, however. "Shake out your shoes. Scorpions like to crawl into warm places. Their bite is pretty harmless, though painful," says the doctor.

The most dangerous spider is the black widow, Dr. Young cautions. "You can identify the female black widow if you turn her over and see a red hourglass figure. You are not able to recognize the male, but then the male is less aggressive."

The symptoms of a black widow bite include pain that travels from the bite area throughout the system. "It can put you out of commission for several days, [but is] hardly ever fatal," Dr. Young says. Being out of commission for a few days, however, could render fatality to the story you came to cover.

"Black widow bites are most dangerous to children and older people with cardiac conditions," he explains. Some new cardiac conditions appear to be developing among the reporters as Dr. Young continues his briefing. Our medical adviser, however, seeks to soothe our stress. He expects, he says, "to only be treating cuts, bruises, and hangovers."

He cautions us not to kick anything. We might unearth a snake, he warns. Be especially careful at night. Use a flashlight. Snakes like to crawl next to sidewalks, where it's warm. Why bring on excruciating trouble? On the other hand, snakes are usually more afraid of people than people are of snakes, he adds.

Wanna bet?

Riding the Rio Grande . . . .

The wildest of the "wilderness experiences" is the 11-mile, six-hour, 24 rubber raft journey, weaving through Mariscal Canyon, paddling at the breakneck speed of two miles per hour, as we squeeze our way down the narrow, shallow Rio Grande River that separates Mexico and the United States. Two rafts with 150 box lunches containing fried chicken and cold chicken are floating down the waterway ahead of us.

En route, the first lady receives shouted greetings from four Mexican nationals on the Mexican side, who, unbeknownst to Mrs. Johnson, are waiting to smuggle goods across the river to the United States.

Secretary of the Interior Stewart Udall is piloting the raft that includes his wife and Mrs. Johnson. At one point, Lady Bird takes pity on the secretary and commandeers the ship with Mrs. Udall. She enjoys the sense of accomplishment, "just the feeling you have enough strength to paddle ... to get out in the open ... to come to term with things."

I am trying to come to terms with recording this escapade on my tape recorder while preserving Metromedia's expensive equipment from a watery grave. As I am narrating a one-minute broadcast of our adventures into my microphone, my efforts to convey the wildness of our journey are nicely dramatized as our raft collides with another raft, crashes into a canyon wall, and a man goes overboard. All in 60 seconds!

Former journalist Liz Carpenter is so pleased with a raft-load of "wilderness experiences" being captured in a one-minute report that she insists it be played several times for the entire press corps.

As we fly out of Big Bend Country into Lyndon Johnson land — Austin, Texas — Mrs. Johnson tells her explorer entourage that the supreme compliment from a Texan is to be described as "a man who will do to ride the river with." She says to her muscle-sore crew, "You proved you will 'do to ride the river with.'"

Final broadcast from Big Bend . . . .

At the close today of Lady Bird Johnson's conservation/ exploration trek into Big Bend country ... America's so-called last frontier ... her huge press corps began taking a poll as to who had had the greatest "wilderness experience." Originally defined as a communiqué with nature ... it came to include possible injuries from wildlife or wild exertion such as our six-hour, 14-mile bump-and-glide raft ride down the Rio Grande River. We constantly consulted Assistant White House Dr. James Young for reference. He reported minor cuts, bruises, a blister on his own hand, and supreme irony. A magazine writer broke his ankle, falling out of bed, to answer the phone in his hotel room! This Is Peggy Smeeton, reporting for Metromedia Radio.

Spring 1966, Potomac, Maryland . . . .

I am having dinner with a lawyer from the Internal Revenue Service (IRS) at a favorite dining destination for Washingtonians in Potomac, Maryland, the Normandie Farm Restaurant. On the other side of the room, Bill Stanton is sitting across the table from a pretty blonde.

"Peggy," says my lawyer date, "I know you're not going to be serious about me, but isn't there anyone in your life you could be serious about?"

Without looking at the congressman across the room, I smile ambiguously, "Well, possibly."

Probing no further, my generous date extracts a resolution from me.

"Promise me something," he urges, "Just give it a chance."

He is completely unaware that the man to whom I might "give a chance" has just passed by our table. Never breaking his stride, or saying a word, Bill runs a finger across the outside of my dress, from the nape of my neck to the middle of my shoulder.

Shortly after the Normandie Farm encounter, I receive an invitation that affords me the opportunity to "give it a chance."

And I keep my promise to my friend from the IRS.

And what was Bill thinking that night at Normandie Farm? "I knew the woman I was going to marry was in that room and I wasn't with her."

Never trust a reporter

Bill and I are having a late dinner, our date having been delayed by a special White House briefing with President Johnson. I ask Bill what was discussed at the briefing. I am stunned by what he tells me. I can hardly wait for the dinner to end, so I can write a report. I finish typing up the story and broadcast it early the next morning.

The United States has been studying the possibility of building a wall between North and South Vietnam. The study has been under way for 18 months, according to top-level sources. The plan came to light at a secret White House briefing for congressmen last night. The president called 35 legislators from Capitol Hill to the White House to hear their thoughts on the Vietnamese war. All of the men had visited South Vietnam. One of the senators present was Edward Kennedy of Massachusetts. Kennedy reportedly expressed serious reservations about the air strikes near Hanoi and Haiphong and the danger of escalating the war. President Johnson countered by asking the senator what he would do. Kennedy then wanted to know if the administration had considered the possibility of building a wall between North and South Vietnam. The reply was that such a plan had been under study for 18 months and that so far it has been deemed impractical. One big reason: the number of men it would take to police the wall. Top White House spokesmen say the estimates run as high as 2 million men. This is Peggy Smeeton, Metromedia News at the White House.

No sooner has the story aired than phones begin ringing all over Washington. Kennedy's office dutifully denies the contents of a classified briefing. Jim Randolph calls me at the White House. "Are you sure of your report?" he asks me. I call Bill off the floor of the House of Representatives to check my facts.

"Oh, Peggy," he gasps, "you didn't report that on the air!" There is heavy breathing on the other end of the phone.

"Uh, yes I did."

He then informs me the briefing was classified — a fact he had neglected to mention. A fact I should have checked.

Sometime after the dust has settled, Senator Joe Tydings of Maryland, a participant in the briefing, sees Bill and I together at a reception.

"It took me the *longest* time to figure out *how* you got that story!" he laughs.

June 21, 1966 . . . .

"Zepha! Zepha!" Lyndon Johnson's full Texas twang bellows to his housekeeper, Zephyr. "Ah got two ladies outchar, but don't you tell Bird!"

The two ladies "outchar" are legendary UPI White House reporter Helen Thomas and me. "Outchar," or "out here" in more conventional English, is the second floor of the White House where reporters seldom trod. We have been invited there by President Johnson after an unexpected ride in the presidential limousine.

It is apparently a custom for the president to parade a visiting potentate around downtown Washington, giving the guest a brief view of the nation's capital.

At the conclusion of today's event, President Johnson drops King Faisal of Saudi Arabia off at Blair House, the guest residence for state visitors. Helen and I are among the press corps observing the dignitaries. As King Faisal disembarks from the presidential limousine, the president holds up the car's departure. He looks in my direction and nods for me to come to the car.

I look around. He must be beckoning someone else.

The president keeps gesturing in my direction. I still hesitate, and am embarrassed by the attention this is causing, but I finally start to walk over.

Then a Secret Service man calls Helen Thomas. Now I think I have presumptuously misinterpreted the president's intention, and I am even more chagrined. But after Helen gets in the car, LBJ continues to wave to me, and the Secret Service man joins in.

I get in, finally. Now everyone is eyeing the scene. Chief of Protocol Jim Symington waves to us as the limousine pulls away.

The president keeps up a steady conversation as we drive past the crowds, never forgetting the political salute. He urges us to do the same. "Wave to the people," he commands. So we do, mentally conjecturing that the crowds are wondering, who *are* those women? They sure don't look like Luci Baines or Lynda Bird.

President Johnson points out the spot where his pet beagle Him was killed. He says the whole beagle tribe has been fraught with tragedy. He recounts how Lynda Bird came into a congressional meeting with "water in her eyes. I thought Mrs. Johnson had gone down in a crash." He says Lynda tells him she has to help Luci. "Luci cried for three days."

When the limousine pulls onto the White House grounds, we expect our new best friend to bid us goodbye, but no, he invites us up for a sherry in the family living quarters.

We sit on a couch facing the president, and the conversation inevitably turns to the current national agony — the Vietnam War. Speaking of the North Vietnamese, LBJ proclaims, "You got to tell them, you can just go so fur and no further, right, Helen?"

"But, do they believe you, Mr. President?" I interject.

"*They don't think they can win anymore*," he asserts. A startling and therefore very newsworthy revelation, which I cannot wait to broadcast.

Appointments Secretary Marvin Watson walks in with a sheaf of papers for the upcoming cabinet meeting. The president looks over the material. A second visitor — the mayor of Topeka, Kansas — arrives with a portfolio of aerial photographs portraying the devastation visited on his city by a recent tornado.

President Johnson calls Helen and me to join in the look-see, and we are all photographed viewing photographs — photographs autographed by LBJ that the White House later sends to me.

As we are leaving, Assistant Press Secretary Bob Fleming tells Helen and I that our entire visit is "OTR" — *off the record*. This means I cannot report the juicy piece of news that the president of the United States says the North Vietnamese do not think they can win the war. The rule of thumb in press relations is that OTR is to be established *before* a conversation takes place, not *after*. Technically, we have the right to disregard Fleming's admonition. Frustrated though I am to give up such a scoop in memory of the conflagration set off by the Vietnam wall story, I honor it.

When we arrive back at the press room in the White House, the entire press corps applauds our entrance. In memory of King Faisal, Bob Fleming presents us with the Arabian flag.

Two weeks later, President Johnson holds a news conference. The headline from the conference reads: "*President says, 'North Vietnamese don't think they can win anymore.'*"

It reminds me of the old cynical joke, "No good deed goes unpunished."

July 1966 . . . .

I sign a five-year contract with the ABC News network, becoming ABC's first female news correspondent in Washington. Not quite two years after my arrival in the nation's capital, my goal to become a network journalist is realized, thanks to a recommendation by Bill Lawrence, former New York Times reporter, now ABC's White House correspondent, who has observed

*my work covering the White House for Metromedia.
There are so few young women news broadcasters, it's
hard not to be noticed, simply by virtue or "vice" of
gender. "If you can't be the best, be the first" is my motto.
But the ABC contract is facing a collision with
another contract.*

Re-enter Auntie Mame. Pat Sullivan has resigned her job
with NBC, where she knew exactly what she was doing, to buy
and run an old clapboard inn in Rehoboth Beach, Delaware,
where she has no idea what she is doing. That, of course, is
part of the fun.

Rehoboth is a two-and-one-half-hour drive from the
nation's capital and the summer shore, where many Washingtonians love to plant themselves for a cool weekend escape
from D.C.'s 90-degree temperatures. Pat's many friends are
more than happy to offer free labor for free room and board.
My roommate, Carol Owens, and I are two of them. One
weekend, we are assigned the job of decorating the inn. Start-
ing at the top floor with our paint buckets, we brush every
stick of furniture white till we reach bottom.

Our one other contribution is nomenclature. We title the
hotel the "Patrician Inn" after its charismatic innkeeper.

One weekend, Bill Stanton joins the Washington pilgrimage to Rehoboth and rents a room at the Patrician Inn. Spying
he and I having lunch in her bright, white dining room, Pat
observes to "Doc" Law, the current beau, "I think we can get
a wedding out of this."

I am not so sure. Realizing the train is traveling too rapidly down the track, I take a long walk on the beach by myself,
asking myself difficult questions. Marriage to a man 15 years
older than I presents the very likely possibility that I could face
an early and long widowhood. I decide a few years with a man
of Bill's quality would be far more preferable to a long union
with a younger, perhaps lesser man.

The more difficult question revolves around a promise
made to myself based on a quote from Jacqueline Kennedy:

"I think if you bungle raising your children, nothing else you do in life will matter very much." The remark made a deep impression on me, not because of who said it, but because of the wisdom in what was said. Knowing that my competitive nature might inevitably overtake my maternal instincts, were my career occurring simultaneously with motherhood, I realize that when and if I became pregnant, I would have to give up a job as demanding and unpredictable as being a television network news correspondent.

What would I be giving up? After all, even as wife and mother I could write stories for newspapers and magazines on a freelance basis. I could write books, none of which would garner the attention, admiration, and immediate access to power that appearing on nationwide television does.

What I would be giving up is fame and all its attendant perks. Could I walk away from all that?

The answer would come weeks later in the most unlikely of settings.

August 6, 1966: "Well, it's white." . . . .

I am sitting at a tall table on the South Lawn of the White House with one of television's most distinguished anchors, ABC's Frank Reynolds. Cameras and microphones are positioned in front of us. We are about to broadcast an historic social event: the first White House wedding in 50 years.

Luci Baines Johnson's marriage has become the American equivalent of royal weddings in Great Britain. For months since Luci broke the news to the world on Christmas Eve 1965 that, at age 18, she would wed Patrick Nugent, newspapers, magazines, radio, and television news outlets have reported every detail that could be extracted from the East Wing of the White House, the first lady's domain.

When I arrived at ABC for my first week at the network, just six days ago, I was shown a thick notebook of wedding details that are required reading for anyone who will be involved in the live coverage the following Saturday.

"Don't bother with it," I am told. "You won't be covering the wedding. We're sending you up to New York this week." I will be subbing for Marlene Sanders on her midafternoon newscast. And while it will be nerve-racking enough to be performing anchor chores for the first time before a nationwide audience, it will be child's play compared to spontaneously hosting a multi-hour presentation of an historic event from the White House.

So I am greatly relieved that my inaugural week with one of the three major networks will not include such a challenge.

The relief ends on the Thursday before the wedding. I receive a phone call from the Washington bureau. After my final news broadcast on Friday in New York, I am to board a plane back to Washington. I *will* be co-anchoring The Wedding.

Stunning news. I am totally unprepared, and unable to even cram Thursday night in New York. The bulging briefing book is in Washington. I will not be home until Friday evening, the night before the event. I conjecture my news anchoring in New York has, in fact, been an audition for anchoring the wedding.

Not to worry, I am reassured. The notebook will be right there at the anchor table and my co-anchor is unflappable Frank Reynolds, who hosts the ABC nightly newscast.

So, instead of a good night's sleep, I opt to have dinner with Bill Stanton, who has become a very steady presence in my life. Happy to see one another after a whole week's absence, we dine much longer than wisdom dictates.

Bill later relates that he is well aware, as he sits on the floor of his Virginia apartment Saturday morning to watch the wedding, that he has kept me out too late on Friday night; so he is more nervous than I am. In that case, clearly a candidate for a cardiac attack.

There are three network anchor desks set up on the South Lawn. CBS, NBC, and ABC are each vying for the nationwide audience, which, after eight months of nonstop news coverage of the "royal event," is massive. I look over at the NBC desk to see that I am competing against the woman who inspired me in my junior year in college to become a network news correspondent, Nancy Dickerson.

Information on Luci's wedding dress has been more classified than the nuclear codes. Lady Bird's chief of staff and press secretary, Liz Carpenter, delivers the details of "The Dress" to the anchor desks to be shared with our viewers only at the moment Luci emerges from the White House.

Unfortunately, Liz is one "poop sheet" short: mine. Frank does not realize this, so as Luci appears at last, with the nation breathlessly watching and awaiting a lace-by-pearl review of the mystery gown, he says, "Peggy, would you describe Luci's dress?"

From where we are positioned on the South Lawn, Luci is the size of my thumb. "Frank," I whisper, "I can't see her."

"Look at the monitor," he returns the whisper, hopefully low enough that millions of viewers can't hear him. To my dismay, the monitor, which is positioned on the desk to our right, shows a close-up of the beaming bride, rendering Luci only visible from the chin up.

"Well, it's white," is my stunning "scoop." Now Frank realizes we are in trouble, and he is stuck with a rookie. This is my debut before one of the largest audiences any network will ever have, and I have blown it.

Convinced I will be fired, I relax. I figure I might as well enjoy my last day on the air and say whatever comes to mind, as does Frank. Lacking the pertinent information of the moment, we begin to fill what would otherwise be empty air waves with inside White House tales.

When it is all over, I go home, convinced that, despite the just-signed five-year contract, my ABC days are over. The next morning, reviews of the wedding coverage come out in *Variety*, the bible of the news and media world. *Variety* compliments ABC's story swapping and says the best "quip" of the day was "Well, it's white."

A telegram is delivered to my front door. "Good job," it reads. "Elmer Lower, President, ABC News."

Roosevelt Raceway, New York · · · · · · · · · · · · · · · ·

"Don't I know you?" The question comes from a lady I have never seen in my life as we are washing our hands in the ladies' room of Roosevelt Raceway where I have watched one of Bill's horses run.

"I don't think so."

"Well, you sure look familiar to me."

It dawns on me where this stranger may have seen me — in her living room on her television screen. But I keep that insight to myself, and the lady gives up the identity search and departs.

So is this what fame is going to be like? Are the perks worth the pain of no privacy? Is this really what you want?

I had achieved my goal. I was now a network news correspondent, in fact one of the first in the country. Shouldn't I feel euphoric, exuberant, and proud?

Why was I looking in the mirror over the wash basin and asking my image, "*Is this all there is?*"

Labor Day weekend 1966 · · · · · · · · · · · · · · · · · · ·

The wind is howling off black, turbulent waters. Bill and I are buffeting the blows from Lake Erie, standing on the stone deck in front of Bill's parents' Madison, Ohio lakefront home. Having proposed to me at the Jockey Club in Washington, D.C., and having won my approval, Bill has invited me to Madison, Ohio, for parental approval. Apparently, having gotten it, he pulls two brilliant diamond stones from his pocket and tells me to choose which I prefer before he has them placed in a setting. Tempted to choose the larger, but cautioned by conscience, I choose the smaller, which is more than large enough.

Once the ring rests on the third finger of my left hand, official Washington takes delighted note. Bill is one of the rare bachelors to enter the House of Representatives. Most new members arrive with well-established families. When Lady Bird Johnson meets Bill for the first time, she says, "Ah understand you're a bachelor." To which Bill replies, "Yes, ma'am, I am." Whereupon the first lady prophesies, "Not in this town, for long."

The impending wedding of the congressman and the TV correspondent reminds some Washingtonians of another Capitol romance between the bachelor senator from Massachusetts and the inquiring photographer from Virginia.

September 23, 1966

We are on assignment at the LBJ ranch. The president waves me over to the fence. "I understand you are getting married."

"Yes, sir."

"Well, you know you didn't consult me about that."

"No, sir."

"Who is this fella?"

"You know him, Mr. President, Congressman Bill Stanton. You're always holding up our dates with those darn White House briefings."

"Well, bring him around. Let me look him over, before I give my consent."

Sunday morning, we trail the president and the Johnson family plus movie star George Hamilton, Lynda Bird Johnson's current beau, to church. After the service, the president and the Johnson family greet parishioners at the after-service coffee. As I come through the receiving line, he asks, "Where is that man? Did you bring him?"

"No, sir. He's back in Ohio. I won't tell you what he's doing."

The president chuckles. Six weeks away from the midterm elections, he knows exactly what a congressman is doing.

Later, he strolls over to me. "So, he's back there campaigning, eh?"

"Yes, sir. You don't mind me marrying a Republican, do you, Mr. President?"

"I don't approve of that at all."

November 18, 1966 ·

Fifteen days before my wedding, I am part of a small pool of reporters invited to the White House for the celebration of the Johnsons' 32nd wedding anniversary, supposedly a surprise party for Lady Bird.

Mrs. Johnson and Mrs. Humphrey take me aside and tell me I will "love every minute of political life." Mrs. Johnson advises, "Get to know five people in every precinct very well. How many counties are in his district?"

"I don't know," I confess, "but I will learn." Mrs. Johnson laughs at my ignorance.

Mrs. Humphrey asserts, "You'll love it. You like people. He will go far with you, I am sure of it."

Lady Bird adds, "You've been on the other side of the fence. Now you know how we feel."

Mrs. Humphrey relates that when the vice president was the mayor of Minneapolis, he told her to "say nothing." The best wife is the dumb wife.

"Things have changed," she says. "But it's hard to get out of that frame of mind."

LBJ weighs in on the marital discussion. Commenting on the recent elections, he notes that, since I was marrying a GOP congressman, I must've known it "was going to be a Republican year."

It must qualify as unique to receive marital advice from the first and second ladies of the land one night and a federal offender the next. At a reception the following evening, I run into a once lionized, now disgraced Washington celebrity who has recently served 18 months in prison for tax evasion after being embroiled in and the center of a major Capitol Hill scandal.

This man takes me aside to tell me I am about to embark on the greatest experience of my life: marriage. "There's just something about watching a child growing up." His wife, he says, is "more exciting" to him now than when he married her 18 years ago. Was that why, I wonder, he needed a girlfriend?

He married his wife, he continues, because "she was the only good woman I knew." Maybe, he counsels me, "you could have as much or maybe more fame and glory as your husband, but marriage is more meaningful."

Remarkable the wisdom one picks up in prison.

December 3, 1966, Georgetown ....

Washingtonians, Ohioans, and Wisconsinites fill the pews of Epiphany Catholic Church to witness the rare union of media and politics. Auntie Mame's current beau, Doc Law, is assigned to drive me to the Washington Club where I am to dress. I discover I have forgotten to clear the top bureau drawer in the bedroom, so I grab a paper bag in which to empty the remaining undergarments, which then spill out onto P Street as Doc and I are crossing to his car.

The day is not beginning well. But then, there should be no surprise. The courtship has been anything but ripple free. I am assigned to cover LBJ in Texas on the weekend that Bill has planned our engagement party in Washington, and I am forced to ring his office from the side of a Virginia highway to call the festivities off before the invitations go out in the mail. It is an election year and Bill is also wooing his constituents in Ohio. I am assigned to cover the George Wallace campaign in Alabama. En route to catch a plane, I stop at my doctor's to obtain a prescription to ease my aching throat. He sends me to the hospital instead of the airport, diagnosed with mononucleosis and a staph infection. Bill flies in from Ohio to surprise the patient and leaves an hour later to return to campaigning in Ohio.

So why should I expect the wedding to be snafu free? So late do I arrive at the church that Bill's best man, his brother Frank, speculates I might not show up. I am so nervous that my tongue swells and my "I do" is nearly incomprehensible. Bill's close friend, Fr. William McCormack, has come from New York to see us through. Reporters and photographers are recording close-ups, but I do not realize this until I see the two-page spread in Ohio newspapers. How they got shots from the altar past Fr. Bill, I do not know and dare not ask.

As we pull away from the church after the ceremony, I see Ethel Kennedy in the rear-view mirror walking with her two brothers Jim and Rush Skakel; Rush was Bill's college roommate and is a member of the wedding party. The siblings all live in different states, so it is good to see the wedding has provided them a rare and happy get together, unaware that the next reunion will be unbearably sad.

5

AMAZING GRACE

June 6, 1968, Georgetown . . . .

"Peggy! Peggy!" I hear my husband shouting. I am dressing in the bathroom, and he has just tuned in the "Today" show to get the final results of the California primary, a contest between New York senator Robert Kennedy and his Senate colleague from Minnesota, Eugene McCarthy, for the Democratic presidential nomination. Since we know both men, we stay up until 1 a.m. following the returns. We had watched CBS news correspondent Roger Mudd, with whom I had covered stories on Capitol Hill, quiz Bobby. It was, we thought, the best interview Bobby had ever done. A somewhat shy man, for the first time he was relaxed and smiling.

"Peggy! Peggy!" I am puzzled by Bill's urgency at this early hour of the morning. I am totally unprepared for the reality. "Bobby's been shot," Bill shouts when I open the bathroom door.

Not many hours after voter analyses predicted him the winner of the California primary and while awaiting the actual results, Senator Kennedy walked through the kitchen of the Ambassador Hotel where he was staying and was gunned down by Sirhan Sirhan.

From that moment till now, a public vigil has ensued. Few Americans are far from a television or a radio, awaiting every bulletin conveying news of the senator's condition. Reports seem hopeful at first. Doctors who actually know nothing are interviewed. They opine that Kennedy could recover, perhaps within weeks. Finally, a doctor with some valid information, who has talked with one of the operating surgeons, tells the truth. The outcome is likely to be extremely tragic, no matter whether Kennedy lives or dies. From then on, it is only a matter of time.

Monsignor Bill McCormack — the priest who married Bill and me a year and a half ago, a New Yorker and personal friend of Ethel Kennedy — flies cross country to Bobby's bedside in Los Angeles. The senator succumbs at 1:44 a.m. Pacific time.

This can't be happening, I think. The younger brother of the president assassinated four years ago has himself been assassinated. For Bill, it is very personal. Bobby's brother-in-law, Rush Skakel, was Bill's roommate at Georgetown University. He has known Bobby since the days the three of them rode the train together to spend weekend respites from college at the Skakel mansion in Greenwich, Connecticut.

It is personal for me, too. My reportorial interchanges with Bobby on Capitol Hill carry memories of kindnesses from the New York senator to a new young journalist.

There was the evening I had been assigned to try for an interview with him about a late-breaking Vietnam story (a nigh impossible task at the late hour it was assigned). I raced over to the Senate, surprised and elated to find RFK just as he was entering the Senate floor to cast a vote. "Sure," he agreed, but first he needed to vote. As he disappeared behind the Senate doors, I turned to the doorman. "Do you think he will come back out for the interview?"

"I wouldn't count on it," the doorman replied. Doormen know everything.

Time was of the essence for filing a story. If I couldn't get the New York senator whom I was supposed to query, I was determined to have an interview with *some* senator. So as the members of the Senate emerged from their voting in the chamber, I buttonholed each for a comment.

Just as I was questioning elderly Senator George Aiken, my substitute interviewee, Senator Kennedy, strode by, signaling me he was ready. But Senator Aiken, always vocal on Vietnam, was still talking. When the elevator doors opened behind him, I hastily thanked Mr. Aiken, while gently pushing the puzzled man onto the elevator.

Much to my consternation, when I turned around, Bobby had disappeared. How to explain this missed opportunity to my bureau chief?

As I despondently headed for the exit, I heard, "Pssst!" There was the senator in the corner behind a large pillar, sitting on a folding chair with another folding chair situated opposite him that he had arranged for me.

Some encounters were amusing. Over Labor Day weekend in 1965, I was sitting in the office of Senator Joe Tydings, waiting for him to conjure up inspiring Labor Day thoughts for broadcast, when his phone rang. It was Bobby.

"I'm just trying to think up a Labor Day message," said the senator from Maryland to the senator from New York. "Got any ideas?"

Instead of a Labor Day idea, Bobby instructed him to ask me if I would like an interview on a victory won by 26 votes.

"No," Tydings responded, without consulting me, "that doesn't seem to grab her."

I had been assigned to collect Labor Day messages, so I continued my mission. Next stop: Kennedy's office. He threw me a beseeching look. "I really don't have anything to say." A Democrat acknowledging he lacked a fond message for a core constituency was quite an admission. We settled for an interview on an urban center in New York.

The same kind of candor was evident at a swimming party/luncheon he and his wife, Ethel, gave at Hickory Hill, their McLean, Virginia home, for a few members of the press. Since I had assignments to cover after the luncheon, I did not join in the swimming. I merely sat dangling my feet in the pool as I listened to Kennedy talking with other swimmers concerning the masses of articles written about his assassinated brother, JFK. He did not know that one of the former president's secretaries was writing a book until "three weeks ago." The name of the book was *My Twelve Years with John F. Kennedy* by Evelyn Lincoln.

"I asked her if I could see it. She said yes, but I didn't see it until a few days before the *Post* came out ... there were parts of it I didn't care for … but I suppose lots of books will be written." Then he asked me. "How did you like it?"

"I didn't," I replied. I thought it bridged the privacy an employer should expect from an employee.

Then he startled me with this question: "Do you find it an advantage being a woman?

That required some thinking. Did he mean personally or professionally? Now I was the person without an answer.

Ethel Kennedy was equally candid. We shared the dressing room, and we spotted a head of hair lying on a chair. Ethel eyed it appreciatively. "I hardly ever wear my own hair anymore," she confessed. Wigs had become extremely popular with political wives who had to travel extensively *sans* hairdresser. "My sisters-in-law see me practically every day, and they can't tell the difference."

All these remembered exchanges leave me greatly saddened as we await what is very likely to be tragic news.

6:15 a.m. EST, Thursday, June 6, is when we learn Bobby has died. I am making coffee for Bill, who is leaving for the airport. He'll be catching a 7:15 a.m. plane to Ohio to attend to duties in his congressional district. As he heads out the door, he says, "I'll probably be back." When he reaches Ohio, he phones to say we will be leaving for New York tonight. The funeral will be at St. Patrick's Cathedral, Saturday morning. The body will lie in state in the cathedral all day Friday.

Upon arriving in New York, we check into the St. Moritz Hotel on Central Park South. It is after 11 p.m. We walk down to St. Patrick's to pay our respects. The line of people is six abreast. It extends all the way to Penn Station. Bill introduces himself to a policeman, who stops the line and clears the way for us to enter the church. A constantly changing group of six men keep vigil beside Senator Kennedy's casket. Bill stands his turn. At 3:15 p.m. Friday, Bill leaves again for Ohio to deliver a commencement address at Lake Erie College. He plans to be back in New York by 1 a.m.

I walk down Fifth Avenue, inevitably drawn back to St. Patrick's. The lines are still thick and long. Across the street from the cathedral, onlookers watch the mourners move up and down the cathedral steps. I eat in Rockefeller Plaza and walk back to the St. Moritz, the hotel I had chosen to stay whenever ABC called me from my Washington base to broadcast in New York.

Father Bill calls. He says Ethel Kennedy is "remarkable," but he is afraid she might fall apart later. "No," he amends the thought, "maybe not." Just a year and a half earlier, Fr. Bill had been on another journey, bringing back the body of Ethel's brother George Skakel, killed in a private plane crash. Ethel Kennedy has now experienced the sudden deaths of two parents, a brother, a brother-in-law, and a husband.

At age 29, I cannot fathom how a person survives so much tragedy. But Ethel is a woman of fierce faith, and I will witness the astonishing strength such faith brings in the next sorrowful days.

I finish the conversation with Fr. Bill, and the phone rings again. It is Senator Kennedy's office, checking to see whether we have received our invitation to the funeral yet. We have not, I answer. The secretary asks if I will come down to 38th and Madison Avenue to Kennedy headquarters to pick up a replacement ticket. I set out from the St. Moritz, at 59th and Central Park South. At the headquarters, a young man greets me and says he is sorry, but the tickets haven't arrived yet. Would I please come back in an hour?

I have little choice. I do not want Bill going after the tickets at 2 a.m. when he returns from Ohio, which he will do if I don't. At 10:45 p.m., I get in another taxi and head back to 38th and Madison. The tickets are still not available.

I walk across the street to where a hospitality suite has been set up. A distant Kennedy family relative, also awaiting her ticket, joins me. The room is full of expectant confusion, and as the night wears on, it begins to look more and more like a Washington "Who's Who," including famed broadcasters, *Washington Post* columnists, congressmen, and Kennedy satellites. Many of the Kennedy entourage from John Kennedy's administration have reassembled for his brother's funeral.

There is a great deal of hugging and kissing — it feels more like old home week than a funeral gathering. Many most likely feel numb after experiencing the second assassination of a Kennedy. For instance, Hugh McConnell, a close friend of Jack Kennedy, was on the plane bringing Bobby's body back East. I had met him the night before with Bill. Tonight, as he orchestrated my entrance into Kennedy headquarters, he exclaimed about Bill, "What a man! What a man!" One hour later, he looks through me rather than at me.

A former JFK aide introduces himself. In our conversation, he alternates between elation at seeing old friends and incantations of "It's terrible. It's terrible." He says he has been up for three days, unable to sleep since learning of the shooting. While campaigning for JFK, he worked closely with RFK, remembering John Kennedy as a cooler, more reserved personality and Robert Kennedy as a man of passion and compassion.

At last, the tickets arrive. It is after midnight, and now there are no cabs. My new best friend and I walk the 25 blocks from 38th and Madison to 59th and Central Park South, passing St. Patrick's Cathedral once again.

Bill returns from Ohio shortly after I reach the hotel. It is 2 a.m., and he is hungry. We search for a sandwich, only to discover that the "city that never sleeps" actually does.

Saturday, the morning of the funeral, burns bright and hot. We are having breakfast in our hotel room. When we switch on the television, we are shocked to discover many dignitaries are already in St. Patrick's or ascending the steps. We are sitting just blocks from the cathedral in our pajamas, in danger of not getting a seat despite last night's ordeal.

When we hail a cab, the driver advises us to walk, saying it would take him too long to wend his way through all the traffic. We take his advice. As we make our way into the cathedral, the watching throngs eye us as they do all funeral-goers, peering to see if we're famous. We take secret delight that we are not.

Saint Patrick's is nearly filled. Again we run into Hugh McConnell, and we are directed to the "congressional quarters." Bill rubs his nose to indicate that the "Schnoz," comedian Jimmy Durante, is sitting in front of us.

Evangelist Billy Graham is next to him. Directly across from us are many of Bobby Kennedy's Senate colleagues, including the man he defeated in the California primary, Eugene McCarthy. He is sitting next to Senator Barry Goldwater, who would have been John Kennedy's opponent in 1964 had the president not been assassinated. Indiana Senator Birch Bayh and his wife, Marvella, are positioned beneath a TV platform, trying to make all the proper liturgical moves from a crouched stance.

Ted Kennedy's eulogy moves some to tears, particularly when Kennedy himself is so moved. The cynical think it sounds like a campaign speech. There is no cynicism possible, however, when Bobby Kennedy's children process to the altar, bearing the gifts.

At the conclusion of the Mass, singer Andy Williams leads the congregation in singing the "Battle Hymn of the Republic," our voices carrying out to the streets and the ears of the onlookers lining Fifth Avenue. As we, along with Susie and Tom Reynolds (in-laws of Ethel Kennedy's brother Rush) are some of the first to leave the cathedral, we watch as a remarkable parade of famous faces pours down the steps of St. Patrick's. A reporter comes up to me and whispers that Martin Luther King's assassin has been captured. Simultaneously, we can see that Ralph Abernathy, King's successor, dressed in blue jeans, is receiving the same message.

A train with close family and friends will carry the slain senator's body back to Washington, where he will be buried near his brother in Arlington National Cemetery. The Reynolds will ride the train, an exhausting, hot, and extremely emotional journey past waiting crowds all along the route. We tell the Reynolds we will fly back and see them at the cemetery.

We walk back to the St. Moritz in the middle of Fifth Avenue. It feels peculiarly like a pageant. Traffic is blocked off. The sidewalks are brimming with sightseers, so we funeral trekkers have the whole street to ourselves. We have a meal at the Cafe de la Paix in the St. Moritz. FBI head J. Edgar Hoover is lunching with Jimmy Durante. They and we very nearly comprise the entire dinner crowd.

When we return to Washington, we drive with Undersecretary of the Army David McGiffert and his wife, Enid, our friends and neighbors, in his chauffeured limousine to Arlington National Cemetery. Services are scheduled for 5 o'clock, but the train has been delayed four hours. As dusk drops over us, we are given candles, their flickering lights lending an evocative glow to an already emotional scene. There is no choice but to wait.

Finally, we see figures moving slowly up the hill. The train riders have at last arrived. It is 10 hours since we left Tom and Susie Reynolds on the sidewalks of New York. Tom, a Chicago lawyer and a big bear of an Irishman, spots us and twists his face into the loudest silent groan I have ever witnessed, an expression that describes this hazard-ridden, humid trip better than any newspaper story ever will.

Ethel Kennedy, on the other hand, dressed in black and under a black veil, looks remarkably attractive and composed. Jackie Kennedy is stunning in a black dress and black mantilla; Joan Kennedy is equally stunning with a deep tan and long blond hair.

The ceremony is very brief. Ethel's brother and Bill's close friend Rush Skakel stands directly in front of us with his wife, Ann; it's the first time we have seen them through the entire event. Rush asks us to come back to Hickory Hill with he and Ann. We feel we should not. We are not family or close friends, but Rush insists. On the ride to the Kennedy home, Rush says his sister has done beautifully, but notices that after her walk through the entire train greeting fellow travelers, she is on the verge of collapse.

At Hickory Hill, however, Ethel presides with great grace. She sits in a corner, receiving guests without a tear. There are people and food aplenty. Pat, Jean, and Eunice Kennedy sit chatting with former movie queen Lauren Bacall. Astronaut John Glenn comments on being a weary pallbearer.

Robert McNamara sits in a corner with singer Andy Williams. Kennedys and Kennedy satellites dominate the upper half of the patio. Ethel's family, the Skakels, cover the lower half.

The horrible truth of the shooting begins to sink in as I view this surreal scene in front of me. With swelling sadness, I realize I will never ask a question of Bobby Kennedy again. The Kennedy sisters are outwardly able to carry on as if nothing has happened, but Ted Kennedy's usual ebullience is clearly missing.

We stay just a short time. As we are leaving, Bill steers me toward Ethel. He (who has experienced the loss of four young siblings) whispers a strange condolence to her, "Sock it to 'em," and gives her a thumbs up sign. I, who have never undergone such losses, know no such codes. I feel very bereft of comforting words, but Ethel's warmth ends that. She embraces me with a kiss. "I'm praying for you," is all I can manage. "Oh, thank you," she responds. Ethel's brother Jim comes home to stay the night with us. He talks about the senator as if he is alive: "I was telling Bobby the last time I saw him ... ."

The following day, we are invited to Hickory Hill for lunch. Lunch? Ethel Kennedy has not endured enough yet? She is going to host a lunch?

Of all the experiences I've had covering the White House and Capitol Hill, no sights have been more amazing. The lawn is a human zoo. There are bodies in every nook and niche and most of them seem to be on telephones. On some tables, there are two telephones side by side. Every phone has numerous extensions. The house sits atop a rolling hill; the pool, made famous by folk taking a swim fully clothed, rests at the bottom of the hill. The bath house is decorated in bright, joyful colors, as is the main house. Everywhere, there are pictures of "Camelot." The piano is covered with silver framed snapshots of Kennedys. The bathhouse, too, is walled with pictures and articles of the RFKs. We head to the bathhouse where the formally dressed notables of yesterday are now comfortably ensconced around the pool in swimsuits, including astronaut

John Glenn and decathlon champion Rafer Johnson. Mountain climber Jim Whittaker is dressed more for scaling a peak than embracing a wave.

Ethel is remarkable. Her ebullient personality, so typical of the Skakel family, shines. She treats the luncheon as if it were just one of the many she threw when her husband was alive, as if he were just away on a campaign trip.

There are children everywhere, all sizes and ages. A touch football game is in progress at one end of the lawn. The pool is crowded, and feet are flying off the trampoline. Ethel is feeding her youngest child. Finally, at 3 p.m., food begins to appear. "Wouldn't Bobby have a fit?" Ethel remarks about the late arrival of bowls of soup, mounds of fried chicken, and a diversity of desserts. "Lunch was 12:30 on the dot!"

It's almost 4:30 p.m. before we leave. Ethel is on the phone talking to Cardinal Cushing of Boston. "Oh, Your Eminence, your voice was so strong and clear!"

John Glenn, Bill, and I become the transportation service to the airport for out-of-town guests. Ethel wonders if she shouldn't drive, too. We assure her we can handle the crowd. She takes her sister Pat, who lives in Ireland, upstairs for a last chat. After 10 minutes, they return, and as we leave, Ethel again gives me a kiss on the cheek, as if I were the one who had sustained the loss she has endured. It is difficult to wrap one's mind around the courage it takes to host an affair like this afternoon after so much tragedy.

Her close friends attribute it to her deep faith. She believes Bobby has gone to God, where we all are supposed to be headed. No doubt she comforts herself that she will see her lost love again in a land of no assassinations.

It is a lesson a young wife will carry into the future when she faces the loss of her own husband.

6

A SUMMER OF SADNESS

In the third quarter of the 20th century, Americans had no conception of a president being forcibly removed from office. It had not happened in more than 100 years, not since Andrew Johnson was impeached in 1868. Thus, during the summer of 1974, when that possibility hung over the Nixon White House, a surreal smog of anxiety, suspense, and tragedy suffused the nation's capital and its inhabitants. What made it more personal for the Stantons was the fact that Bill Stanton, as a Member of Congress, would ultimately have the responsibility to cast a vote of yay or nay if impeachment reached the House of Representatives.

July-August 1974

We are in a state of suspended animation waiting for President Richard Nixon to decide between two unattractive options: resign or be impeached.

All through the summer, tensions have been building as the impeachment process has been inexorably moving forward. The sentiments of the legislators and the public have ebbed and flowed like the waves on Lake Erie.

The first bombshell dropped a year ago last summer when a young man named John Dean, former counsel to the president, pointed an accusing finger at the president. He and he alone claimed that Richard Nixon participated in the attempt to cover up the Watergate break-in. Not another presidential aide stepped forward to confirm Dean's testimony, but the suspicions and the evidence began to mount.

The next bombshell exploded again in testimony before the Senate Watergate Committee when another former White

House aide, Alex Butterfield, inadvertently revealed that the president taped every conversation in the White House.

Including conversations with John Dean.

At last came the cry, "Now we will know the truth!" Not so fast. President Nixon, claiming executive privilege, refused to release the tapes. This served only to fuel suspicions. If the president were innocent, he should be happy to turn over the tapes.

Each new revelation fires the environs of D.C. until exhaustion or boredom sets in, and then the appearance of normality resumes. Court battles ensue; the president consistently loses. The fusillade that rocks the republic comes to be known as the "Saturday Night Massacre." Special Prosecutor Archibald Cox is fired when he subpoenas the tapes. Attorney General Elliott Richardson refuses to carry out the firing order, so the president fires Richardson and asks the next in line, Bill Ruckelshaus, to fire Cox. Ruckelshaus also refuses and then resigns. Even for the nation's capital, it is an astonishing weekend.

The Saturday Night Massacre bursts the dam. The public becomes furious. Washington is flooded with telegrams, telephone calls, and letters berating the president. "Impeach him" is the cry. From that moment, impeachment becomes a serious possibility. Still, the thinking persists, it cannot happen.

Then the president is forced by court order to turn over 40 tapes on Watergate and he chooses to release them to the public. A new storm sweeps the airwaves. The president claims the tapes will exonerate him. In fact, they accomplish the opposite. The pulse for impeachment quickens. But the House Judiciary Committee grinds on so slowly that patience wanes, tempers fray, and the mercurial Congress swings back toward the president!

To comprehend this strange fluctuation, one has to understand the pain of impeachment. Very few men want to pass public judgment on another man, particularly the president of the United States. They also genuinely fear the damage impeachment will do to America.

So in mid-July, the atmosphere toward impeachment cools again, and folk are predicting it will never happen. And then the judiciary committee turns up the temperature by opening their seven-month inquiry to television and the public.

Overnight the mood shifts again. The committee members conduct themselves like statesmen with a minimum of barroom wrangling so typical of legislative overhauling. The TV audience view men agonizing over a decision they do not want to make. The viewers discover men they had never heard of, and many times they like what they discover. I attend one of the hearings. The committee room is small, so there is none of the circus atmosphere that prevailed during the Watergate hearings. There is an element of dignity and decorum. The drama begins with the first vote on Article 1 of the impeachment resolution. Each vote is cast with solemnity, as if it is being cast in stone. There is genuine pain registered on the face of the committee members.

When seven out of 17 Republican members vote to impeach, the psychological effect on the president's case in the full House is devastating. Ten Republicans stay with the president. They are led by the very bright Chuck Wiggins, who speaks in slow, deliberate, and legalistic tones. He insists that the evidence, "the smoking gun," is needed to convict the president. Circumstantial evidence will not do.

Wiggins is vociferously backed up by New Jersey Republican Charles Sandman and David Dennis of Indiana, and somewhat sardonically by Del Latta of Ohio. Though they lose badly in committee, Wiggins strives to win on the House floor. He is meeting with all congressmen who will talk to him, trying to persuade them to his point of view. But the view now is that Nixon's impeachment is a foregone conclusion.

It is looking like an agonizing autumn. The impeachment debate in the House is scheduled to begin August 19 and last for 10 days. The trial in the Senate will commence in September and could last six months. A long, rocky road is stretching before the country.

Bill vows to read all the thousands of pages of testimony and listen to the tapes before making a decision. He begins staying up late and leaving the house between 6 and 6:30 a.m. just to afford reading time.

Then the Supreme Court rules against the president, stating he must turn over 64 additional tapes to the special prosecutor. The president had insisted that the previously released tapes told the whole Watergate story.

But they had not.

The nail that seals the coffin of Richard Nixon's presidency comes on August 5, 1974, when the tapes he turns over to the special prosecutor become public. The "smoking gun" is dated June 23, 1972. It destroys the president's assertion that he knew nothing of the cover-up until March 21, 1973, when he said John Dean told him about it. The June 23 tape reveals the fact that Nixon not only knew about the cover-up, he participated in it only six days after the Watergate break-in when he tried to get the FBI to cease its investigation of the break-in.

Headlines around the world scream, "Nixon Confesses." His ardent defenders are devastated. Chuck Wiggins chokes out his decision to vote for impeachment on national television. Every member of the judiciary committee, Democrat or Republican, joins that vote. The final tally is 38-0.

The floodgates open. Congressman after congressman announces their support for impeachment. Except Bill Stanton. Though he has no choice, he refuses to make his vote public until he reads all the evidence as he had promised. And he intends to keep that promise.

August 8, 1974 . . . .

The nation's capital is holding its breath. Every radio has been on for three days. Since the release and revelation of the now infamous June 23 tape, all the Republican leaders have been urging the president to resign. As there is no one left in either the House or the Senate to defend him, a trial seems useless.

In a phone conversation this afternoon with Betty Rhodes, the wife of House Minority Leader John Rhodes, I learn that General Al Haig was brokenhearted, as was George H.W. Bush. They had all been at the Rhodes' home on Sunday night. These men who had believed the president were crushed. They felt betrayed. Betty said her husband's announcement was very painful to make.

"I keep thinking," Betty says, "of the practical things. Like how will he leave?" In a lame attempt to lighten a dark moment, I suggest that maybe this will be the first time the horse "Black Jack" will have a rider. Betty says her husband John, Barry Goldwater, and Senator Hugh Scott had a very difficult meeting with the president at the White House, but the president managed to joke. "How many votes do I have in the House," he wanted to know, "10?"

Tonight, the president is scheduled to speak to the American people. It is expected he will announce his resignation. There is, as yet, however, no public confirmation. Then the phone rings. It is Bill. The president will resign, he says. Vice President Jerry Ford will be sworn in at noon tomorrow. Bill relates that the mood in the House of Representatives is "pensive and sad." That is the key word — sad. Everyone, lover or hater of Richard Nixon, feels sad. It is like losing a father, albeit an errant one.

This morning, shortly before noon, my neighbor and good friend, Molly Tully, and her son, John, and I drive down past the White House. As we are nearing the gates, the radio is airing the White House press secretary's announcement that President Nixon will go on television at 9 o'clock tonight and that he is meeting at this moment with Vice President Ford. It is a strange sensation to be looking at the mansion and realize that history is happening within its walls.

Hundreds of ordinary citizens are gathered on the sidewalk outside of the White House, walking, standing, and staring. It's like a death watch.

What emotional tumult must be churning within Jerry Ford as he prepares to take the reins of government out of the hands of his old friend of 25 years, the man who had raised him from congressman to vice president?

Just a month and a half ago, when as vice president he was a dinner guest at our house, I asked him, "Did you ever think two years ago that you might be in the White House?"

"I never dreamed of it," he answered. "As you well know, Peggy, all I ever wanted to be was speaker of the House of Representatives."

August 9, 1974 . . . .

It is finally over. One awakens with an acute sense of depression. The president's televised resignation speech was vintage Nixon. It moved me not at all and I had been prepared to be moved. This morning, however, sorrow washes over anew. "I feel drained," Bill comments as he gets up.

On national television at 9:30 a.m., President Nixon prepares to say farewell to his cabinet and his White House staff. He enters the room smiling. Pat Nixon smiles. Julie Nixon Eisenhower, who publicly defended her father, is strangely composed. As the crowd applauds him, it seems, the veil parts and the humanity we had been denied so long becomes visible.

Richard Nixon stands alone, his advisers who had helped to destroy him gone from his side; their scenarios and plastic images have vanished. Here at last, perspiring and tear-stained, is the real Richard Nixon.

He begins badly with a swipe at the press, but he becomes quite moving as he speaks of the dedication of the people who worked for him. They had made mistakes, he concedes, but they had never made them for financial gain. He reminisces about his father, saying "They would have called him sort of a little man, common man. … But he was a great man, because he did his job." He turns to his mother and her difficult life. "She will have no books written about her. But she was a saint," he chokes, as tears glisten on his eyelids.

Then he reads a passage from the diary of Theodore Roosevelt about Roosevelt's young wife, who died before life's treachery could scar her. This quote stands in contrast to the quote Nixon read the night before in his resignation speech, also from Roosevelt, about "the man in the arena whose face is marred by dust, sweat, and blood" and who "if he fails, at least fails while daring greatly."

As these words emerge, he almost breaks down completely. Pat Nixon's lovely, stoic countenance quivers slightly, as though she fears he might not make it. But he does.

Interestingly, he dons glasses to read that passage. The American public has never seen him wear glasses. He is done with masks apparently, at least this morning. One feels as we felt with Lyndon Johnson; if only we had seen the human side of him before. Both men appear to have been so insecure in their personalities that they had manufactured what they apparently deemed was an acceptable façade, and it didn't work. It ultimately played a role in their dissolution.

The television cameras zoom in on some of the stricken faces of Nixon staff. Henry Kissinger resembles a sad hound dog; Nancy Kissinger shows no emotion. The most poignant face belongs to beautiful Mimi Timmons, her delicate features tilted toward Bill Timmons, her distraught husband.

Out on the South Lawn of the White House, a helicopter awaits to take the Nixons to Andrews Air Force Base. A large crowd stands at attention to say farewell. President and Mrs. Nixon are greeted by longtime friends Vice President and Mrs. Ford. Jerry Ford and President Nixon flank Pat Nixon, Tricia Nixon, and Betty Ford. Jerry has his arm around Betty, whose arm encircles Pat Nixon who has her arm around Tricia. Richard Nixon has his arm around no one — ever the loner. He waves and smiles broadly at the onlookers. The most striking final picture of the disgraced president is the sight of him, arms folded, looking out the helicopter window for a final view of the White House. Then the propellers whirl the helicopter into the sky, and he is gone.

Jerry Ford's face is controlled but agonized as he stands on the lawn and watches his tragic friend depart. The moment is almost too difficult to absorb. Scarcely two hours later, in the very same East Room, with much of the same crowd, Gerald Ford becomes the 38th president of the United States. Betty Ford, in an ice-blue suit, trimmed in white piping, looks remote and serene, but sad. Jerry's face, which is usually wreathed in smiles, is extremely solemn.

His speech is simple eloquence. He addresses the sorrow of the moment. He wants, he says, to talk some straight talk to the American people, his friends. He is, he realizes, the first American president not to have been chosen by the electorate, and while that was a disadvantage, the plus side of the ledger meant that he was indebted to no man and to only one woman: his "dear wife." He then goes on to say:

> My fellow Americans, our long national nightmare is over. Our Constitution works; our great Republic is a government of laws and not of men. Here the people rule. But there is a higher Power, by whatever name we honor Him, who ordains not only righteousness but love, not only justice but mercy. As we bind up the internal wounds of Watergate, more painful and more poisonous than those of foreign wars, let us restore the golden rule to our political process, and let brotherly love purge our hearts of suspicion and of hate. In the beginning, I asked you to pray for me. Before closing, I ask again your prayers, for Richard Nixon and for his family. May our former President, who brought peace to millions, find it for himself.

He touched all the chords with just the right notes.

It is difficult to describe the divergence of emotions coursing through the hearts of Americans today. Betrayal, sorrow, disappointment — and in the deepest recesses of our soul — guilt. Did we drive a man from office unjustly? No. The events unfolded as dictated, the tragic web woven by the victim. The demise of a president, however, is such a painful sight to view that we may weep in memory of it.

Richard Milhous Nixon was a Shakespearean study in the leader with the tragic flaw; I believe Nixon's was his insecurity. Perhaps he didn't like himself, which made it difficult to like and trust others. He couldn't confess his aides' implication in Watergate because he was afraid he would be rejected by the electorate. That insecurity led to the destruction of his presidency.

August 13, 1974: A short honeymoon . . . .

I am surprised by a call from the new first lady. Would I help her plan the congressional guest list for Friday night's state dinner for the King and Queen of Jordan? The task had literally been dumped in her lap by the departure of the previous president and first lady.

Since the royal duo were young and very attractive, Betty wanted the same kind of people from the Congress there to greet them. She wanted the swinging set from both sides of the aisle to come for dancing after the dinner. Unfortunately, the dinner guests had already been invited, so the swingers would have to find their own dining fare. Betty says she will need the list by 10 a.m. tomorrow morning! Since I am departing for a dinner party, it is going to be a sleep-deprived night, but I promise Betty a list by the deadline.

"Do you care if they are older?" I ask.

"No, as long as they are fun."

"Do you care about their philosophical leanings?" I inquire, her husband being a conservative Republican.

"No. Don't worry about that."

So we settle on the criteria: "Bipartisan, young and attractive, or old and charming."

The more glamorous criteria also provide a golden window to a stunning view of a new national unity. With the first lady's approbation, I include Democrats, liberal Republicans, and even, unknowingly, a Republican who voted against Jerry's nomination for vice president! — an unforgivable *faux pas* for which my ignorance of that vote was to blame. Nixon staffers ascended through the roof or descended to the floor in a dead faint when they viewed what became known as "the list."

Since the "swingers" were not included in the dinner, Bill and I arrange to dine at the Sans Souci, a popular restaurant down the street from the White House, with good friends: two Democratic congressmen and their wives and a liberal Republican senator and spouse.

As everyone speculates over the asparagus as to who could have put together such a politically diverse (and dangerous) list, and how they, themselves, could have been invited, I guard my anonymity in the proceedings. It is important that they believe it was the Fords who desired their presence, not merely their friend Peggy. Most at the table had not been invited to the White House in more than five years.

Upon arrival at the White House, the "list" is again the topic of conversation. "Who was the genius who did the list?" Helen Smith, wife of congressman Henry Smith of New York, wants to know. My ego is itching to claim credit, but my guardian angel clamps his wing over my mouth.

"Look at this magnificent crowd," exults Ohio Democrat Lud Ashley. "There are no enemies here!"

Another Ohioan, John Seiberling, who had cast the dissenting vote against Ford's nomination for vice president, expresses regret he had voted thus. He feared the former House minority leader would be too partisan. But, he says, he is changing his mind "because of Jerry's actions as president. ... Tonight [he] shows he really wants to have an open administration. Last week, we ended the Watergate. Tonight we ended the war."

Not quite. In another giant mistake, I included a Republican who had changed his stripes and become a Democrat. Nancy Howe, the president's assistant, says our main job tonight was to keep the turncoat away from President Ford, who explodes, "That sounds just like Peggy Stanton," when he hears I am the one responsible for the gentleman's inclusion in the evening.

Oh, my, I thought, the turncoat isn't the only one who better stay out of the president's way.

That is not possible when he asks me to dance. Anticipating a dressing down, I launch my defense.

"Mr. President, I understand I am in the doghouse." He laughs. "Oh, Peggy, I was just tired when I said that."

I tell him Betty's criteria, among which was attractive wives. The one-time Republican's wife is a stunning example. "On that basis, I agree," Ford smiles.

On a more pragmatic perspective, I add, "Your predecessor had no one but pals here and look where that got him."

"I know. I know," the president agrees.

"But you are wondering what your pals in the cloakroom are thinking."

"That's right! Oh, well, we will have more of these."

I repeat John Seiberling's statement to him.

"OK. OK. You're smarter than I am."

The music ends and President Ford invites me to sit down at his table with the King and Queen of Jordan. I demur. After my exchange with the commander in chief, I am not feeling up to sparring with royalty. "Oh, come on," he insists, when to my relief, Bill arrives with Betty Ford. The president continues to be magnanimous, inviting both of us to join the table. We bow out gracefully. Despite his graciousness, I feel sure the less the president sees of me, tonight, the better.

Whatever Jerry Ford thought of the list, the guests more than adequately fulfill Betty Ford's requirements. Swing they do. There are rock-and-roll dances. There are Charlestons. There is even a Mexican Hat Dance, which is the more bizarre sight of the evening: several large circles of high government officials holding hands and raising their feet. "I've never seen so much 'joy' in the White House," marvels the dignified, famed CBS correspondent Eric Sevareid. I urge him to join the dancers, which he does with delight! America's leaders are letting off bipartisan steam after a summer of collective tension, like a room full of high school graduates at the senior prom.

"Happy New Year!" Senator Mark Hatfield calls to a reporter as we depart the White House.

Two years later, at the annual White House Christmas party for Members of Congress — the Fords final *soirée* before turning the keys over to Jimmy and Rosalynn Carter — Betty takes me aside with a twinkle of triumph in her eye. "Jerry said the best party we ever had was the first party."

7

HELLO, "DALLY"

During congressional recesses, Members of Congress sometimes used the opportunity to better acquaint themselves with issues and political figures across the sea. Spouses were permitted, if there was room on the plane, to accompany the members on the trip. In 1976, the journey provided us the occasion to step outside of the political arena into the unexpected, fascinating, humorous, and somewhat bizarre world of a famous figure from the field of the arts.

"There goes Salvador Dali!" I exclaim to my dinner companions at La Tour d'Argent in Paris. My eyes are following a large entourage that sweeps through the front of the restaurant to a choice table overlooking a spectacular view of Notre Dame Cathedral.

"How do you know?" My husband is doubtful. "You only saw the back of his head."

"From that view, I can see a mustache curling out of the side of his face. That has to be Dali," I insist.

The man in question sits with his back to the rest of the diners, so the controversy does not abate until it is noticed that the entire restaurant staff is ringing his table like courtiers, fussing over napkins, passing out menus, and taking drink orders. Some just stand there.

"Well if it isn't Dali," says Representative Gilbert Gude of Maryland, "then it's *someone*! There's a waiter for every person at the table."

It is 1976, and we are in Paris for interparliamentary legislative sessions on European Common Market problems. After a full day of meetings and a reception, our group decides to deplete our pocketbooks with a trip to one of Paris' most famous restaurants, renowned for its duck entrées, each duck numbered for culinary posterity.

"Let's send a note to the table and offer to buy Dali a drink," suggests Congressman Robert Stephens, a portly, white-haired Democrat from Georgia with a wry sense of humor and a rural appearance that belies a scholarly brain, put to the bench during the Nazi trials in Nuremberg.

"Oh, Bob! Don't be bush-league." The women are aghast. The waiter is not encouraging either. "The master," he warns," can be difficult."

Stephens is not intimidated. He scribbles something on the back of his card and the waiter reluctantly takes it to "Dally" — which is how the master's surname rolls off Stephens' Southern tongue.

Our group watches discreetly as Dali reads the note. Then he, along with his entire assembly, turns around and surveys our table.

The waiter returns with a phone number on the back of a piece of paper. "He says," reports the waiter turned courier, "to call him at this number tomorrow. Not before 11."

Stephens is assured by his companions that he has been given the brush-off. And he deserves it. "Well, I'll bet you," he drawls, "that the number is real. Else why would Dally say 'not before 11'?"

A fair point, we had to agree. The next morning, however, the congressmen are off early to meetings. By lunchtime, they have thought better of the evening's mischief. So have the women.

Grace Stephens had extracted the card with the phone number on it from her husband's pocket and taken it down to the control room. The control room is run by the embassy staff in order to see to it that the congressmen and their wives get to their appointed rounds at the appointed hour.

"Let Maria call," says Pia Anderson, a tall, authoritative Swedish woman. "Maria is very good at this sort of thing."

Indeed. Maria — no one ever learned her last name — was a short, hefty, arrogant Parisian, and a passionate fan of

Dali's paintings. She could hardly wait to get her fingers in the dial. To everyone's surprise, the number belongs to a phone in Dali's suite at the plush Le Meurice hotel, just down the street from the congressional party's much humbler quarters, the Hotel Regina.

The master himself comes to the phone. Twenty minutes of conversation follows. Would the congressmen be in town on Sunday? They would not. That was too bad. Twenty dancers were coming to perform for him in his suite on Sunday. A nice surprise for the congressmen, Dali thought.

How about joining him for cocktails tomorrow at 12:30 p.m. in room 108 of Le Meurice? Maria says she will check with the representatives. Then Dali was concerned. "I want you to explain to them that I am not as bizarre as I am pictured."

"Ohh," coos Maria, "it is your mystery that the ladies like. I am not going to tell them that." Maria has a new friend. Dali insists she must come, too. "Oh, no," she demurs, "I am no one important. I am just a member of the embassy staff."

"You must come," insists the great artist. "You must help translate."

Maria does more than help translate. Early in the morning she has her hair done. She wears a full-skirted organza dress and orders long-stemmed lilies, because Dali's secretary told her he likes them. She has one for each woman to present. She instructs the delegation to be in the Meurice hotel lobby at precisely 12:30 p.m. so that we can all proceed to room 108 as an orderly group.

The following morning, Maria runs a hotline between the Regina and the Meurice. Mid-morning, Dali calls to push our arrival back 15 minutes. Then Congressman Gil Gude appears in the control room requesting admittance to the party. After all, the Gudes, too, had been at the table last evening. In the excitement, they have been forgotten. Maria calls room 108 to negotiate two more visitors.

Two more is too many, Dali balks. He doesn't like crowds. She is sorry, Maria apologizes, but she had not known the Gudes were at the table. "Well, all right," Dali finally concedes, "if they are your friends, let them come."

Jane Gude, unaware of the struggle to get herself into room 108, extends an invitation to Representative Ben Rosenthal, a Democrat from Queens, New York, and the chairman of the congressional delegation. Maria ages two years at the suggestion. It is explained to Maria that it might be inadvisable to exclude the chairman of the delegation. Besides, as a New Yorker, he is probably the only one who understands Dali's surrealistic art.

At 12:30 p.m., per instructions, we assemble in the lobby of Le Meurice. No Maria. "Where is Maria?" The men are annoyed. "She bugged us to be here at precisely 12:30. Now she's not here." The congressmen are not nearly as intrigued with the intrigue as their wives. This is their only afternoon off from two-and-one-half days of meetings, their only chance to view some sights.

"I think I would rather be at the Palace of Versailles," Gil Gude mutters.

"*Anybody* can go to the Palace of Versailles," a wife retorts.

An apparition of long-stemmed lilies and camera equipment suddenly appears. It is Maria. "I don't think we ought to take pictures," someone whispers. "This isn't a political convention." The congressmen wear resigned expressions of men going to face irate constituents.

"Where is the chairman?" Maria is checking heads as she passes out lilies.

It is difficult to tell her that Ben Rosenthal has backed out upon learning from an indiscreet staffer that Dali was annoyed with the additions. Rosenthal, tall and lean, has the look and air of a man who has seen it all and done it all, and he probably has. "I don't really like these things anyway," he says by way of exit.

Maria looks weak, but pulls herself together and the group proceeds to room 108. We are greeted by Dali's secretary, a handsome, garrulous Spaniard. Behind him stands the master.

At first it is hard to focus on the painter because of the surrounding environment. Four cut-glass swans dominate the corners of the room. In front of the fireplace is a motorcycle with a pair of distended iron hands gripping the handlebars. On a radiator crowned with pink and red roses is a miniature shark in full yawn. An alligator stands on an end table balancing a gold bar on his brow. On closer inspection, he turns out to be a lamp. On the far-right wall hangs a picture of Dali with rays of light beaming from his eyes. The mantelpiece is crowded with aging long-stemmed lilies.

It is difficult to guess Dali's age. He could be 65. He could be 75. He is in fact, 72. His face is red and mottled. The few remaining strands of his graying hair hang in greasy strings down to his shoulders. His famous trademark, the starched mustache, juts out of the side of his face and curls back to his nose. He is costumed in a zebra-striped jacket and a rhinestone vest.

He greets each member of the group with a solemn, unsmiling handshake, then asks who the most important woman in the room is. "Protocol," he explains. Grace Stephens, whose husband has the most seniority in Congress, is pointed out. He instructs Grace to stand to his right while Maria takes their picture.

Next, he moves to a red velvet couch and asks Congressman Gude to sit next to him. Gude accepts the invitation, ducking his tall frame under a spreading swan wing to avoid a crack on his skull.

Conversation is a problem. Dali understands English but chooses to speak Spanish most of the time, which none of the Americans understand. Nobody understands his paintings either. A common topic is elusive.

There are several lame starts with equally lame finishes. Dali abruptly arises from the couch and walks to the other side of the room and sits down in a high-backed chair that appears to be his throne.

A quick brain-racking. "Ask him about the movie he's making," someone suggests. Maria relays the question in Spanish. In kind, Dali replies that it has something to do with

Mongolia and his impressions of Mongolia, but that is about all that he can say on the subject because he doesn't know yet what his impressions of Mongolia are.

Someone says that he has been in San Francisco lately and has enjoyed Dali's paintings there. "Oh that was a long time ago." Another topic retired.

Finally, in a deliberately booming voice, Ohio republican Representative J. William Stanton instructs Maria to ask Dali what his politics are. Dali seems startled, but he replies that he has admired two politicians, Mao Tse-tung and Franklin Roosevelt. He goes on to relate that he had done some work for Mao in China and that he would "like very much to do something for America." Clearly he has never been asked.

Ever one to play the fool to excite the moment, I suggest, "Why don't you do a mural depicting the 200-year history of our country? For our bicentennial."

"Where would you like it?"

I clear my throat. Dali is showing too much interest. "Oh, the nation's capital would be a nice place."

"No problem. You pay, I paint." Suddenly the Spaniard is speaking English.

"You mean, first I must get the *dollars?*" Didn't he want to make a donation to such a grand event?

He did not.

"Haven't you heard about the terrible recession in our country? And the inflation?"

He nods, but not in sympathy.

The whole thing is getting out of hand. "Well, when we cure our economic problems, I'll call you."

The humor escapes the translation. His secretary steps forward and gives me his card. "I'll wait to hear from you," he says.

Dali has disappeared into an adjoining room. The group concludes that the audience has terminated and heads for the door. "No, no, no," his secretary puts a halt to the parade. "You must wait to say 'bye-bye.'"

The secretary is extremely gracious and speaks good English. While we wait for the master to reemerge, we chat about Mrs. Dali, one of the master's favorite canvas subjects. She has just departed, the secretary says, "to take her relax at the castle." Her husband is following in three days. Summers are spent in Spain.

Dali does indeed return to say "bye-bye," his most picturesque farewell being to Maria. He lifts her hand in the air as if he is going to invite her to minuet and then dips his knee.

As we are going out the door, Dali's secretary taps me on the shoulder and says, "I'll be waiting to hear from you."

He is still waiting.

8

A DIFFERENT IDEA
OF FREEDOM

*The congressional trip to Cuba was as far removed
from the atmosphere and tone of Paris as Salvador Dali
and Fidel Castro were removed in looks, temperament,
personality, and purpose. What the two world-famous
characters did share was social distancing made possible by a multiplicity of handlers. No masks were visible.
They were there nevertheless.*

As Air Force Two touches down, the American flag emblazoned on its side, we can see Cubans lining windows and
doorways, staring with great curiosity at the rare sight of a
United States government plane landing at the Havana airport
in 1978.

We are the largest official U.S. government delegation to
visit Cuba since the revolution in 1959. A mix of representatives
from several different congressional committees, State Department and Treasury Department officials will meet with Cuban
officials with an eye toward a normalization of relations between
the two countries. Among the congressmen is silver-haired
Italian Sil Conte of Massachusetts; scholarly Henry Reuss of
Wisconsin; humongous Henry Hyde of Illinois, towering of
build and brain; and my husband, Bill Stanton of Ohio.

One of the major stumbling blocks to normalization is
the Carter administration's acute concern over the presence
of 24,000 Cuban troops in Africa; thus a primary goal is a
personal encounter with Fidel Castro himself, to inquire as to
the purpose of those troops.

There has, however, been no assurance of such a meeting,
and Castro has just harangued the U.S. government in a very

recent speech. Even if a meeting should occur, knowledge of it may not be revealed until minutes before it takes place.

Fidel apparently has great concern for his personal security, which is the reason given for his unannounced comings and goings as well as the myth that he never sleeps two nights in the same house.

According to a source very close to Castro, it is not true that he is in a different residence every night. The president has about three or four houses, one very close to the presidential building. It is claimed that they are very simple, but no one knows because their whereabouts are never revealed. There have been 89 bona fide assassination attempts against Castro, says this source, the last one in Chile. Castro has nothing to fear in Cuba, the source maintains. Still, it is in Cuba where all the secrecy is practiced.

We are greeted by Cuban banking and commerce personnel and their wives, many of whom never leave our side for the duration of the trip.

Inside the Havana terminal, we are presented with the unusual combination of daiquiris and information forms, which we are required to fill out behind locked doors. Once our vital statistics are recorded, we are unleashed and board buses that take us, without hotel pause, directly to Cuban fishing-fleet repair shops financed by the Soviet Union.

We are bundled into fat, insulated jackets and invited into the huge fishing refrigeration facilities. A member of the delegation quips that word is being sent to Fidel, "We've got the 10 American congressmen in the deep freeze. Shall we shut the door?"

From the fishing port, we reboard the bus, which is outfitted with a bar and waitress, a circumstance that seems at variance with the much-heralded Cuban austerity program. We are unable to determine whether the constant presence of rum mixed with any number of liquid companions is a habit of the Cubans or what they imagine to be a habit of the *gringos*. Wherever we have a gathering this first day, be it a school, governors' meeting, or an airport, a new concoction is proffered. We take to sniffing before sipping in order to retain some measure of our wits. Since a bottle of rum costs 20 times the price of a kilo of rice, refusal is akin to turning one's back on a gold bar from Fort Knox.

Our next meeting is with Óscar Fernández Mell, the governor of the province of Havana. He is also mayor of Havana city. Governor Mell tells us he has problems with housing, traffic, sewage, and transportation. "But we have very good education and public health." Havana, he points out, was "an overdeveloped city in an underdeveloped country," so when the Castro regime took over, "the city had to wait." He brags that, before the revolution, the Cuban illiteracy rate was 30 percent. The revolutionaries launched a huge campaign to teach the people to read and write. The result, the governor-mayor claims, is an illiteracy rate of zero.

When Governor Mell is asked about drugs, he says the problem doesn't exist in Cuba, because "when authorities are not pleased with a situation, it can be gotten rid of." Indeed.

We leave Governor Mell and board the bus for the U.S. mission, which was once the American Embassy until diplomatic relations with Cuba were severed in 1961 via the aborted Bay of Pigs invasion. The head of the U.S. mission, Lyle Lane, takes us to the only definitely secure room in the building, meaning it is the only area where we can be reasonably certain the walls do not have ears.

The mission has just been reopened in September 1977 with the hope of reestablishing relations with Cuba. Fidel Castro, according to Lane, is a very charismatic leader with no serious opposition. "There is no question that Fidel will have his say."

Cuba is basically a single-crop economy, the majority of its revenues coming from sugar. The Soviets, who pay 30 cents a pound for sugar, which is 23 cents above the world price, and sell the Cubans oil for $6 a barrel, $8 under the world price, in effect, subsidize the Cuban economy to the tune of $3.5 million a day.

There are 10,000-plus Soviet families living in Cuba, 2,000 medical advisers, and 6,000-8,000 civilian advisers. It is the U.S.' best judgment, however, that Cuba does not pose a strategic threat.

Finally we are taken to the Havana Riviera, a modern hotel that predates the revolution. It has pleasant accommodations and an interesting billing system. If you are Cuban and honeymooning, your room rate is $6 a night. If you are American and representing your government, the same room cost $75 a night; our staff, however, chipped $25 off the original tariff. I am unable to learn what the hotel charges the Russians, who are everywhere present.

Hotel management makes a point of keeping the Communists and the Capitalists apart during dinner, the Russians being assigned one restaurant and the Yankees another. One wishes they had taken the same precautions on the elevator. There is no mistaking the presence of a Bolshevik in a lift. The nose is immediately assaulted by their underarm hygienic austerity program. Whew!

We never see a menu in Cuba. Our meals are either buffet or served without curiosity as to our preference. We eat at a prescribed hour both morning and evening. The dinners have some variety. But breakfast is always a ritual of ham and mushy scrambled eggs.

The Cubans seem to be fond of close encounters of the nocturnal kind. After a 7:30 p.m. dinner in the hotel the first evening, we attend a 9 p.m. meeting with representatives of the National Bank of Cuba and the Cuban minister of finance.

The next morning, we are on the bus bright and early riding out to see the pride and joy of the Cuban educational system, the countryside school. The name of the school we are taken to see is Vladimir Lenin. Lenin is such a hero in Cuba that you see more of his face on Havana buildings then you do Fidel's. As a matter of fact, one sees very little of Castro's visage until Santiago de Cuba, the home of the revolution.

We watch a film with a screen full of the wisdoms of revolutionary hero José Martí as they are flashed before our eyes, which pretty well typify the Cuban educational thinking of today.

"The New World needs a new man."

"It is necessary to substitute the literary spirit with the scientific spirit."

"The pen must be used in the afternoon — the hoe in the morning."

The latter phrase explains why vocational schools, as opposed to totally academic schools in the country, are the elite educational facilities for Cuban young. Children are educated with an eye toward the needs of the state; thus they are trying to work as well as study. For instance, we watch some girls laboring at sewing machines and some boys making baseball mitts.

All of the students are learning some kind of trade at the same time they are hoisting the books. Revolutionary general José Ramón Fernández has some philosophical thoughts of his own: "A man with a good education and good health can enjoy all the good things of life. Cuba places a priority on education and health over unnecessary consumer goods."

"Work is essential," Fernández continues. "The man who does not work with a social aim is actually a parasite. Man needs to work like he needs food and water. Maybe you did not feel the happiness of the students because of the language problem. ... But they are very happy because they have just made their production quota."

Everywhere we went from the fishing port to the mayor's office, some group of workers were being praised for "just making their quota."

During the Q&A, Fernández is asked if religious education is allowed. "We do not interfere," he replies, "but education is for the good of the state and religion cannot push forward educational tasks. We do not motivate religion. We do not believe in it. But we do not interfere" — a statement we later find disputed.

When I ask why Cuba seems to have so little problem with kids using drugs or liquor, Fernández points out that it is "uncertainty in life that brings on such problems. Drugs, particularly marijuana, flourished in the '20s, '30s, '40s, and '50s, but Cuba has no problems today, not because of repression, but because the young people are too busy."

History, Fernández explains, is taught a little differently in Cuba than in the United States. It is the "movements" (i.e., the revolution) that are important, not the individuals. That is why a former vice president of Cuba visited the school and found that the children had never heard of him. If educators were to talk of past Cuban leaders, Fernández says, they would have to tell the children about a lot of crooks. "Would you call that history?"

One doubts, however, that Fidel will be ignored in future classes.

There is, however, one individual, along with Che Guevara and Lenin, whose history is anything but ignored, and surprisingly he is an American: novelist Ernest Hemingway. "Papa" spent many years of his life living in Cuba and his *casita* is about 10 miles outside the city limits. It is now a carefully preserved museum.

As we are driven around Havana, every Hemingway haunt is carefully noted. We are passing Hemingway's favorite stop, Sloppy Joe's Bar. Standing on the balcony of the downtown museum, a Cuban proudly points to a window with a broken shutter in a nearby apartment house. That is where Hemingway wrote *For Whom the Bell Tolls* — a fact that Fidel Castro later disputes.

Two of the favorite tourist restaurants are the ones the famous author used to frequent. There is considerable irony in the thought that free-spirited, high-living Hemingway, who would have rebelled against the austerity of today's Cuba, is now so revered by the Cubans. But the adulation is more by design than accident. It is clearly fostered by their leader and his hero worship of Hemingway. Some think this provides some of the most revealing insights into Castro's complex personality.

"Will we or won't we meet Fidel?" becomes a kind of parlor game in Cuba. And if so, where? In recent months, it is reported he has been seeing all comers from the United States in the interest of furthering normalization of relations. But on December 24, just four days before our arrival, Castro had delivered a fiery fusillade at the United States.

He is annoyed with the U.S. for criticizing his military troops in Africa. He is not, he said, about to remove them. He has fought with five presidents, and he can fight with the sixth, etc., etc. The U.S. mission here is now wondering if *El Presidente* will deign to see us, and if he doesn't, it will be a very negative signal as to the normalization of relations.

Even when Fidel does intend to see a visitor, the visitor is not informed of the privilege until minutes before the event occurs or he is summoned. Two congressmen who preceded our visit by a month did not get the word until 2 a.m. in the morning that Castro would grant them an audience. They were with him for two hours, leaving for the airport at 4 a.m.

Our people are given no substantial clues. There has been much haggling about numbers, if and when Castro should appear. The Cubans are arguing for a very small audience, the banking committee and State Department staff insisting on the entire delegation. The current feeling is that we will be spirited away from the National Bank of Cuba cocktail party arranged for the quaint hour of 9:30 p.m. All those suspicions, however, could prove fraudulent, and Castro might greet us at a housing development project tomorrow.

As we are dressing for dinner the second evening, a knock comes on the door. It is a member of the staff arriving to inform us that we will not see Fidel tonight after all. He has invited us to a reception at the Presidential building tomorrow afternoon at 1 p.m.

There seems to be great excitement about this turn of events. First of all, because the invitation has been issued hours rather than minutes before the occasion. Secondly, because the visit is going to be a reception at the Presidential building, a very rare happening, and thirdly, because Castro has agreed to see everyone in the delegation: members, wives, staff, dogs, and children. Clearly, relations between the U.S. and Cuba have not grown as thick with ice as Lyle Lane had feared.

We are delighted that a status quo, if not a warming trend in U.S.-Cuban relations, is indicated by this gesture, but it definitely takes the edge off the evening and a little bit of the romance out of the rendezvous. After all, *anybody* can meet a president in a *mucho grande* hall. And most do. But how often do you gather clandestinely under a coconut tree or Sloppy Joe's Bar with a national leader? International nuances be damned — we crave a little intrigue.

However lacking in intrigue, the 9:30 p.m. cocktail party provides a conversation concerning religion that is revealing. Central Bank Director Rafael Hernandez insists that religious freedom *does* exist in Cuba. He points out that the Catholic Church in Cuba was not nearly as strong or deeply felt as it was in many other Latin American countries. It was more of a social tradition than a religious experience, thus it was not hard to wrest it away from many of the people. They had very little to lose. In Argentina, the papal nuncio says the faith was not firmly affixed due to a lack of clergy, a mixed culture, and the influence of tourism for pleasure.

The people who do retain their faith in Cuba are generally old and very poignant. One morning we attend a Mass in the church not far from our hotel. There are surprisingly more parishioners than I expect, perhaps even 100. Almost all are senior citizens with the exception of two teenage altar boys and six young choir singers whose strident voices are singing hauntingly beautiful Latin hymns. Part of the beauty comes from the courage it takes to be singing religious songs in a communist country.

Across the aisle from us is a very ancient couple. The wife has cropped, uncombed white hair. Her black coat hangs loosely around her thin shoulders, and her nylons dangle around her ankles. Her husband, whose suit could claim 50 years, guides her carefully around the church, trying to pilot her into a pew with some difficulty. Her dark eyes are framed

by brows that arch straight up into her forehead in an attitude of resignation. "There's a face with a thousand stories,"
whispers Bill.

When the couple finally find a home, the husband keeps
talking softly to the wife, who knows she is in church, but
seemingly little else. The old gentleman is very thin; his
hooded, hallowed eyes, iron gray hair and aquiline nose hint
of a former aristocracy.

Behind a curtain that is drawn during the Mass, there is
a splendid crèche as complete and three dimensional as any
I have ever seen. Congressman Henry Hyde and General
McMurray attend another church, which remains nameless, in
order to protect the integrity of the priest who speaks out so
freely to them concerning religious freedom in Cuba.

After Mass, Congressman Hyde and General McMurray
ask the priest if they can speak with him. He says certainly, but
he makes sure they are standing in the middle of a parking lot,
free of walls with ears, before he begins to talk.

He says religious freedom is technically a fact, in reality
a myth. The churches are allowed to celebrate one Mass a
day, then required to be locked up. A Cuban family known to
be "religious" is likely to have their food rationing curtailed
and the children withdrawn from school — even if they are
only attending the less prestigious street schools. It is virtually
certain they will not be invited to attend the elite countryside
school, no matter how talented they are, and their chances for
a career in government are annihilated.

The priest is a Spanish Capuchin. His church has formally
been run by the Jesuits, who are now gone, as are all native
Cuban clergy. Ironically, Fidel had been baptized Catholic at
age 8 and attended Jesuit-run Dolores School in Santiago, and
a second Jesuit institution, El Colegio de Belén in Havana.
Priests fought with him in the Sierra Maestra mountains, and
the archbishop of Santiago de Cuba pleaded with Fulgencio
Batista, then president of Cuba, to save Castro's life when he
was jailed after his failed 26th of July movement. The archbishop's efforts are not mentioned when one tours the Santiago

Revolutionary Museum. The guide credits a police lieutenant for sparing Castro's life. We ask Fidel's interpreter, Juan Ortega, why the archbishop's intervention is neglected. The interpreter claims that the archbishop is just one of the many authorities who acted in Fidel's behalf and that his influence was minimal.

Upon Fidel taking over in 1959, the churches were shut down and not allowed to reopen until the mid-1960s. When the Spanish Capuchin came to Cuba 12 years ago, he had 600 parishioners, but the subtle government pressures have apparently taken their toll. He now has only 150 church members. Ten years ago, he had 60 to 71 First Communions. This year he had one. There are about 20 churches open in and around Havana. The Capuchin is allowed to preach, but if he says anything that annoys the government, he hears about it. The Church today in Cuba, according to the Capuchin, is rather monastic and introspective.

The Cuban bishops seldom speak out because, number one, they might cease to exist if they did, and number two, they would probably have little influence. Seminaries are allowed to operate, but none of the seminarians are allowed to work together.

There are a number of evangelical sects in Cuba and they, says the priest, get along better with the government than the Catholic Church.

Fidel has done some good things, the priest acknowledges, but the subtle oppression of varying beliefs is not one of them. As Fidel himself put it to us, "We have a different idea of freedom than you do."

One has to smile reading some of the Cuban Chamber of Commerce brochures with which we are surfeited. Cuba is described as "the pearl of the Caribbean ... new excitement, new experiences and new attractions in the nation that is open to fun and amusement. ... The island of the gay sunshine." We saw a lot of sunshine, but we saw little gaiety with the exception of New Year's Eve.

Cubans today are very serious, almost introverted people. There is much speculation that they are not happy. I would not say that I thought they were as sad as they were subdued and sober. According to a number of prerevolutionary visitors with whom I spoke, Cubans 20 years ago were very happy-go-lucky, volatile, inquisitive, and unrepressed.

Today Cubans do not gather in the streets chattering and laughing as do citizens of Bogotá, Rio, or Santiago. We often see large crowds standing silently waiting for buses, which are old and dirty and teeming with riders. A bus ride costs 5 cents. There are few modern cars in Havana; most are 1950s vintage, some remarkable for still being able to move.

Parts of Havana resemble a postwar metropolis. The buildings are scabbed, scarred, and peeling paint. The saddest sites are once-lovely Spanish style homes, now boarded and vacant or dwellings for the poor. "Are those your slums?" I start to ask one of our Cuban bank friends. The question is curtailed by an urgent jabbing from Bill, who whispers, "They consider that improved housing."

Twenty years ago, a prerevolutionary tourist told me, Havana was called the "Paris of the Caribbean." The Malecón, a roadway that extends from our hotel along the ocean, was once a magnificent thoroughfare, bulging with elegant cars and people. The shops were full and expensive. The buildings were sparkling, clean, and well maintained. There was art, music, and culture. There was also gambling, rampant prostitution, crime, corruption, and the presumed presence of the mafia.

Today, Havana's shops and department stores are either nonexistent or poorly stocked. The goods in the window have a dusty, out-of-style "Second-Hand Rose" look to them. The Cuban man's sartorial splendor is rationed to three shirts and two pairs of pants per year.

As for food, Cubans are allowed to purchase no more than three-fourths of a pound of meat every nine days, and shopping days are circumscribed by the government. José's meat-purchasing days might be Monday, Wednesday, and Friday, while Rafael must confine his shopping to Tuesday,

Thursday, and Saturday. Thus, if on Tuesday, Rafael finds that José has bought up all the meat on Monday, he must wait until Thursday to try again. Milk, vegetables, and fish are not rationed.

Cuba was ripe for communism 20 years ago, because it was ruled, in banking committee staffer Dr. Paul Nelson's words, by one of the most oligarchical systems in the world. About 1 percent of the population controlled the wealth in the government. They lived in Havana, and Havana literally milked the countryside. That is one reason the revolutionary government, in its attempts to get rid of illiteracy, disease, and unemployment, went to the rural areas for its improvements, while letting the city wait.

There is some evidence, however, that the government feels they have waited long enough and will have to rehabilitate Havana if they are going to appeal to foreigners; and since they are trying to encourage tourist income, it won't do to have Havana remain a showplace gone sour.

Havana was of course once famous for its nightclubs and floor shows, and we are treated to one on New Year's Eve. It is one of the most varied shows I have ever witnessed. There is modern dancing, Cuban dancing, rock singing, Hispanic singing, and trio singing. There are even trained monkeys. There is no dance floor, but the Cubans are the only people I have seen who can rumba sitting down. When they like the music, a whole booth full of shoulders quiver up and down, left and right.

The serving of drinks and dinner is apparently designated for a specific time, because Congressman Charlie Wilson and his wife, Jerry, arrive at 9 p.m. and cannot get so much as a glass of water for 45 minutes. Every request for a cocktail is rebuffed with "*uno momento.*" We, too, sit for a long time without service, even though we wait to arrive until 10 p.m. Finally we are given one rum drink and a pork dinner (no options). That is it. Unless you happen to be sitting with the head of the Secret Service, where we note three drinks and a bottle of rum are served.

Fraternizing with Fidel ·······················

At 12:30 p.m. we leave the hotel by bus for the Presidential building, a huge modern edifice that makes the White House look like a guest cottage. The décor is lean and spare, though the rooms are enormous. We stand in a large reception hall, waiting for himself. I have a small tape recorder. One of the congressmen inquires as to how I got permission to "get that in here?"

"Never ask," I smile. "Never give security the option to say no, because they always will."

After about 10 minutes, Castro emerges from a far door on the left side of the room, flanked by an entourage. His familiar green khaki uniform is immaculately pressed. His hair is mostly black, though not as abundant as in more youthful days. His eyes are brown and very alert. His hands are tanned and smooth, the nails carefully rounded and white. He is smoking a small, lean cigar during the reception, which I am told he immediately substitutes for a huge Havana stogie in the later private meetings with three of the congressmen. The famous beard is the only flaw in his grooming, rather thin and straggly; there seems to be no attempt to shape it, perhaps because it symbolizes the condition of his chin when he emerged from the Sierra Maestra.

Fidel is well over 6 feet tall, perhaps 6-foot-3 or 6-foot-4, but somehow he does not appear overpowering. As he greets each member of the delegation, he says little, appearing almost shy. After the salutations, we move into an adjacent room where healthy daiquiris and assorted 20-year-old rum drinks are served along with a buffet that includes Cuban crayfish (which Texan Charlie Wilson admits are larger than Texan crayfish), lobster, stone crabs, rice with squid, and superb wine and coffee.

As Castro moves around the room, he is surrounded by a small circle of questioners. It is during these exchanges that Fidel comes to life, but in a surprisingly low-key manner, distinctly at variance with his usual volatile, arm-waving, vibrant podium manner. Instead, he converses in a very soft, husky voice that is sometimes difficult to hear. He is far less passionate in his pronouncements than his interpreter, who sometimes gets quite carried away with her message.

Fidel listens intently, answers gently, allows interruptions without irritation, and sometimes answers questions with his own questions. He seems an intensely curious person with a wide variety of interests. He talks with equal ease and presumably knowledge about education, construction, the economy, employment, fishing, hunting, and Ernest Hemingway.

There are many questions about Africa. "In general," says Castro, "our relations with Africa have nothing to do with economic interests. We have no multinational enterprises nor investments over there."

"Would you be satisfied to leave a country like Angola," I ask him, "as you said, soon, if you did not leave it a socialistic government?" Castro looks at the recorder in my hand but says nothing.

"We do not set any conditions for assistance to them. We are there because of agreements that we have signed with them. ... They are agreements that we cannot violate because they are sacred to us. ... Of course we help them, because we feel that they are honest, progressive, and revolutionary people. Otherwise we would not have any motive to help them, you know." Castro repeatedly insists, "We have not set any condition on the kind of government they have to create there. We supported them to obtain their independence."

"But," I counter, "as someone who believes passionately in the revolution, can you resist the urge to encourage the revolution in these other countries?"

"See, the revolution cannot be imposed."

"How about encouraged?"

After a pause, Castro replies, "Encouraged? I think you can encourage it by your example. ... Besides, no country and no leader would like to be told what he should do. We don't like to be told and we don't think anybody likes it, and that's why we don't say to people what they should do in our opinion. Rather, if they request an opinion we just give an opinion."

"Does not the presence of military troops, as opposed to medical and technical advisers, make the opposite kind of statement?"

"We don't have troops everywhere. We have advisers. We have instructors. So not in every place do we have the same situation. We have doctors in other places. But we want the problems to be solved. We do want the problems to be solved, and we would like them not to need army, military personnel. ... That is our expectation, that is our wish. It's more satisfactory for us to send a doctor than to send a soldier."

"Why do you not tell us how many military troops are there?"

"Are you a journalist?"

"I am just the wife of the congressman from Ohio."

"You ask very intelligent questions."

"*Gracias, Señor Presidente.*"

"I'm telling you seriously. It is not a courtesy. It is not a compliment."

"I confess to being a writer. I write books."

"Ahh, that's why. A writer is a very good journalist. Hemingway was also a journalist, you know."

"*Si. Si.* But you didn't answer my question, *Señor Presidente.*"

"No, because that is not a journalist or a writer question."

"I'll be glad to put on whatever hat I need to ask it."

There is much laughter all around, but still no answer from *Señor Presidente.*

Many thought Fidel revealed more of himself talking about his hero, Ernest Hemingway, than with any other topic. He went to see Hemingway's home after he died, the house which has now been turned into a museum.

"I was concerned. I remember, shortly after Hemingway died, I went to see the house. And now I go, and I find the house better than it was at that time. ... Everything is the way he used it, just the same way he used it. Because that was organized by the people who used to work for him, so they know where he used to keep everything, you know. He used to write standing, you know.

"They try to reflect what they saw there. I, myself, sometimes I remain with a book, I don't want to leave it aside, so I leave it nearby, when I'm sleeping. When I'm not sleeping, I take it up again. Maybe I keep it on the bed, you know." Castro is alluding to reading material left on side tables in Hemingway's house just where the writer left it.

"Did you fish in *Señor* Hemingway's contest?" I ask.

"*Sí.* I did."

"Did you win?"

"Yes, I did. It was lucky, you know, because I had no experience in that field at that time. But there was someone going ahead of me. And about one hour before the tournament was over, I was lucky enough to fish one. But after that, I read a book by Hemingway's brother, where it was insinuated, you know, that I cheated. I did not. The first day, it was like that. The first day I got three. The second day, I got two. And the third day, I got one, almost at the end, just one hour before the tournament was over. There were eight. They were not big, but they were calculated on the amount of fish you captured.

"It was quantity," I joked, "not quality."

"Yes," he agrees, "But ... the captain of the boat you are fishing [on] is very important," he stresses. "I had a captain who is an experienced man. And that is important, because they know the area in which the marlin fish goes. Generally, they can see from far away. They can detect where the marlin fish is. Then they tell you, 'Marlin! marlin!' And they maneuver with the boat. The person who is handling the boat is very important. Actually, that day, everybody that knew a lot about this was leading a different boat, so I was not especially favored by that. I had a good captain, but there were others."

"Was Hemingway in the contest himself?" I wanted to know.

"No, he wasn't. At the end of the afternoon, he gave the award. He gave the cups."

"A cup? With a daiquiri in it?"

"No," Castro laughs, "but it would have been better, you know. But Hemingway used to like both. He used to like fishing. He was really fond of that. Really fond of fishing. All his life. Fishing and hunting. He also liked the martinis. The daiquiri, the martini, whiskey, all that. He was a tremendous character. His own life is a novel, you know."

I was curious. "What do you most admire about Ernest Hemingway?"

"Actually, I like his personality. [He was] that kind of man who used to face things. He had an adventurous spirit. And I have a little bit of an adventurous spirit, myself, you know. And then his love for nature. The whole struggle against the forces of nature. As a writer, the realism with which he writes. The fact that he says what he has lived. He wrote everything he lived … and the monologues."

"What book do you like the most?"

"The one I like the most is *For Whom the Bell Tolls*."

"I thought you would say that."

"That's the one I like the most. It's considered one of the most famous books by him, and it's really a tremendous book. Also, *The Old Man and the Sea*. He did write that in Cuba. And he got inspiration from (those) who did live here in order to write about that."

"There is a legend promoted by guides that Hemingway wrote *For Whom the Bell Tolls* in a downtown apartment building. The tour guides even point to a specific room."

Castro debunks the tale. "I think no. Because he went to the war in Spain [the Spanish Civil War]. … and he stayed in Madrid. He used to like to go to the front lines. He liked to talk a lot with the people. I think he got that from reality, you know. The reality of his life at that time, there. He was a journalist, you know, so he wrote very good reports. He wrote very good stories. It seems to me that it's also a very good book, *Death in the Afternoon*. Almost everything I know about the bulls, I learned it from his books."

One cannot help but ponder how the fate of Cuba might have been so very different if this charismatic man had chosen a different hero than Ernest Hemingway, if he had chosen a man whose life was also full of adventure, whose life also read like a novel, though it was fact and the subject of history's all-time best seller. What would Cuba have been like if Fidel Castro had admired Jesus Christ as much as he admired Ernest Hemingway?

From Cuba to Brazil

Next stop on our journey: Rio de Janeiro, and an interesting encounter with a Brazilian reporter, who asked me, "Did I think Brazil could achieve democracy?"

I replied that two-and-one-half days in the country hardly qualified me as a judge, but that indeed, I thought it was certainly possible — "if you are brave enough," I added. "Freedom is a big task, demanding great responsibility. It takes courage to get it and wisdom to keep it. If democracies of the world do not pay more attention to the concerns of the poor, they are opening an inviting niche for communism.

"Communists don't create a need," I concluded. "They fill one that already exists."

PART TWO

For, though I knew His love Who followed,
Yet was I sore adread
Lest, having Him, I must have naught beside . . .

   — Francis Thompson, "The Hound of Heaven" (1909)

9

MAKING TIME FOR THE MASTER

The two decades and two years between Part One and Part Two go by with the speed of a bullet train.

Taking on the job of motherhood with a background in journalism, instead of a degree in home economics, proves to be a steep learning curve. Proud as I am of my beautiful little daughter, Kelly, who is born 11 months after our wedding, I keep my resolution to resign my broadcasting job to raise my child. Mental photos pop out of the memory file: Kelly toddling into the Montessori school at age 4; Kelly crowned the May Queen in Our Lady of Victory grade school; tumultuous years at Georgetown Visitation "Visi" high school; and insisting to Bill that any further travels overseas must include Kelly. By the time she is 20, she has seen Paris, London, Rome, Berlin, Tokyo, Beijing, Shanghai, and Nairobi.

I also remember 16 years of campaigns and elections — Bill winning big, despite being a Republican in a Democratic district, and my hostessing and attending lavish parties. I remember Bill's momentous decision to move, after 18 years, from the national to the international stage: from the United States Congress to the World Bank, whose stated goal "is to end extreme poverty in a sustainable way." I recall seeing the world from Africa to Atlanta; from Haiti to Hollywood; and from Paris, France, to Painesville, Ohio. At that time I veered from the field of journalism to found and head Creative Solutions, a special events and public relations business with offices in a client's Georgetown hotel. My partners were Kappy Leonard, wife of CBS News chief Bill Leonard, and Doris McClory, wife of Illinois congressman Bob McClory. Senate and House wives took on part-time assignments as seminar leaders.

The firm affords acclaim from satisfied clients and easy money, but no real sense of purpose; the lack thereof is amplified one day by a spontaneous stop in Epiphany Catholic Church, where Bill and I were married. Standing in the aisle I had walked down as a bride 22 years ago, I suddenly hear, "I did not put you on this earth to make money." The voice is not audible, but the message is loud and clear, and so unexpected that I am completely taken aback. I look around. There is no one else in the church.

That I can see.

Despite my frequent Mass attendance (largely motivated by my father's daily attendance), I was *in* the pew, but not *of* the pew. I realize the amount of time consumed by growing a business has resulted in growing a chasm between my Creator and me.

It would seem I am not following the plan for which God had designed me. Perhaps that accounts for the emptiness I feel in the very few moments of silence allowed in my life.

But what *is* His plan for me?

Afraid to hear the answer, I walk out of the church.

The Fairlamb School of Fine Art

The voice and the message heard in Epiphany Catholic Church echo the emptiness that has arisen from boredom with an enterprise grown old. It seems a clear message to move on from Creative Solutions. But to what? Could it be the gift I have most neglected? Perhaps I should investigate the art world. Do I have any serious talent or am I just a cartoon artist?

The chance to find out suddenly manifests itself when a fellow parishioner, a rather elegant Georgetown resident named Doris, happens to tell me she is studying art in a downtown studio. Intrigued that such a place exists in the center of the nation's capital, I accompany her to a lesson.

Doris introduces me to the "master" of the I Street studio, Guy Steele Fairlamb, who invites me to join his students. I am still running Creative Solutions and I tell him I am concerned I don't have time to pursue art lessons. He is having none of my excuses. "You don't *have* time," he says, looking me sternly in the eye, "you *make* time."

So I do.

If I have a client luncheon, I often walk the half-hour distance from Georgetown to downtown in my business finery, fur jacket, and heels, pausing at Guy's studio en route for my art lesson, then resuming my walk to meet the client. This entails leaping 50-cent-size cockroaches to climb four steep staircases to the top of an ancient townhouse on I Street between 17th Street and 18th Street.

At the top of the final set of stairs, a sandy-haired man gazes out at all visitors with a jaunty eye from a crooked canvas. Surrounding the figure on the canvas are various colored clown masks with the face of the sandy-haired man. The painting is a self-portrait of Guy, or "the old master" as his largely older students like to refer to him.

With his fine brown hair rakishly askew and curling over his neck, his square jaw, and his flip manner, Fairlamb conveys the casual air of the sportsman more than the intensity of the eccentric artist. He strides among his students in a long white medical coat over a turtleneck sweater. "Guy, you look more like you're doing going to attack a kidney than a canvas," quips one of his students.

Whatever is lacking in the old master's personal eccentricity is more than made up for by the appearance of his studio. There are three main rooms and two bathrooms. There's an ancient tile fireplace and two tall, very dirty windows overlooking I Street. Crammed on the windowsills and hanging from hooks are a variety of real and plastic plants in various stages of disintegration.

Along the opposite wall is a slanted desk, laden with pencils, papers, erasers, brushes, coffee cups, straw baskets, and food. Doting students supply the fare for mid-morning coffee breaks; half the time it is donuts or rolls. One day it is raisin plum pudding from a Puerto Rican recipe. Another morning, it is an Indian breakfast concoction and one large dish with several spoons, which is enjoyed communal style.

One week there are million-calorie caramel chocolate chip bars. "What are you doing to me?" Guy moans as he helps himself continually throughout the morning.

In almost every available corner of the main room are large, paint-spattered wood easels. Next to each easel is a rickety TV table, which serves as support for the artists' paint equipment. There is much squirming and jostling as students vie amiably for position.

In the adjoining smaller room, there are two or three easels and a telephone, a skeleton, skulls among the coffee cups, a set of lips, Grecian heads, tired old pieces of lace, paper towel rolls, scraps of newspaper, rags, smocks, and canvases propped up against walls.

I have a hard time believing I am actually enduring the happy squalor, but I persevere because I find I love learning to paint; when I become completely engrossed in perfecting a picture, the clock by which I usually live often disappears.

I could not have journeyed further from the plush dining rooms where I head to meet my clients, who are usually bankers. But when class is over and I shed my paint-smattered smock to don my fur jacket, slip back into heels, and finish the luncheon trek, no client is the wiser.

My yearlong odyssey into the art world, however, eventually takes me from Washington's downtown to Alexandria, Virginia's Old Town, where a 76,000-square-foot World War II torpedo factory has been turned into a flourishing art center. Sometime in mid-January I feel I have outgrown the cramped quarters of what I had dubbed the "Fairlamb School of Fine Art." So I investigate the Torpedo Factory in Alexandra and begin studying under a very talented portrait painter, known to her students simply as "Tommi."

Tommi is a plump, dark blonde, perpetually clothed in jeans and shirttails. With hair hanging straight to her shoulders and cheeks blooming like a German *fräulein*'s, she looks 30 but is actually 41. She is very eclectic in her ethnic tastes. For five years, her beau was an Italian sculptor about 20 years her senior. There was an interlude with a Jew, and she is now in an oriental phase with a Chinese painter named Chang. During each class as she demonstrates how to paint or pastel, there is usually a running narrative of new episodes in the life and times of Tommi, all highly amusing.

There is, for instance, the saga of helping her mother steal china from an ex-husband's home. The rationale for the thievery — the fact that the china actually belonged to her mother, a gift from her mom's prior ex-husband.

There are the adventures with Alfredo the sculptor, whose demise in her affections is the result of womanizing. "He is still in love with me," Tommi explains, "but that's just the way he is." They remain good friends, and Tommi still lives in the $250,000 house Alfredo purchased for her.

There are her laments about odious commissions, in particular the $30,000 portrait that caused her unending grief. The picture was of a five-member family. Only one out of the five gave her a problem. The mother continually requested changes in the portrait. She wanted herself facing out instead of in profile; she wanted an arm or a hand change; and she even asked Tommi to repaint an exquisitely rendered American Beauty rose into a Peace rose. Finally, Tommi had had it. She refused to make any more changes and refused to sign the painting.

The class is made up of assorted middle- and old-aged folk. There is Meg, who wears T-shirts and baggy tan fatigues, who gets commissions for watercolor portraits. She is a Radcliffe graduate who works for $15 an hour as a housekeeper for her "clients" in order to support her art and studio. "The difference between a Radcliffe cleaning lady and a Salvadoran cleaning lady," summarizes a fellow student sardonically, "is the Salvadoran works for her 'lady' and the Radcliffe graduate has 'clients.'"

There is a 70-year-old former sculptor, the class clown, who has held down 32 different jobs and paints like a primitive because he can't see very well. There is the professor with a Ph.D. in economics who is "not ready yet" to abandon academia for art.

Then there is former TV correspondent, still and always a journalist, who is examining the possibility of becoming a portrait painter and who decides the time has not been wasted whatever the art outcome. The characters she is sharing studios with are supplying her with rich writing fare.

She finds the area of a portrait she most enjoys rendering are the eyes. It is an election year, and she begins studying the eyes of the presidential candidates, since it is said the eyes are the windows of the soul. If that's true, what would we learn about the candidates if we only focused on their eyes? The concept becomes her first one-woman exhibit in a Georgetown gallery, called "Eyes on the Presidency," attracting wide, even international media coverage. Our newly-elected president in 1988, George H.W. Bush, sends a handwritten thank-you note for his portrait. "The Eyes have it!" he writes.

Creative Solutions is closed. A new career is launched. A senator commissions a large portrait of his grandchildren. AT&T asks the artist to create a painting for the bicentennial of the U.S. Capitol in 1994, of which lithographs are made by AT&T and presented to every member of the House and Senate.

She is very pleased with the upward trajectory of her artistic endeavors, never imagining the direction they will go as the result of a journey she will one day reluctantly undertake.

10

1988: FROM TERROR TO WONDER

May 2, 1988 — Paris

There is little to recommend 1988 as a very good year for international travel. Ships are being sunk, cities are being bombed, and planes are being hijacked. There is, however, no visible sign of angst in Paree, as I sit solo and jet lagged in the Hotel Regina bar, eating a chicken sandwich and watching the world go by. The streets are thick with tourists; there are crowds of young people festooned in sloppy chic: cascading hair, baggy pants, and blouses over skinny pants. It seems there are more motorcycles than I have ever seen here before — or is it that I am noticing them nervously, wondering if a hostile rider might toss an unfriendly plastic bag into the crowd?

I am keeping my eyes open and my mouth shut — an unnatural position for the latter. But on this first beautiful morning in Paris, menace from the skies or from the streets seem very far away indeed. I leave the hotel and walk through the Tuileries to the Grand Palais on the Champs Élysées to see a beautiful exhibit of the Dutch Masters Vermeer and Rembrandt.

If the crowds are cavalier about their safety, the police clearly do not share that nonchalance. The security around the Place de la Concorde near the American Embassy is heavy. Steel-fence barriers are being set up on either side of the street. There is no one resembling a terrorist anywhere in sight. But then who knows what they look like?

From Charles to Leonardo

We are flying out of Charles De Gaulle Airport just days after another bombing of a plane in Sri Lanka, originating in London — 31 killed, 41 injured — but there is no discernible angst among the passengers. I am, I joke to Bill, considerably relieved to be seated next to a Catholic priest. Maybe I can get the last rites on the way down.

It turns out the priest is a cardinal and one of the highest ranking in the Church. He is the official in charge of choosing bishops. His name is Cardinal Bernardin Gantin and he heads the Congregation for Bishops. He is from Benin in West Africa. When Bill asks Cardinal Gantin how he likes his bishop-picking post, he replies, "It is a very difficult job. I try. Please pray for me."

As the plane touches down in Rome, I compliment the cardinal, "Thanks to you, Your Eminence, the plane landed safely."

"Thanks to *you*," he responds graciously.

Could be true. The Lord did say He came to save the sinners, not the righteous.

At Leonardo da Vinci Airport, where a bomb went off a few months ago, nervousness is very much in evidence. As we come up the escalator, we are greeted by a soldier with a machine gun. Every few feet there are more security officers, some visually obvious, some in plainclothes.

We see police halt two young men in a car, demanding to see their IDs, and guards in shop entrances with machine guns on their hips. In contrast, Romans and tourists seem engaged in one continuous party with an air of nonchalance and gaiety on the main streets, the side streets and back streets belying any sense of lurking danger.

St. Peter's — the Papal Palace

There are just five of us in the Pope's parlor waiting for John Paul II's entrance. Bill, who is the World Bank liaison between the bank and the Vatican, has arranged this private meeting between the Pope and the president of the World Bank, Barber Conable, and it has come close to cancellation because John Paul has just returned from one of his extensive and exhausting papal journeys. Also present are Barber's wife Charlotte, and a young Mario Draghi, then a World Bank employee.

When this once athletic Pope finally totters into the room, I am alarmed by the visible fatigue he exhibits. Nevertheless, he soldiers through the meeting, chin resting on his curled hand, no doubt grateful that President Conable is such a garrulous extrovert. John Paul, who is accurately portrayed as a superb listener, does mostly that. As Conable talks volubly about the bank's work in the Third World, John Paul says quietly, "And then there is the fourth world." The president of the World Bank pauses, puzzled by a possible reference to the supernatural, and then resumes his monologue.

When the half-hour meeting concludes, the Pope presents us with Rosaries. In my large black bag are four silver Rosaries that I have purchased at the base of the Spanish Steps to give as gifts. I gather up my courage and ask the Holy Father if he will bless them. John Paul looks at me quizzically and says, "More Rosaries?"

I nod toward my black bag. Without asking to see the Rosaries, John Paul raises his hand and blesses the entire bag. Not one of us in that room, including the Pope, can envision the dramatic transformation those silver Rosaries will undergo.

New York, JFK Airport, July 31, 1988 · · · · · · · · ·

It does not seem quite rational that I am, once again, boarding an overseas flight in a world awash in international terrorism – to of all destinations, a Communist country!

"This is so weird," Kelly says, "this whole experience."

Mixed feelings might be the best description of my own emotions at the moment: fear, anticipation, wonder, belief, and doubt. Part of the weirdness is traveling under such difficult circumstances. We are already five hours from departure and as Kelly points out, we've gotten nowhere. Well, not entirely true. We have gotten from Washington, D.C., to New York.

"I warned you," I remind my blonde, smoky blue-eyed daughter, "this adventure would not be for sissies." She groans, "I know." She also knows she is the reason we are sitting in Kennedy Airport in the summer of 1988, in the midst of chaos. For once, we are on the road at her instigation, not her parents'. And since the blame — or credit —belongs to her, she grows silent.

It certainly is not her mother's idea of a vacation: traveling 26 hours to a remote mountain village, in communist Yugoslavia, a village with no hotels, where one stays in a peasant home and shares one's bathroom with strangers! Never mind that millions of people, including movie stars and millionaires, have done exactly that since 1981.

"People go there," reported one high Catholic prelate, "and they come back different people." Exactly what I am afraid of. I love my life and have no desire to change it. Medjugorje sounds like a spiritual Magic Kingdom, achieving results with souls unheard of in modern times. As one writer put it, "Medjugorje is conceivably the greatest happening of the 20th century or perhaps its most persuasive hoax."

Famed former movie queen Loretta Young is reported dining on bread and water in a Hollywood restaurant, explaining to puzzled companions that she has been to Medjugorje and is now fasting three days a week! The Rosary is making a comeback. Prayer groups are forming. Lapsed Catholics are returning to the fold. Protestants are developing a love for the Virgin Mary, a woman they had previously regarded with suspicion.

Many people are hearing an interior message basically telling them, "You are called to go to Medjugorje," so the story goes — personally invited by the Holy Mother. Congresswoman Lindy Boggs of Louisiana accepted the invitation readily, she said, "because I thought it would be rude to turn her down."

Some of us are slow to recognize an invitation and even slower to accept it. The first time I heard of this strange village, Medjugorje, I struggled just to pronounce it. A friend, Ann Buckley, wife of former New York senator Jim Buckley, returned from two trips to Medjugorje full of enthusiasm and excitement over the alleged apparitions. I listened to her revelations about revelations with polite interest and more than a little skepticism.

It's not that I didn't believe in heavenly warnings and apparitions. Such famous shrines as Lourdes in France and Fatima in Portugal attest to the fact that periodically the Creator sends direct and visible communicators to visit His creatures when they are getting particularly off track. How could He be considered a merciful God if He did not send messages that we were heading toward a disaster, as He did when He sent the Blessed Mother to Fatima in 1917 during World War I?

As she did at Fatima, Mary comes to Medjugorje bearing secrets, 10 in all, none of which can be revealed until Our Lady gives permission. The visionaries have chosen a priest to announce them to the world three days before the events are to occur.

The visionaries have kept the secrets since 1981, a miracle in itself. What *is* being revealed are Mary's messages to the world, which are delivered on the 25th of each month to one of the seers, Maria Pavlović. Within 24 hours, the message goes global through the internet.

One of the first messages was, *"I have come to tell the world that God exists. He alone is the fullness of life. To enjoy this fullness and obtain peace, you must return to God."*

The messages are offered in the simplest language, presumably so all mentalities can comprehend them. They always begin with the salutation *"Dear children."* They are strangely moving, albeit repetitive (what mother is not repetitive?). They are so maternal, so loving, that it is hard to imagine teenagers devising them.

But for every genuine apparition, there are often dozens of false claims of personal visits from a heavenly being, usually the Blessed Mother. Ann Buckley, however, is far removed from the above category. She is as delightful as she is devout — athletic, pragmatic, in possession of an infectious and uproarious wit, usually fielded at her own expense.

Ann saw none of the "miraculous" phenomena that so many pilgrims have claimed to witness. "Do you think the apparitions are authentic?" I asked her. "Yes," she answered.

"Why?" I pursued. Ann believed in the visions, she said, "because of the people."

The villagers, it seems, have been transformed under Mary's tutelage. They had been churchgoers, but prone to complain if the Sunday Mass services extended beyond 45 minutes. Now they are in church daily for three or more hours. To an inhabitant of the Western world, albeit a daily Mass attendee, this sounds extraordinary.

Ann gave me a book about Medjugorje, which I dutifully placed on my nightstand without cracking a page. It lay there, submerged from sight by "important" secular reading for two years. But the subject refused to disappear. It loomed again at the close of a speech I was delivering at the Hay-Adams Hotel in Washington, D.C., on a subject not remotely juxtaposed to anything Yugoslavian.

A lady in this audience of banking spouses timidly raised her hand during the Q&A to inquire whether anyone had ever heard of Medjugorje. Most of the audience had not, but the speaker had. The lady went on to recount that she was in possession of a picture taken of the Virgin during one of her appearances to the children in Medjugorje. The photographer did not see the apparition. He merely pointed his camera in the direction the children were looking and when the film was developed, there was the Madonna!

I listened intently. A photograph of the Mother of God? Medjugorje finally had my attention. The journalist in me saw the potential story value of such an occurrence. But despite the lady's promise to send me a copy of the picture, it never arrived.

Interest again subsided until ABC News, my former employer, aired a filmed report on the village relating extraordinary occurrences in this remote mountain town. I began passing the tales on to my 20-year-old daughter, purely as a generic faith booster.

Thus, I was totally unprepared for her proposal. "Let's go there." Go? Go? This is something one talked about, ruminated about. One didn't *go* to such a strange destination. "Why not?" Kelly was insistent. "We go everyplace else." Indeed we had already taken her to China, Japan, Hong Kong, Taiwan, and Europe several times.

"I am at a very vulnerable time in my life," she said by way of persuasion. How true. She was a senior in college, recovering from the dissolution of a long-term romance, wondering what she would do with the rest of her life.

"You can't say no," my husband declared later. It was fine for him to say. It wasn't going to disrupt *his* schedule. He was going to hear about the trip from this side of the Atlantic.

Kelly's traveling window of opportunity was very small. Due to her scheduled return to college, she stipulated, "I can only go the week of July 31 to August 7." The date of her request was July 15. Surely, that was my escape. How could one organize a journey to a communist country in two weeks' time? Not possible.

I was troubled, though. On one hand, one can hardly deny a young American steeped in materialism the chance to have a spiritual experience. On the other hand, Medjugorje had not received official Church sanction. What if it were a hoax? Or, at most, innocent mass hysteria? The experience would then be faith-weakening rather than faith-strengthening, and the only motivation for my going would be to deepen Kelly's faith.

The dilemma brought me to my knees in the most sincere prayer I had ever uttered. *"Lord, tell me what to do. If You are there, I am willing to go through the inconvenience and expense of the trip in order to strengthen Kelly's faith. But if You are not there, please do not let us go through all of this. It would be such a disappointment."* I asked for obvious guidance. *"I will take it as a sign if there is a trip available between July 31 and August 7,"* I concluded.

A tough assignment, I thought confidently, even for the Almighty. After all, I had never heard of any travel agency booking trips to Medjugorje. All too soon however, I learned of an agency in Cleveland, Ohio, which devoted itself to the destination. The agency did have a trip going to Medjugorje the first week in August, but it was fully booked and had been since June. That was that, I assumed. The Cleveland group was surely the only travel agency with trips to "where?"

I called Kelly with the disappointing news. Just not meant to be, I said, trying to hide my relief. I was wrong. Only a few days later, as I was walking out of Holy Trinity Church in Washington, D.C., I overheard a woman telling a friend about her trip to Medjugorje on August 15. She was not traveling with the Cleveland tour group. She had booked with an agency in Chevy Chase, Maryland.

Amazing, I think. There are actually two travel agencies in the United States going to this remote village! Obligatory guilt sent me to the telephone. A trip just one week removed from Kelly's window of opportunity had to be investigated. Once again, rejection. The August 15 trip was sold out. I gave the agent my phone number, "just in case you get a cancellation."

A few hours later, the agency called. "We don't have a cancellation for the trip on August 15," reported a lady named Nancy, "but we do have some space on a pilgrimage leaving *July 31*, returning *August 7*!" How could you be booked for a trip later in the summer but open for seats in a group leaving in just two weeks? I wanted to know. Nancy hastened to relate they had thought this journey was also booked, but suddenly discovered "two seats we did not know we had."

I could hardly withhold a gasp nor a request for those two mysteriously available seats. As a priest to whom I later related the story commented, "I don't know how much more direct an answer to prayer you want."

"Just go with an open mind," I constantly counseled Kelly, "and don't expect to see miracles."

Here in New York my open mind begins to close after a session with Yugoslav Airways, also known as JAT. According to our travel agency, we are supposed to pick up our tickets to Sarajevo at the JAT office in New York. But JAT has no tickets. We are sent to the Pan Am ticket office by JAT representatives. Pan Am knows nothing about our tickets. They send us back to the JAT representatives where the tune has changed. They now mysteriously unearth our tickets.

Boarding is scheduled for 5 p.m., but there is no sign of movement and it is long past five. We have yet to see a leader. It is a mob scene here at gate 6, and a JAT representative indicates that we might not get a seat. Nonsense, says a yellow-shirted nun named Sr. Bettye. She assures us even communists do not make you stand all the way across the Atlantic.

It is an eclectic group of pilgrims assembled in Kennedy Airport: a snappy suburbanite in white slacks and shirt; teenage boys in jeans and tank tops toting a videocassette recorder; a man in a navy blazer, yellow shirt, and bright red pants; two brunette girls in pink sweatshirts emblazoned with iridescent skyscrapers on their chest; not to mention grandmothers, grandchildren, and men in shorts.

Conversations come easily under duress. A tanned blonde lady from Pennsylvania is a particularly friendly pilgrim. She went to Medjugorje last October. "My life will never be the same," she states. She claims to have seen the silhouette of the Madonna to the right of the sun, a sight many people are alleged to have seen. A priest who has been coming to the mountain village for years says he has never witnessed any extraordinary phenomena. We decide God is very selective.

Perhaps I grilled the Pennsylvania blonde too skeptically, because she concluded our conversation with, "I hope you get something out of this. You don't seem too enthusiastic." She apparently deduced this when I responded to her tales of vision with, "My, they must be having fun up there."

Kelly is so unnerved that she has to have a cigarette, and she has just given up smoking! Mother Mary, what kind of influence is this? Noise, confusion, airport TVs blasting. For the first time but not the last time on this journey, I ask myself, "What am I doing here?"

However direct the answer seemed during that telephone conversation, the clarity begins to fade amidst the cacophony at gate 6 in Kennedy Airport. Two of Kelly's former classmates from Visitation Convent School in Washington come to chat with Kelly. They, too, are going to Medjugorje. "We just couldn't believe it was you," exclaimed classmate number one. Indeed, Miss K. demonstrated her independence from parental and scholastic authority during her senior year in high school, and the effort nearly cost her a timely graduation from Visitation. "They think they have seen their first miracle," I whispered to Kelly, "Kelly Stanton in Medjugorje."

I hear a rubber ducky squeaking above the TV fray. It is now one hour past the announced boarding time, and we are still ground bound. One gray-haired lady says she has been in the airport since 11:15 a.m. "This is peace?" I ask the woman who identifies herself as the "Queen of Peace." I think longingly of the back pew in Epiphany Church in Georgetown, the church where the ABC network correspondent married the handsome bachelor congressman from Ohio and where, 22 years later, I am still most comfortable worshiping.

Finally, we begin to board the plane. We are in a row with four other people. There is no air conditioning. My face, my hair, and my neck are damp. Kelly's face is aglow. The red hair on the head of the young man seated next to Kelly is wet. Kelly feels the need for another cigarette. She looks at me. I can hardly blame her, and I swallow my speech. I have vowed to leave the preaching to the Heavenly Mother on this trip.

I think of the heat that a tiny nun, encased in full black and white habit, must be feeling. "The Lord isn't making this easy for us," I attempt to sympathize. She gazes back at me. "That's usually the way," she retorts with a benign smile. I settle into my seat on the aisle. Kelly sits between me and a young man named Michael. He is red haired with angular features and a lean build. He is, he announces, gay, a former cocaine addict, and an alcoholic. With that headline-grabbing preamble he also relates that he is a graduate of Harvard.

Michael initially gets our attention by producing an alleged photograph of an apparition. The photo is in soft focus. People are visible in the foreground, albeit blurred. One can make out the site as Mt. Podbrdo, the mountain of the first apparitions. One can also distinctly see a female figure in a white veil and long gown. The face is rosy brown, but the features are not discernible. I ask Michael if I may show the picture to a wisecracking Irishman from Long Island, Mr. Milroy, who is seated in front of us. "Oh, my gosh," the New Yorker gasps. "Look at this!" he commands his wife. They examine the photograph for several minutes. "Thank you for sharing," Mr. Milroy says as he returns the picture. I had seen a black-and-white reproduction of the same photo in one of the books about Medjugorje, the only photographs cited as possible evidence. The photographer was a Yugoslavian woman from the village of Mostar, 12 miles from Medjugorje.

Michael says his Rosary turned to gold as he was saying it one evening. This is his second visit to Medjugorje in two months. It has, he asserts, changed his life. Until very recently he was a nonpracticing Catholic, unfamiliar with the Rosary and the Church in general. Since his sophomore year in college, he has been an alcoholic as well as a cocaine addict. He regales us with wild tales of his "drinking and drugging years," replete with crashes to the bottom and rises to resurrection, followed by reversals to Death Valley. Finally, three-and-one-half years ago, he found Alcoholics Anonymous and has been chemical-free ever since.

He tells us his first trip to Medjugorje so moved him that he prayed for the means to return and "here I am," he says. He speaks of the profound peace that settles over one upon entering Medjugorje. "You will feel it," he promises. I'll need it, I think, but refrain from saying that. "While you're here, you will hear all kinds of stories of people meeting Mary on the road," Michael continues. How for instance, a group of pilgrims making the Way of the Cross up Mt. Križevac kept noticing a young woman in pink lying prostrate at each station, who seemed to appear and disappear. The phenomena was so peculiar that they begin to speculate as to whom she might really be. Later that day the same group visited with one of the visionaries, Vicka. They told her they had just finished making the Stations. "Yes," Vicka replied, "I know." Apparently Vicka had just had a visit with the *Gospa*, which is the Croatian title given the Virgin.

I had heard similar stories, but they do not impress me. I'm inclined to think people are so anxious for a mystical happening that they will attach heavenly significance to almost any occurrence.

Michael says he had to take instructions to learn how to pray the Rosary. Now he recites it daily. "I love it." Kelly is listening to Michael with profound interest. "I am much more excited than I was," she tells him. As he concludes his biography, this young gay man of 27 pulls out his Rosary and a devotional book without embarrassment and begins to pray. How does Michael merge his gay lifestyle with his newfound religion, I ask? "Not easily," he admits. A few minutes later, Kelly reaches into her purse and takes out her Rosary. I feel sure that watching the sun dance in Medjugorje — a phenomenon many pilgrims have claimed to witness — will not stun me as much as seeing two young 20th-century Americans praying the Rosary on a transatlantic airplane flight.

Sunday morning, August 1, 1988, Sarajevo ....

We are about a half-hour out of Sarajevo. The stewardesses on our last flight have the sourest façades I've ever seen on airline hostesses. One fears they would just as soon pour the coffee *on* you as *for* you.

In Sarajevo we are delayed another two-and-one-half hours. Suitcases have been lost and we are waiting for all luggage-less pilgrims to report their losses. Michael is one of the victims. He shrugs, "I don't care, I really don't." Indeed, all of our compatriots are remarkably sanguine for having endured nearly 20 hours of flights, delays, and now a three-hour bus ride. From this vantage point, it is difficult to imagine anyone undertaking a second trip to Medjugorje. Yet people are returning there two, three, four, and even 10 times.

Having traveled to destinations as far removed as Shanghai, China; Dakar, Senegal; and Jeddah, Saudi Arabia, I am at a loss to recall any ventures absorbing as many hours as this journey. When skeptics inquire why the Blessed Virgin would choose such a remote locale, I respond, "What a way to demonstrate divine 'drawing power'!" Certainly nothing else could prompt so many millions from all over the world to undertake such a difficult sojourn.

Kelly is deeply regretting dancing until 3 a.m. the night before departure. She is feeling comatose and is presently stretched across two bus seats in attempted slumber. Michael is two rows up in a similar occupation. A hand with lavender fingernails joined to a wrist wearing a white plastic watch is dangling under my nose. It belongs to a female pilgrim in her 20s. She is traveling to Medjugorje with her brother, and it is clear that he is the believer and she is not.

Behind me is a young couple with a 3$^1/_2$-year-old mentally and physically handicapped child. "We came for our son," says the mother, who has short, dark curls and a New Jersey accent. She tells me that she and her husband are, of course, hoping for a cure, but if the request is not granted, she hopes God will give her the strength to bear the years ahead.

"Hello there!" A female voice suddenly booms from the front of the bus. "My name is Linda, and Aida and I will be with you through Dubrovnik." At last we have a leader. Linda is slim with short, unruly, very black hair, arched brows, and a ready smile, one of the few we have seen on a Yugoslavian face. Linda is with Kompas Travel, the native travel agency handling Medjugorje trips. Linda completes roll call and discovers all pilgrims are on board. She thinks Kelly is *Mr.* Stanton and we are too tired to disabuse her of the idea. She warns us it is very hot in Medjugorje. The reliable Kompas Travel agency had told us the temperature would be about 80 to 85 degrees. Linda says it is 110. I take out my Rosary.

From behind me I hear the voices of the young couple with the handicapped child praying, "Hail Mary, full of grace" as their afflicted son croons and giggles. I think of Mary Anne, my own brain-injured sister. She is high on my list of petitions. Thoughts of bringing her had occurred but were dismissed for lack of courage and faith.

11

MEDJUGORJE

Sunday evening, August 1, 1988 . . . .

Medjugorje at last! It is 5:15 p.m. I do not know whether or not the sun pulsates in Medjugorje, but I can certainly testify that it fries! Washington, D.C., from whence we came and where the average temperature is 95 degrees, feels like Anchorage, Alaska, compared to the heat we are experiencing here. We are in the process of dispersing pilgrims to the various guest homes, and the progress is incredibly slow. It feels as if the "greenhouse effect" has advanced to a unique level in Medjugorje.

Our next rude awakening is the entrance to what used to be a peaceful village. Now both sides of the road are decorated with makeshift gift shops under bright orange canopies, full of plastic statues, glass Rosaries, and white tennis or sun hats with the *Gospa*'s image on the front. Sandwiched between the gift shops are equally improvised cafés. All this in front of the famed twin towers of St. James Church. The communist government, being atheistic, is promoting such secular development while denying the Franciscan priest who pastors the church the right to build more spiritual quarters, we are told.

When our transportation finally pulls in front of a three-story, white stucco dwelling with wooden, alpine balconies on the second and third floor, we stumble down the stairs to be greeted by the Vasilj family. They stand in the front yard, smiling and greeting their exhausted boarders. There is Shima, with short, black hair, rosy-brown skin, and deep blue eyes fringed with thick black lashes. There is her husband, Ivan, short, sandy haired, tanned, and clothed in khaki shorts and nothing else. There is "Papa," but of whom he is Papa, I never learn — maybe Shima, maybe Ivan, or maybe us pilgrims.

He is jolly, bald, large bellied, and clothed exactly like Ivan. In 110-degree heat, who can blame them? The Vasiljs are housed on the first floor. Papa and a very sick wife have the number one bedroom, while Ivan, Shima, and their two children are in the adjoining two bedrooms. They all share one small bathroom.

On the second floor are four bedrooms to house eight pilgrims. The beds are just pale wood slats. A fellow pilgrim of considerable bulk soon decimates her bunk and spends the rest of the week sleeping on a mattress on the floor. Our room has two beds, one small table between the beds, and one armoire for our clothes. There is a crucifix on the wall. To find a mirror, one has to repair to the one bathroom when seven other competitors are not challenging your position. I find 4 a.m. a nice, quiet, leisurely period to get showered and shined. All told, Shima hosts nearly 20 people for whom she cooks breakfast and supper every day. She prepares all the food with Papa and Ivan lending somewhat lame hands. Papa, however, is very good at getting ice water, which lives in a huge square bottle he unearths from a mysterious location. As we are perpetually thirsty, Papa is very busy.

One comes to greatly admire Shima. She juggles children, parents, and pilgrims with serene equanimity. Her tiny kitchen is always crowded with family or visitors. It appears not to trouble her. An indulgent earth-mother smile almost continually plays about her full rosy lips. According to legend, the Blessed Virgin told the visionaries that soon they would be receiving visitors from all over the world and that the residents were to graciously house them, which the villagers did, originally charging nothing. But when the Yugoslav government began collecting taxes on the tourists, the hosts were forced to exact a toll from their guests, even then only charging $25 a day for a room and two meals.

Shima's dining room is a large square room with rectangular tables arranged in a U-shape. On the end of one of the tables is a television set that is on just two evenings during the week we are there. The only viewers are Shima and Ivan's small son, who falls asleep in the middle of the program. On one wall is a huge wooden Rosary, on another, a luminescent face of Christ.

The evening meal (as do most meals) consists of very well-cooked pork chops, cucumber and tomato salad, well-buttered mashed potatoes, and bread. One night there is chicken, and it turns out to be the house favorite. The heavily salted food, in combination with the heat, soon swells the ankles beyond recognition.

The pilgrims gathered around our table are from all parts of the United States: Maryland, Georgia, Washington, D.C., Washington State, Massachusetts, and California. There is even a mother-daughter team from Latin America. Almost none of us have known one another before embarking on the journey to Medjugorje, but we are like family after just one shared meal, everyone on a first-name basis, with last names all but forgotten. Our residence houses all women. I am shell-shocked one evening when two teenagers from Los Angeles comment on how much there is to do in Medjugorje: "In Los Angeles, we are always complaining there is nothing to do!"

Our first church service in Medjugorje, coming only a short while after we arrive in the village, fielding nearly 26 sleepless hours, is a spiritual disaster. We are hot. We are exhausted. We haven't eaten since breakfast and will not eat dinner until 8:30 p.m. The service begins with the Rosary, recited in Croatian, as is the Mass. One of the Franciscan friars leads the Rosary on his knees, 10 decades before the Mass and five after its conclusion. All the Franciscans seem to possess low, husky voices that pray very softly into the microphone as if they are whispering into the ear of the Almighty.

The timetable is this: Rosary at 5 p.m., Mass at 7 p.m., followed by the conclusion of the Rosary and the healing service — all told nearly three hours! Nonetheless, every seat in the church is taken. All the side aisles are filled, as is the middle aisle. The overflow sits on the stone steps in front of the altar. Outside, services are piped over the loudspeaker to the crowds who respond in their own language.

Allegedly, the Virgin makes her appearance at 5:40 p.m. to the children in the church choir loft. The mind has a difficult time digesting the idea that apparitions can be scheduled. On the other hand, if Dan Rather can broadcast on the minute, why can't the Mother of God?

When 5:40 p.m. arrives, the majority of the parishioners do not even look up at the choir loft. They keep right on praying, which is, of course, what they are supposed to do, answering Rosary prayers with fervor and singing lustily. I, of course, with thoughts of Lot's salty wife whirling in my brain, do turn around and I see absolutely nothing but a very humble choir loft.

Monday morning, August 2, 1988 . . . .

It is 7 a.m. and I am walking through the winding dirt roads of Medjugorje to the adjacent village of Bijakovići where the apparitions first began on the small mountain known as Mt. Podbrdo. New construction is shooting up on both sides of the road. It all seems so ordinary, so lacking in Divinity, even though the back streets of Bijakovići are quietly charming. The white stucco houses have balconies festooned with brilliant varieties of flowers. Nothing, however, smacks of incense and holy water.

"What am I doing here?" I whisper to the Creator. "I've felt Your presence so much more in other places."

After breakfast, Kelly and I climb the large mountain of Mt. Križevac, sometimes called "Jesus Mountain" as opposed to the smaller mountain, which is His Mother's mountain, Mt. Podbrdo. We make the Stations of the Cross while climbing to the summit, where a 14-ton cement white cross stands atop the mountain overlooking the valley. Theresa, a 29-year-old nurse from Seattle, Washington, joins us. This is Theresa's second journey up Mt. Križevac in 100-degree-plus tempera-tures. It is a stony, steep hike over jagged and loose rocks. The sun is merciless and very close, it seems. When we reach the station where Jesus says, "I thirst," I commiserate. "I know just how you feel, Lord." I guess that's the idea. Trekking this primitive, difficult path, sweating in the sun, and parched of tongue, makes Christ's sufferings a shared physical reality — something impossible to glean in the comfort of an American church. Theresa has borrowed a meditation book from St. James Church, and we take turns reciting a reading before each station.

As my daughter reads slowly and thoughtfully, I can hardly keep from staring in open wonder.

Up and down the path we pass other pilgrims of all nationalities, ages, and dimensions. Some scale the rocks in their bare feet. And some of those feet are very old feet!

From the Stations we go to the English celebration of the Mass, which is just as crowded as last night's Croatian Mass. With a full night's sleep and food in the pipeline, and a language which we can understand, the Eucharistic Liturgy becomes a beautiful experience. All week long, we will savor services more moving than any I have witnessed in my lifetime, redolent with joy and enthusiasm seldom seen in America.

En route, we stop at the home of one of the visionaries, Vicka. She is casually standing on the porch talking with a number of pilgrims as she does every day. Several spontaneously kiss her on both cheeks and she endures the intimacy with great charm and even enthusiasm. She is completely without affectation, warm and friendly with an infectious grin that bursts from her lips continually. Now in her 20s, Vicka has medium brown hair and dark eyes alive with curiosity. She is dressed in pants and a loose gray shirt with an American flag on the breast pocket, perhaps a gift from a visiting American pilgrim.

Sometimes Vicka's cherubic smile issues a chortle of embarrassed merriment at some of the questions she is asked. We hear that Americans have the reputation for posing the dumbest queries. Nevertheless, Vicka maintains an almost playful joy. She is an able Marian emissary. The qualities she radiates are far more impressive, I am thinking, than whatever showers of light emanate from the sun.

The sun phenomena is handled well by the Franciscans. Father Philip Pavich, who conducts the English Masses,

Typing up my
script for the
ABC evening
newscast.

Publicity photos were part of both TV and congressional life.

On my wedding day, Dec. 3, 1966, I am flanked by my favorite men: my brothers "JBS" and "TR" (to my right) and, on my left, my new husband, Bill.

Stanton Takes Bride In Wedding of Year

By FRANCES SULLIVAN
County Editor

WASHINGTON, D. C. — Lake County lost its most eligible bachelor this morning when U. S. Rep. J. William Stanton of Painesville exchanged wedding vows here with Miss Margaret Marie Smeeton.

MARRIAGE of the dark-haired, dark-eyed REP. STANTON District and the fair Miss Smeeton came after a year's courtship. The freshman congressman from Ohio was introduced to the television news commentator by Rep. William A. Ayres of Akron when she was covering Capitol Hill for Metro Media.

She now is reporting news from The Hill and the White House for American Broadcasting Co.

The daughter of Prof. and Mrs. C. Brooks Smeeton of 6391 N. Prospect Ave., Shorewood, of Lake Shore Drive, North Madison, and the late Mr. Stanton, were wed in the Church of the Epiphany in Georgetown, District of Columbia.

as maid of honor. Bridesmaids were a sister-in-law, Mrs. Thomas Smeeton, of Annandale, Va.; Mrs. Thomas Goehrt of Wayland, Mass.; Mrs. Philip Jennings and Mrs. David Cannon, both of Milwaukee; Mrs. Susan Obey, Miss Kathleen Day and Miss Sirius Gallagher, all of Washington.

The attendants' gowns were of velvet in a cherry red color. The coat-style dresses were floor length and were fashioned with long sleeves and cape backs. Striking accents to the red of the gowns were the white fur muffs carried by the attendants.

Francis F. Stanton of Painesville served his brother as best man. Ushers were Patrick Lonch and Robert Rothfuss, Painesville and now residing in Lake Wales, Fla.; Rushton Skakel of Greenwich, Conn., college roommate of the bridegroom; William McGloon of Kensington, Md., and two brothers of the bride, Thomas Smeeton of Annandale, Va.; and John Smeeton of Milwaukee.

IMMEDIATELY after the ceremony, a reception was held at the Washington Club at DuPont Circle. Three hundred guests were

The bride was graduated with a bachelor's degree in English and political science from Marquette University, where her father is

Greeting Jerry Ford, who was then Minority Leader of the House of Representatives, aspiring to be Speaker, and never dreaming he would one day be President of the United States.

To Peggy and Bill Stanton — with our best wishes for a wonderful life together , on this happy day December 3rd 1966 Lady Bird Johnson — Lyndon B Johnson

This beautiful, framed engraving was personally delivered from the White House; a wedding present from President and Mrs. Johnson, even though LBJ didn't approve "at all" that I was marrying a Republican!

Picture taken in the living quarters of the White House after LBJ gave Helen Thomas and I a ride in the presidential limousine.

Very proud parents of beautiful baby Kelly, who seems a bit
startled by the camera. She quickly got used to it!

When President Nixon campaigned in Bill's congressional
district in 1972, we could not foresee that his administration
would end in infamy just two years later.

Pat Nixon was perhaps one of the most stoic of America's
First Ladies, managing to preside at White House functions
with dignity despite the ordeals she endured.

Attending our Great Gatsby-themed party (thrown to say
farewell to celebrated host and presidential advisor,
Peter Flanigan), Vice President Gerald Ford was just
weeks away from becoming Commander-in-Chief.

Every patriotic holiday in Ohio called for the
Congressman's participation in a parade.

When Democrats and Republicans in Washington were
friends … legendary Speaker of the House Tip O'Neill and
Massachusetts Congressman Eddie Boland.

Hitching a ride on Air Force One with
President George H.W. Bush.

Salvador Dali greeting us in his suite at
Le Meurice hotel in Paris.

Kelly and Theresa scaling the rocks as they make the arduous
climb up Mt. Križevac, also known as "Jesus' Mountain,"
on our first trip to Medjugorje.

Kelly (center, in red dress and straw hat) stands in one of
Medjugorje's always long lines for Confession, often held
under trees surrounding St. James Church.

My painting was inspired by Joseph Hooker's actual Easter Sunday photograph (inset) of "Christ in the Clouds" over Mt. Križevac. Note the "lamb" at the Lord's right shoulder and the shepherd's crook over the lamb's ear.

A silver Rosary I bought in Rome turned gold in Medjugorje.

There was no electricity around the cross on Mt. Križevac. It was 10:30 at night. We climbed the mountain so late because the *Gospa* was supposed to be appearing. The cross was barely visible. My camera had no flash. There was no fire at the base of the cross. It made no sense to take a picture. But when the film was developed, this was the result. I titled it "Fire of Love."

Vivacious visionary Vicka Ivankovic (second from right) welcomed myself, Theresa, and Kelly on her front porch.

I was inspired by this little girl, praying quietly in the fields around Medjugorje, to paint her portrait.

Our hostess that first trip to Medjugorje, Shima Vasilj, with her husband and children. Shima, always smiling, cooked breakfast and supper for 20 people every day.

PICTURES
TO THE EDITOR

Letters to the Front

"These pictures are from a refugee camp in western Herzegovina. A child in that camp, Slavica Remjlak, wrote to our foundation, asking, 'Please write.' So we started SLAVICA: Sending Letters and Voices in a Children's Alliance. If American kids send letters to SLAVICA, we'll see that they're delivered."
—Peggy Stanton, President,
The Mary Anne Foundation, Project SLAVICA
2818 Pennsylvania Avenue NW
Washington, D.C. 20007

Using pictures I took of refugee children during the Balkan War, The Mary Anne Foundation launched the "Letters to Slavica" project through *Life* magazine. Some 3,000 letters poured in from all across the United States, the largest reader response *Life* had ever received since becoming a quarterly magazine. The enthusiasm led to the Kids for Peace Pilgrimage Week.

The first feature of Jesus to appear on my "canvas" were His eyes. The painting eventually "grew" to be 7 ½ feet tall and was displayed at the first celebration of Divine Mercy Sunday at the Basilica of the National Shrine of the Immaculate Conception in Washington, D.C.

When Bill left Congress to go to the World Bank, he often
attended meetings at the Vatican, affording us, on several
occasions, the great privilege of meeting the future
saint, Pope John Paul II.

As Dames of Malta, we are afforded the honor of escorting
malades (French for infirm) annually to Lourdes, France,
for physical and spiritual healing in the miraculous
waters and inspiring services.

"Victor for All People":
Jesus celebrating His victory
on the Cross with His Father
and children of the world, many
the faces of Balkan children
exhibiting courage and joy
despite the terrible challenge
of living during a brutal war.

"Mother of All People":
The message is that we, all
races, religions, and cultures
are one human family under
God. On the Cross, Christ
gave His Mother to the
entire human race – to all
generations to come.

"The Road
Not Taken":
painted during
the first Gulf
War, after
the failed
international
prayer event.

Dear Bill and Peggy. *God bless you Mc Teresa mc 13-5-96*

Mother Teresa, at age 83, dared "speak truth to power,"
electrifying a National Prayer Breakfast audience in
Washington, D.C., with her unabashed plea to
preserve the tiny life in the womb.

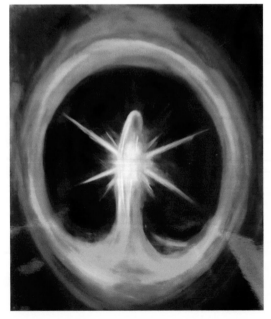

A Pennsylvania
pilgrim, Nikki
Murphy, photo-
graphed the sun
"dancing" in Med-
jugorje. When the
film was developed,
she was astonished
to see an image
of the Madonna
and Child stand-
ing inside what
OB-GYN Dr. Matt
Bulfin identified as
a womb! I painted
the image in pale
and deep blues and
titled it "Madonna
of the Unborn."

cautions pilgrims not to gawk at the solar disc. A dancing sun, in theological terms, is not what the Catholic Church can document as a miracle. "Please do not look at the sun. We are getting some very sad stories of 50 percent eyesight loss. So it is a mixed witness."

Father Philip may as well drop his pastoral concern down a well. Few pilgrims can resist sneaking a peek. Kelly is among them and is now concerned that one eye is hurting. There is a "sun theory" as espoused by Fr. Sal, a short, dark-haired priest from New Jersey, whom we met in Medjugorje. If you look directly at the sun and it is doing its dance and your eyes do not hurt and you do not see sunspots, then the Lord is protecting your eyes. If, however, you look at the sun and none of these things are happening, you should cease and desist immediately, as your eyes are at risk. This is not your gift.

I, being an artist and writer, value my eyes perhaps more than most and so I do not care to test Fr. Sal's theory. Fortunately, I do not have to do so. Fellow pilgrim Amanda Borghese has actually captured the event on her videocam. She did not witness all the action with the naked eye but when she trained her camera on the sun it gave a performance.

I watched the playback three or four times to be sure I was indeed seeing what I thought I was seeing. First, the rays formed a cross in front of the sun; then a larger, darker disc seem to engulf the original paler sphere. The sun lurched backwards and forwards. At the conclusion of the video, the lower left and right edges of the sun appeared to bulge and pulsate like a human heart. Amanda says the event took place about 7:30 p.m. during the Croatian Mass.

After viewing this phenomenon, I formulate my own "Son" theory; a viewer is not seeing the *sun*, he or she is seeing the *Son*, Jesus, in His Eucharistic form moving over the solar disc, and that is why eyes are protected at select times.

All kinds of mystical sightings are being reported. One of our housemates, Celia, a middle-aged Korean woman, claims she saw the mouth of the Madonna statue in the apparition room move. Kelly thinks two of our silver Rosaries are turning gold in color. Something *is* definitely happening to them. The two Rosaries are the ones I purchased at the base of the Spanish Steps in Rome and had blessed by Pope John Paul II. They were bright silver when we arrived; now they are dull. Kelly's began to change before mine, and the difference was visible. By the end of the trip, my Rosary is a bright gold.

At a café, we learn that an apparition may occur at about 11 p.m. The source of this information is a friend of Ivan the visionary, who says that Ivan's prayer group will be meeting on Apparition Hill tonight. While there are no guarantees of a heavenly sighting, the *Gospa* apparently frequently shows up at Ivan's evening mountain prayer sessions. For someone who was taught by nuns, the casual scheduling of a sacred visitor strains credulity. Nevertheless, like a bunch of children anticipating Christmas Eve, the pilgrims grow excited. The news spreads through the valley with the speed of wind blowing through the tobacco fields that surround the village. All interested pilgrims are to gather at the foot of Mt. Podbrdo at 10:30 p.m.

And so we do. Our Indian priest director, Fr. John, ordained a Jesuit just two years ago, is very low-key in his enthusiasm, though a believer in the visions. Father John says he does not need a dramatic sign, but he would like to witness one of the seers in "ecstasy."

From a distance, watching the trail of lights winding up the mountain is quite a sight. All ages and sizes, flashlights in hand, are making the climb, which is difficult by day and potentially hazardous by night.

Midway through the climb, just as we are passing a café, Theresa has a "G.I. stress attack" and runs back to the comfort station in the café. Kelly sits down on a rock to wait for Theresa's return, and I start to join her. "Please, Mom," Kelly pleads, "don't you stop, too. I'll just die if we both miss something!" I can see she really means it, and of course I don't want to miss anything either, so I begin making my way over the stones in the dark. Theresa has our only flashlight. Soon I draw even with a lady named Dee, who graciously shares her illumination before I tumble down the mountainside.

When we reach the apparition site, I am shocked. Ivan has quite a prayer group! Hundreds, if not thousands of people are all praying the Rosary in Croatian. When the Rosary concludes, there is sudden and total silence from the crowd. You can hear a paper clip drop. I am standing about 20 feet from an aluminum cross that presumably marks the spot where the *Gospa* appears. The silence signals her arrival.

The silence continues for about five minutes, then Ivan speaks to reveal through an interpreter what the *Gospa* has said. She is very happy tonight, according to Ivan. She wants all of us to be joyful and to pray hard in preparation for her birthday. She asked that each of us pray the Glorious Mysteries of the Rosary before going to sleep.

I have no physical or emotional "vibes" as the apparition takes place, no sense that a mysterious presence is among us. But when her message is read, I find myself moved. It is very simple, and yet so full of love that one has to ask who but a caring mother is speaking? These words do not sound like the thoughts of an awkward teenage boy.

Friday is the *Gospa*'s birthday and it is also one of the weekdays she requests fasting. Ivan indicates that the *Gospa* says we should have a "good time celebrating, but not too good." There is an appreciative chuckle from the crowd.

After the apparition, there are prayers for the sick. The young couple with the afflicted son has carried their child all the way up the mountain in his stroller, but are unable to reach Ivan for a prayer.

The pilgrims begin to filter down the mountain, some singing "Ave Maria," some praying the Rosary, some just silent. Michael and Fr. Sal are with me. I cannot find Kelly and Theresa. We stop at what I call the "Cousin of Ivan Cafe" to refresh. The verandah is filled with pilgrims and local folk, including Ivan! He lingers just long enough to get a soft drink. (If he had ordered a beer, I would have gotten on the next JAT airliner home.) Close to the café are a number of taxis. It looks as if a Broadway show has just let out.

Michael goes to the bar to retrieve some Cokes for us. I sit near a stone wall observing the descending crowd, trying to comprehend the evening. "The mind will not compute," I say to Fr. Sal. "First, we get the word at the local café that the Mother of God will appear. The apparition is scheduled for 11 p.m. Then we repair to the local watering hole after this heavenly visitor departs. Hardly our grade-school image of Mary — solemn, eyes downcast. This is a Mary of flesh and blood who smiles and sings and speaks of joy and peace. Delightful, I admit, but can this be the Mary of my childhood?"

"What's wrong with going to the café to discuss what happened?" Fr. Sal challenges me. "This is the center of village life. The difference here is everyone is talking about God! They are discussing Mary's message. What did she say?

"What we are groping with," he continues, "is God walking among men. It is easy to deal with God's divinity. It's His humanity with which we struggle."

This is a profound and unique perspective. It leaves us to speculate had we lived 2,000 years ago, whether we would have accepted Jesus Christ — son of the carpenter Joseph — as the Messiah? I had always assumed I would. Now I wonder. For the first time, I comprehend the Jews' disbelief. After all, we humans expect nothing but utter solemnity and grandeur from God. How could the Almighty take the form of a mere tradesman? He, the Creator of Kings? It is humbling to realize we might well have been among the unbelievers.

"We would have had one improvement over tonight," I say. "At least we would have seen Him." I asked if anyone felt "a presence," adding that I had not.

Michael says he did. I conclude that the *Gospa* is really giving Michael the treatment.

Father Sal confesses to a strange reaction on the mountain. He had the urge to leave. "Why?" we ask. Father finds the reason difficult to articulate. It has something to do with his responsibilities to the people back home. They will look to him for guidance on Medjugorje.

In two days, at another mountain gathering, I will come to a dramatic understanding of Fr. Sal's emotions.

Father Sal has touched on what sets Medjugorje apart from the rest of the world and why it draws visitors from all over the globe. God is the center of life here. He is the "Main Man," the "Mayor" of this town. Rosary beads dangle from hands of farmers as they walk down the road with their cow. They hang around the necks of children, women, and even a devastatingly handsome male model. In Medjugorje, one goes to Mass as frequently as Americans go to Starbucks, not because one feels obliged, but because it's the best action in town and one is afraid of missing something. Two Masses a day would be unheard of in America. Not in Medjugorje.

This evening is a case in point. Having attended the 10 a.m. English Mass, I thought I would pass up the 6 o'clock Croatian Mass. Amanda Borghese and I walk over to the Kompas Travel Café.

The conversation is fascinating, and at any other time and in any other setting — Paris or Rome, for example — we would've enjoyed it immensely. Somewhere in the midst of the dialogue, however, we can sense in one another that we would rather be someplace else.

Just across the field, we can hear the Croatian hymns drifting our way. Both of us stand up and begin to move toward the music. Had we been in the U.S., our movement might have been motivated by guilt. Our feelings this day have nothing to do with guilt. They are powered by desire.

Theresa and Kelly comment that they are not praying enough. When they total up the Rosaries, the Eucharistic Adoration, the spiritual talks, the Stations of the Cross, they accumulate three-and-one-half to four hours! At home God is fortunate to get three-and-one-half minutes. The *Gospa* once told the visionaries they should daily spend four hours in prayer. To the children's expressed astonishment, she allegedly replied, "That's only one-sixth of your day."

As I ponder these reflections, our guest house is totally dark. All pilgrims and residents are asleep, and I am writing, literally by the light of the moon. This evening's mind-bog-gling event has left me unable to sleep. It is a mystical evening. The moonlight shimmers across the small Swiss balcony on which I sit. Just below and to the right of the moon is a very bright star that I cannot identify.

To the left of the moon is an even brighter star, equally lacking in identity. The Big Dipper, which was visible on Mt. Podbrdo and while we walked home through the vineyards, seems to have retired for the evening. A dog is baying in the background and other dogs are responding. The only compet-ing sounds are crickets chirping.

In the moonlight, I can see the village houses dark with slumber and the new construction amid mounds of dirt, tools at the ready for the morrow's labor. I squint at my wristwatch. It's 3:40 a.m. Suddenly an extraordinary sight passes in front of our house, a group of village women in dark scarves and skirts walking down the road, reciting the Rosary! Shortly, they are followed by another group of women. They are headed in the direction of Mt. Križevac. Had they been a group of nuns, I would not have been on the verge of cardiac arrest. These were not women of the cloth; these were local, hardworking women with farms and families to attend, giving up precious sleep to pray!

The following evening, not to be outdone by the natives, three visitors — Kelly, Theresa, and I — scale Mt. Križevac in the dark ourselves. We are not alone. Many others are proceeding or succeeding us: couples, families, and singles, praying the Rosary in French, Italian, German, and Austrian. The mountain is more treacherous at night, the path strewn with small and large rocks, many worn smooth by the army of feet that have passed over them. Just as I was thinking it, one of the girls suggested, "Let's say the Rosary as we go up the mountain." I'm beginning to understand Michael's statement on the plane: "People seem to read your mind here." There have been so many expressions of simultaneous thought, it seems to me as if God, the "Master-mind," must place the same idea in His creatures' brains at the same moment in order to enable them to act in concert.

Standing at the base of the cross, preparing to descend the mountain, my eyes fashion on a sight that will haunt my memory long after I return to America. To my right, *beneath* not *above* my gaze, I am looking at a huge spherical object, nearly close enough to touch. It takes several minutes for the realization to sink in. I am looking *down* on the moon! The shadings are so emphatic that the lantern of the evening has a three-dimensional quality totally absent at ground level. For years, whenever a full moon illumines the sky from a faraway post, my mind will hug the recall of proximity felt at this moment.

Part of the insight gained atop Mt. Križevac is that from the perspective provided at the base of the cross, one's eye can span the entire valley of Medjugorje as well as the surrounding villages and Mt. Podbrdo, where the *Gospa* originally appeared. I speculate that this is perhaps the way God sees the world — in the round and all at once, past, present, and future.

What is the miracle here? The miracle is love. To quote my recent confessor, the Madonna of Medjugorje is different from Our Lady of Fatima or Lourdes. She is smiling. She is joyful. Perhaps, he speculated, in Fatima, she was distressed about not one but two world wars and that Russia and communism would take over a large part of the globe. "But," he added, "we are supposed to be a religion of joyfulness."

A priest from Sioux City, Iowa, put it rather well at Mass this morning: "It is when we embrace the Cross — and we all have one — that it grows light in the bearing. The mystery of Mary is that with Christ's gesture of generosity at the close of His Passion, when He said, 'Woman, behold, your son!' and then, 'Behold, your mother!' [Jn 19:26-27] God gave us a Mother who would never stop loving us, and He gave her children for whom she would always feel responsible. Like earthly mothers, who are torn asunder emotionally when their children are in distress, Mary is heartsore when she sees her charges losing the race."

The most amazing miracle in Medjugorje is the enormous number of confessions, a sight not seen in any other church in the world. There are so many penitents daily that St. James

Church cannot accommodate them. Visiting priests are pulled into duty where they and the Franciscans sit on folding chairs outside the church, hearing confessions for hours. Father Sal tells me one day he has listened to sins for four hours, "and these were not laundry-list type of confessions," he says.

Neither is mine. It has been so many months since I have been to confession, I forget how to say the Act of Contrition. By total coincidence, I wind up unburdening my sins to the same priest who listened to Kelly's confession, a confession she had vowed never to make. After an unfortunate encounter in the confessional box in the U.S., Kelly announced to her parents that she would remain a Catholic, but would never again go to confession. Thus, the sight of her standing in line is stunning indeed. "What took you so long?" Kelly asks me later when I finish telling my sins, with perhaps just a touch too much glee.

What takes so long is a philosophical discussion with the priest about Mary. I ask my confessor why I struggle with devotion to the "BVM," as we used to call the Blessed Virgin Mary in high school. Why have I felt no need of her, as if she were "the caboose on the train of salvation" as the Sioux City cleric so aptly put it? My confessor says he, too, had the same problem, "an intellectual problem" with Mary. Then his life got kind of "messed up" and he started praying the Rosary. After about five years of recitation, he began to straighten out. Why? Because "we need a mother's love. It's different from Christ love."

"How would you describe a mother's love?" I ask him.

"Unconditional, nonjudgmental, forgiving, no matter what her children do. Christ has to judge us at the end of our lives. Mary does not. Christ had the Father create a Mother for Him because He needed her and we need her."

12

MARY'S BIRTHDAY

August 4, 1988 . . . .

It is the eve of Mary's birthday and St. James Church is filled to overflowing. Services are piped over a loudspeaker to those of us on the piazza or in the fields. It is stirring to pray in the fields under the dome of the Creator's cathedral, surrounded by mountains, trees, and lush crops, while watching the glorious Medjugorje sunset. It is particularly majestic this evening, the crimson ball shooting its rays above and below passing clouds. The sky has been mercifully gray all day, threatening a storm that never materializes.

The pilgrim crowd has swelled considerably from midweek; many new arrivals are here in anticipation of Mary's birthday. The Catholic Church has always designated September 8 as the Virgin's birthdate, so Catholics question why Medjugorje celebrates it on August 5. "It is fine if the Church wants to celebrate Mary's birthday on September 8," was Ivan the visionary's response. "She prefers to celebrate it on her real birthday."

There has been an air of expectancy all day that Mary will ask her Son to do something spectacular to commemorate the occasion; or shall we say it is the hope. More impressively, there is an air of deep reverence during all the services. I am particularly moved by Eucharistic Adoration. During this service, we are actually seeing the Lord in His Eucharistic form rather than His human form. He is, in fact, physically among us.

It is one thing to intellectually accept a concept and quite another to experience it. Even we Americans who believe in transubstantiation don't live it. Eucharistic Adoration does not fill the churches. So I am certain that this will be one time when St. James will be relatively empty. Surprise! At the start of the event, the seats are almost all taken and as the service progresses, the aisles fill. Pilgrims are even spilling over the steps in front of the altar, much as the scenes must have been when the Lord was preaching in human form 2,000 years ago.

One young man is on his knees with his torso bent low over them, his head touching the floor. He remains in that position for more than an hour. Other young people kneel on the stone steps for the duration of the service.

As the priest slowly raises the monstrance to bless us, the phrase "The King of Glory is here" pops involuntarily into my head. It is not a sentence I ever remember vocalizing. I drop to my knees and do not rise for 45 minutes. Tears slide down my cheeks. In all the many years I have attended Eucharistic Adoration, no such emotional response has ever occurred. Theresa reports a similar reaction. "I couldn't believe I was on my knees for so long," she says later.

The Lord's promise, "I am with you always, to the close of the age" (Mt 28:20), springs to mind. So *this* is what He meant!

At the conclusion of the ceremony, I walk through the fields to the cemetery, reciting yet another Rosary. A small knot of young people from different countries are praying the Rosary and singing. From this site, one can view the surrounding mountains; the tobacco fields; the vineyards, lush with green leaves; and white stucco homes with terracotta roofs.

I return slowly down the dirt path from the cemetery back to St. James. The husky voice of a Franciscan friar can be heard reciting the evening Rosary. It is inspiring to listen to Hail Marys and Our Fathers said in German, Italian, French, and Croatian, in unison. I take a seat on the sidewalk between two Western Europeans. They are answering a Croatian Hail Mary with a Holy Mary in French and Italian, and I in English. The words are different, but the prayer is the same.

The man seated next to me is Italian — tall, muscular, and perhaps a construction worker. He hardly looks like a cultured type, but he is praying softly, head bowed. It is hard to wrap one's mind around the fact that so many people can be beyond the boundaries of church walls and conversing with no one but God. Even children running up and down a nearby haystack are playing silently.

One does strange things quite naturally here, such as falling to one's knees in the middle of a tobacco field at the site of the cross on top of Mt. Križevac, not the least concerned that people are strolling by.

As the services progress, I join Amanda Borghese and her friend from Venezuela, Auretha, who are sitting in the middle of the fields, watching the setting sun shoot magenta and gold rays through gray clouds as it dissolves into a red ball. The fields are well populated; there are prayer groups under trees, and penitents confessing to brown-frocked friars beneath the shade of a tobacco leaf. We are riding a kind of spiritual high. Little do I suspect that I will soon come crashing to the ground with a swiftness of a cocaine comedown.

A birthday party for a Queen

Kelly and Theresa have decided they want to spend the night before the *Gospa*'s birthday on Apparition Hill. They have invited Fr. Sal, Michael, and anyone else who might be interested to join them. Thus, when a pretty, dark-haired teenager approaches me in the fields to report that "Maria" will be appearing on the mountain tonight because Ivan's prayer group will be there, I try to dissuade her of this idea, thinking she has mistaken Kelly and Theresa's prayer gathering for the visionary's group.

"No," she replies very firmly, "It is Ivan's group that will be there."

Still skeptical, I nevertheless pass along the latest village intelligence to the girls. Despite my carefully pooh-poohing the source, Kelly and Theresa's excitement meters rise several degrees. Dinner is skipped. Meeting Fr. Sal is forgotten. Since I am valiantly trying to stick to my internal promise not to preach, I go along with their plans. I am less altruistically motivated by the fact that Theresa possesses our only flashlight. Besides, I am a little afraid I might miss something myself.

As expected, early arrival provides prime location — just about six feet from the aluminum cross marking the spot where Mary first appeared. We are, however, far from being alone. A knot of young people is seated around a brightly burning campfire. And very soon, more pilgrims begin coming. And coming. And coming. Perhaps on the theory that the last shall be first, the last pilgrims push their way past the first, crawling over the early arrivals. I am amazed at the charity of a man next to me, who rather than curse a Johnny-come-lately stumbling over him, lights the tardy soul's way to a choice seat.

Our small group attempts the Rosary, but the surrounding cacophony of competing prayers in Belgian, German, and Italian so distracts us that we cease our efforts. We are very annoyed. What are all these strangers doing on "our" mountain? Suddenly a very loud Croatian voice stills the verbal chaos by first singing, then praying the Rosary. Her arms are extended toward the cross in the Our Father position. Amazingly, this old, harsh woman has succeeded in bringing the crowd together; that is, until the guitar-playing young people, seated to our right, begin the "Alleluia" chant.

"*Shhhhh!*" comes the severe admonition from the Rosary reciters. For a few minutes, the singers pay heed. Then they attempt "Ave Maria," and this overwhelms the Rosary. The valiant Croatian woman keeps trying but eventually she is drowned to silence. Alleluias ring out. Then the swelling chorus of "Ave Marias." An American woman near us moans, "This is awful." Indeed, it is more like a tailgate crowd than celebrants anticipating a supernatural arrival. I express my displeasure to Kelly and Theresa. Having been hunched on a small rock for almost two hours, I feel the need to stand and shake galloping arthritis out of my joints. From a full body stance, I am able to see what I could not see from a crouch. The crowd is swelling on all sides.

Hordes of people had climbed the mountain and were still climbing the hill behind us, all with some kind of illumination that gave the effect of a mountain aglow with fireflies. While I am standing, a soft but persistent wind, a kind of

caressing breeze, begins to blow through my hair. It is somehow comforting. I, who dislike wind, remain standing, just
to be enveloped by it. Now I am less troubled by the lack
of reverence. The midnight sky seems to have exploded into
small-, medium-, and large-sized stars, millions of them. One
tiny star in particular fascinates my eye as it throws a ray of blue
light all the way to the earth. "Does she travel by moonbeam?"
I only half-jokingly query myself.

Across the valley from us, I can see the large dark mound
that is Mt. Križevac. Suddenly, a vertical bar of light, joined
by a horizontal bar of the same brilliance, flashes on and off
against the black sky. I stare at this bizarre spectacle, trying
to comprehend what it is. Could this strange marvel be the
white cross on top of Mt. Križevac? Just last night our housemates had told us they had watched the cross lighting up. I, of
course, had given them my usual correspondent quiz. Under
ordinary circumstances, the cross is almost invisible at night as
there is no electricity on the mountain.

The skeptic now madly tries to hitch her zoom lens to
her camera, frustrated by haste making waste. Fingers fumble badly. They botch the attachment until it is too late. Mt.
Križevac goes dark as suddenly as it lit up. Kelly is unimpressed
with my "vision." She claims she saw a much more spectacular
display at the previous Monday evening apparition, the evening she had waited for Theresa while I had gone ahead. Both
girls said they witnessed a fire go up the cross and a ball of fire
descend from it. They also claim to have seen a light "dance"
across Mt. Križevac. Kelly said she was grateful Theresa had
been with her or she would have doubted her own eyes, just as
I doubted mine now.

There is something about viewing an out-of-the-ordinary
event that makes you question your vision, if not your sanity.
But in a future pilgrimage, my camera will unwittingly produce
an astonishing photograph verifying the sight Kelly described.

It is now close to 11:30 p.m. and Theresa has had it. She
wants to go. I have mixed feelings. Something in the air, the
wind, and the stars has erased much of my earlier negativity. I

throw a quick question to the *Gospa.* "What should I do?" And there is an immediate thought response, "*Do what the children want to do.*" Is that a thought from me or someone else, I wonder. "Children" is not the way I refer to girls in their 20s, but the *Gospa* refers to all mortals as "children."

The "children" are clearly ready for departure. They are on their feet. Leaving is an ordeal. We trip over knees, elbows, hands. I cut a finger on a sharp thorn bush and the blood flows freely. There must be 10,000 people charging this hill; 9,997 are traveling up and only three are traveling down.

"*Poor fools,*" we are thinking patronizingly. "*Little do they realize they are hiking on false information. The Mother of God would surely never appear in the midst of such a rowdy atmosphere.*" The site of an occasional priest or nun in the middle of the fray should give us pause for thought. But no, we just assume they are naïve.

Finally, we reach bottom. The road before us is strewn with automobiles and taxis. "Oh, well," Theresa philosophizes as we trudge through the moonlit vineyards. "She may come. I hope she does come, but I don't need to see her."

Quite a statement from a young lady who has been seeking Mary behind every bush and who, hours earlier, insisted we skip dinner so as not be late for the apparition. Another Medjugorje miracle! Instant maturity.

When we reach our guest house, we find fellow boarders who had declined the climb seated on the second-floor balcony, watching the twinkling lights on Mt. Podbrdo. The scene reminds one of Ronald Reagan's favorite phrase, "The Shining City on a Hill."

"Did she come? Did she come?" our housemates ask breathlessly. "There were so many lights. We figured something must be happening."

"No, she didn't come," we reply. "And if she had shown up in that atmosphere, I would have less respect for her," I add.

We relate life on Mt. Podbrdo, complete with my tape-recorded sound effects of the cacophony. God must look down and shrug, "Oh well, what can you expect? They are only humans." Then I speculate how the Creator would have fun with His creatures. "When everyone is asleep, He will throw up a massive *aurora borealis* and only Fr. Slavko Barbarić, stepping out for some fresh air, will see it." The balcony resounds with laughter.

Finally, we all retire. We are asleep only two hours when we hear the two German ladies, residents of the adjoining room, returning from the hill. In a split second, Kelly and Theresa are in the hallway. I am right behind them. "Did she come? Did she come?" The girls are almost breathless with curiosity. "Yah! Yah! Yah!" Their rosy German cheeks are bobbing with excited assent.

"What time? What time?" The *fräuleins* do not comprehend the question.

The Americans point to their watches. The Germans point to the number 12. It appears we just missed the Mother of our Savior by a few moments and a lot of impatience. The next day we will hear that two teenagers who were seated close to our stakeout broke into tears during the apparition because they saw a head and a crown of 12 stars.

The Blessed Mother was reported to be very happy, the German ladies informed us. "She was happy?" I am incredulous; I expected at least a short sermon on crowd control.

None of us sleep well the rest of the night. Theresa and Kelly are upset. I am upset. We are like children sent home from the party before the ice cream and cake are served. We are confused. We thought we were the reverent ones, leaving due to a perceived lack of courtesy. Wasn't that admirable? Why had God punished us? Kelly wanted to know. "God didn't punish us," I respond. "We punished ourselves. If Mary is truly appearing, we were extended an invitation and we turned it down." I think of the pretty teenager who had informed me that "Maria" would be on the mountain tonight. I had not believed her.

It is odd how depressed this leaves all of us feeling. Why, I'm not sure. After all, we had been to one apparition on the mountain. We have been present during several apparitions in the Church. We saw nothing. This occasion very likely would have been no different. We would not have seen her, even if we had been only six feet away. *On the other hand, if she was there, she would have seen us.*

As I toss and turn, I ask myself, "Why are we so blue?" It is not rational. It is not adult. It is immature. I try asking the Lord that direct question and this thought returns to me: "*Because you turned your back on My Mother.*" I never figure out whether that is actually His response or the answer I *think* He would give.

Am I down because I, who had proudly prayed before arriving in Medjugorje, "Don't bother sending me a sign because I don't need one," now find that I *do* need a sign? Am I down because I have been so critical of the crowd — even mocking it — and God fixed my clock? Am I down because I was so up all day? Am I down because the journalist in me hates having left the scene of the story? Am I down because the girls are down and might go home with less faith than when they started?

A combination of all the above, I conclude, with emphasis on the latter. I cannot deny I feel anger at Theresa for insisting on departure even when I pointed out we were inconveniencing all the pilgrims over whom we had to crawl to accomplish our descent.

August 5: The Queen's birthday

I am still awake at 5 a.m. when Theresa knocks at the door wondering whether Kelly and I intend to keep our promise to the *Gospa*. We had decided making the Stations of the Cross would be a fitting birthday present. Disgruntled as I feel toward the young woman, something urges me to reconciliation. "Yes," I tell Theresa, "I will come." Kelly is sleeping too peacefully to arouse. I feel sure Mother Mary will understand.

Attitude is everything. This morning the route up Mt. Križevac is truly a Way of the Cross. I am not nearly so moved as I had been. The heat feels even more oppressive. My skin is damp. The climb seems deeper. There are many more pilgrims than we have previously encountered.

"Did the BVM ask all these people to make the Stations last night?" I quip to Theresa.

Several of the pilgrims smell like deodorant is a stranger to them. Many are older, heavier, and are moving very slowly. I keep looking at my watch. I am terribly thirsty, too thirsty even to sympathize with the Crucified One. Father Slavko Barbarić, whom we have seen every morning and whose meditation book we are using, sails by us. He is dressed in a T-shirt and slacks.

Theresa seems to be feeling all the reverence that has left me. She wants to pray the Rosary out loud together. I prefer to say it to myself, but my conscience forces me to reluctantly agree. She wants to read the meditations out loud. I want to read them to myself. She is stumbling with the readings and they are going very slowly. She apologizes for the errors. I tell her it's no problem, but I don't mean it.

We finish the last station. I charge up the rest of the mountain without waiting for Theresa. Wednesday morning, I had been so moved at the sight of the cross that involuntary tears had glistened my eyes. This morning my eyes are dry. I say a quick prayer and stand overlooking the amazing vista of the valley and villages. Even this scene leaves me cold.

When Theresa finally appears, I notice her knees and arms are skinned. She has obviously fallen. She kneels on her wounded knees on the dirty stone steps in front of the cross and prays for several minutes. When she finishes, we begin our descent in silence, bucking a continual and growing stream of ascending pilgrims. "Does it seem more difficult this morning?" I ask Theresa. "Yes, it does," she admits, "I'm kind of glad we don't have to do it again." Two days earlier, this young woman had walked twice in one morning. The fact that Theresa seems to share my "down syndrome" saddens me even more.

All week I had watched two young Americans, born and bred in materialism, blossoming in spirituality, as they recited the Rosary, which they had seldom said before, and attended church services willingly, even eagerly. Now they seem disillusioned. The whole reason for the arduous, inconvenient trip is to increase Kelly's faith. If the vibes at the close of the journey are negative, it might end it.

I suddenly feel very angry. I shower and dress for the 10 a.m. English Mass with the anger building. It continues to increase as I walk to St. James. The heat is stifling in the church. This liturgy I had so loved, now seems saccharine. The songs have lost their melody. I can barely answer the prayers. Tears begin creeping down my cheeks. I am horrified. *Oh no*. This is the "tear thing" that I have heard overcomes so many pilgrims. *No, please God. Not me. Don't let me embarrass myself in front of all these strangers.* But I have no control; it's a fate worse than death for someone who has prided herself on remaining calm and cool in the eye of the camera before millions of viewers on nationwide TV.

The tears refuse to stop. They flow even more freely. I can feel actual sobs in my chest. This is ghastly, unseemly. I cannot believe it is happening to me. I take Communion, but I wonder if I should. I slide to my knees, hoping to hide my distress behind the legs of standing pilgrims. I, of course, have no handkerchief, no Kleenex, only the palm of my hand to wipe away the moisture. I am grateful for my large sunglasses. They, at least, partially camouflage my shame.

I begin a dialogue with the Host on my tongue, the Eucharistic Jesus. "How can this be happening? I don't believe in the *Gospa*; I mean I believe in your Mother, but I don't believe she is appearing here. I hate Medjugorje!" Then I am being urged on by some mysterious force to reject Christ Himself. For a terrible moment I am just a hair's breadth from doing just that. *But it is a step, no matter how disturbed and how disillusioned I am, that I cannot take.* "I still love You, Lord. I still believe in You. Please don't ever take my faith in You away."

The tears are streaming now. How can there be anything good, I ask myself, about a place that can shake the faith of someone who has believed for so long?

I remain kneeling. I don't dare stand up, though I am aching to leave the church. "*I've got to get out of here*" is a desperate recurring thought. There is, however, no quick escape. The crowds are too thick. I am forced to thread my way to the door, all the while trying to cover my anguished face.

At last I am outside. I am supposed to meet Kelly at 11 a.m. to purchase bus tickets for the trip to see the legendary Fr. Jozo Zovko, who suffered torture from the communists for his belief in the apparitions. But I head for the field instead. I dare not let Kelly see her mother in such a distressed state. I have to regain control of myself. But control is not coming. Instead, my condition is getting worse. My shoulders are shaking. My chest is actually heaving with sobs. I have never experienced such an emotional outburst, not even in my teenage years, wailing over a lost love.

High above the valley in front of me, the cross on Mt. Križevac stands impassive against a cobalt blue sky. I focus on it. "You want prayers of the heart? Well, you're getting them. I don't understand you! Why am I behaving like this? Why am I crying? So what if we walked out on the BVM? We meant well. Why should such a small thing cause such a large upset? Why are the girls let down?

"Why would you let us come all this way to lose our faith?"

I stare defiantly at the cross as I rush down the path, wanting to tell it, "Do something! Twirl. Change colors. Do all those things I said I did not need. I *do* need something."

Suddenly, I hear a feminine voice at my left shoulder. "Hello," says the voice. I turn. I can't believe my eyes. The owner of the voice is the pretty teenager I had seen in this exact spot 24 hours earlier, the girl who had told me with such certainty that "Maria" would appear last night, the girl I had refused to believe. How does she manage to be nowhere in view at one moment and at your elbow the next? "How are you?" she asks sweetly, but not intrusively. If she has witnessed my distress, she gives no sign. "I'm just fine," I fib, still stunned by her presence. She smiles again and indicates she is headed toward a group of young people gathered in prayer under a tree.

As she departs, I come to the startling realization that the small exchange of conversation with the mysterious young woman has stilled the sobs that were uncontrollable only minutes before. I continue toward the cemetery where young people have been holding daily Rosary gatherings.

I can feel the Rosary in my pocket. The *Gospa* claims it is one of the most powerful prayers, but I do not feel inclined to say it. I duck under some propped-up boards that form a decrepit entry to the cemetery. There are two or three people here, a man saying the Rosary and a couple reading the tombstones.

I feel the Rosary again in my pocket — the Rosary that has gone from brilliant silver to dark gold in a few days' time. Well, all right. One decade. I sit on the edge of a tombstone facing a larger monument. I find myself staring into the eyes of Jesus, who is looking at me from a holy picture pasted on the grave. I gaze at those eyes as I run my fingers over the beads, and as I pray, the war on the battlefield of my soul seems to cease. So I say another decade of the Rosary. When I conclude, the anguish is gone. I am as peaceful as if the previous hour had never occurred, though I am totally mystified by the fact that it did. I put the Rosary back into my pocket and start through the fields toward St. James to meet Kelly.

"Mom, where have you been?" Kelly demands impatiently when I reach Kompas Travel to purchase the bus tickets. I evade an answer. How can I explain to my daughter an event that I do not understand myself? This is certainly the afternoon to see Fr. Jozo. We have been told time and time again we must not miss a talk by Fr. Jozo, who was the pastor of St. James when the apparitions began. One day in the future, Fr. Jozo's story will be told on film with movie star Martin Sheen playing the Franciscan.

We have heard so much about the saintly Fr. Jozo that I do not know what to expect, but I am surprised by what I see. Fr. Jozo is a young man, somewhere in his 40s. He is about 5-foot-10 in height, perhaps 155-160 pounds in weight. He has short black hair; a handsome, tanned face; and a very wide, infectious grin that he uses sparingly. His new parish in Tija-lina, surrounded by low mountains, is much smaller than St. James, hardly more spacious than a chapel, with bright white walls largely unadorned but for a statue of Mary standing to the left of the altar.

While we are waiting for Fr. Jozo to begin speaking, many pilgrims hasten up to the statue of Mary to take a picture. When Fr. Jozo tells of how the statue wept, I realize what has occasioned the photographic rush.

A lady from our pew volunteers — rather insists — on acting as translator for Fr. Jozo, who does not speak English. He has his own translator, but does not want to hurt the volunteer's feelings. While the three are negotiating at the altar, I chat with a nun named Sr. Jane, who is on my left. She shows me a photo, another alleged picture of Mary. It is just a head-shot; the features are in very soft focus, revealing a dark-haired woman in a white veil, beautiful but rather somber.

This is the same picture I witnessed being presented to Ivan, one of the seers, for inspection at another time. After examining it for a while, Ivan says it is too blurred for him to positively identify her as the Madonna and then adds that no camera or painting could ever do her justice.

As we are sitting in the church, I become aware of a very beautiful fragrance filling the air. I look around for its origin. No one new has entered our pew.

The fragrance is luscious. Certainly it is not from Sr. Jane. I cannot resist sniffing as surreptitiously as possible, wishing I knew the wearer, so I could inquire as to how I might purchase a bottle of that perfume for myself.

Finally, Fr. Jozo begins to speak. The volunteer translator has her hands raised in the air as she interprets. Unfortunately, it does not aid her skills. One has to strain to comprehend her speech. We are, however, mesmerized just watching Jozo's performance. He speaks with his eyes closed in a husky whis-per. We know he is telling us the roots of the Medjugorje story as he lived it, but the translator's translations are more myste-rious than the Madonna, so we only capture bits and pieces.

Father Jozo eventually realizes our struggles and as kindly as possible, he reverts back to his own interpreter. He smiles his very white smile and takes the blame for the difficulties. "I feel very ashamed that I cannot speak to you in your own language," he apologizes, gracefully saving the pushy pilgrim from embarrassment, with his simplicity and humility.

"Don't be scared," Fr. Jozo's quiet voice intones, "don't be scared. Go toward the light." The phrase touches hearts because we are all a bit frightened by the oft-repeated line, "You have been called here."

"Pray with the heart," Father tells us. "Without the Holy Spirit, we cannot pray. Prayer from the heart means accepting your cross." Father Jozo then relates a story of an Italian priest who arrived with a group of pilgrims, all of whom had a picture of Our Lady. One picture was crying. Everyone witnessed the crying. "They called me," he continued. "I came. I wanted to see if it was fake. I took the picture with me. I called the bishop. The bishop saw the same thing."

The reason for the *Gospa*'s sorrow, claims Fr. Jozo, is "the sickness of priests. They do not feel with the Church." He asks a series of rhetorical questions: "How come priests become sick? What has happened that priests do not feel with the Church? How come those who lead and protect have lost their faith? How is it possible to heal priests?"

People forget, the friar continues, to have feelings and pray for priests. "I feel you Americans have a good heart." We apparently do not criticize priests as much as they are criticized in Europe. "Your priest is always a prophet; even if you hate him, don't leave him. Don't throw him out of your heart. Pray more for your priests. Invite priests to your home so kids can talk to them … just as Jesus had a special place at table.

"We need your love, not your criticism. Put us in your hearts." Many years in the future, when the clergy scandals rock the Church, Fr. Jozo's words will take on the aura of prophecy.

Father Jozo turns his attention to the Bible. "This book is different from any other book. … After 75 years the Bible is coming back to Russia." He tells us we should have a statue of

Mary in our house. There should be a cross on one side and the Bible on the other. The Bible is, Fr. Jozo explains, "God talking. Don't liberate Jesus' Word from the Bible. No one else talked like Jesus did. Nobody else wrote the Bible like God wrote the Bible. If you are looking for power in your life, it's in the Bible. You need a night when you don't sleep, when you just listen and just talk to God."

Thinking of the previous evening, the last admonition hits so close to home, I almost draw a loud breath. Kelly and Theresa are sitting directly in front of me, and I wonder if Fr. Jozo's words seem as prophetic to them.

"Everything is possible with God," Fr. Jozo reminds us. "Why is the Rosary important? The Rosary is the mystery prayer. You cannot [just] repeat the prayers. Prayer is always different. Like a river. It always has new energy, new life, new power, [a] new gift. To pray with the heart is to pray the way God wants us to pray. *With prayer you can do anything.*" He says it's like the story of David and Goliath. "David had just one rock." Father Jozo holds up the Rosary. "With this, we have five rocks."

"Pray with your heart," he repeats, "with the bottom of your hearts, not just your lips. Don't be scared of the light. Whenever you pray, you have to feel with the Church. Prayer is not a product from the human brain. It is a gift from God." Medjugorje, he indicates, has infused the Church "with a new atmosphere of happiness and love."

He finishes with a very sobering conclusion. "We have a role of prophecy. 'I choose you.' Can you imagine that Mary said that? 'I invited you because I need you. You are important.' You are not here by chance," Fr. Jozo insists. "You are here because God and Our Lady have great plans for you." Eyes still closed, the friar lifts a wooden cross above his head and blesses us.

It is one of the most compelling spiritual presentations I have ever witnessed, and is needed to be seen to be fully appreciated. When Kelly tells me he has spoken for an hour-and-a-half, I am astounded.

Pilgrims rush out of the pews to surround Fr. Jozo. Father Sal tells me he has the gift of healing. I am intrigued because I have never seen a healer before and usually connect healing with fraudulent evangelists under the big tent. Father Jozo moves very solemnly down the line of pilgrims kneeling at the altar rail. He puts a hand on each head, over a heart, sometimes on the back. How he knows where the problem is located is not apparent since no one seems to tell him. Suddenly we hear deep sobs, much like the pilgrim shown breaking down on ABC's "20/20" television news program after praying with a visionary. These sobs come from a man in a blue-and-white-striped shirt. The woman next to him gently holds him.

Watching the man's eyes fill up, Fr. Jozo says nothing. He merely turns and quietly leads the rest of the pilgrims out of the church so that the man can experience this spiritual moment by himself. It is a great act of kindness.

In the courtyard, Father continues to bless people. I do not go near him. My recent bout with "internal combustion" is quite enough for one day, thank you very much.

We are bused back to Medjugorje. It is time for the Rosary service. The church again is teeming with congregants. I position myself shamelessly at the door. Maybe the Lady will show herself to the whole church this night as she once did when the apparitions first began. After all, it is her birthday. I cannot resist clocking the time, with apologies to the Lord for my curiosity, reminding Him He gave it to me. The same gentle but firm wind of last night begins to sweep through the trees just as it swept across the mountain. Again, I, who detest wind, love the feel of this one. It brings to mind a message attributed to the Blessed Mother: "*The wind is my sign. When you feel the wind, you will know that I am near.*"

I move away from the church door and stand on the fringe of the crowds surrounding the piazza. Suddenly there is a luscious fragrance passing under my nostrils, the very same scent I had noticed in Fr. Jozo's church. What is that? I ask myself. Nobody told me perfume was a staple product of the valley. I keep sniffing, but there is no apparent source. I walk to the fields. I can hear a soft Franciscan voice intoning "*Drago Maria.*" Other voices answer in French, Italian, German, Gaelic, and Croatian from the piazza, the steps, and the fields. There is unity amidst the diversity, not the discord of the previous evening. Sheep with a shepherd are behaving like lambs.

As the bells begin to toll for the evening Mass, I notice lines of people along the right side of the church staring intently at the sun. "*Darn screwballs,*" I think to myself, "*they never listen.*" Father Philip warned them they could damage their eyes. I give the sun a quick glance. It is very bright, and I am afraid to chance the second peek. An artist goes mute without eyes.

More and more people are staring at the sky. Cameras are focusing. There is no shouting, no excitement, no finger-pointing. Rather, everyone just peers at the sun as if in a trance. I am so concerned, I attempt to tug at the sleeve of one very intent sun spy. She seems not to know I exist. "Let them go blind," I say to myself. "No one will listen to reason." I walk away feeling incredibly rational.

Once again, the laugh is on me. The pilgrims are apparently gaping with good reason. The sun was doing its dance. "I saw the sun! I saw the sun!" Fr. Sal exclaims excitedly later. He must have seen *something*, because he had not been caught up in the sun mania. He, like me, has been ignoring the sun with the proviso, "If the Blessed Mother wants me to look, I'll just happen to look and God will protect my eyes." Apparently the *Gospa* had given the nudge. But despite viewer raves, I am strangely not sorry to have missed the show. And it will be years before I am a reluctant but awed witness.

As we gather this evening for our last meal in Medjugorje, Theresa is the missing link. "Where is Theresa?" my housemates ask. "I guess in church." It proves to be a sage prophecy. Theresa arrives in the dining room about 9 p.m. "Was there a storm during the Rosary service?" she wants to know. "No," we tell her, "a strong wind came up, but no storm."

"There was no thunder?" Theresa persists. "None," I respond, "and I was standing right outside the church during the Rosary."

Theresa's sizable brown eyes grow a trifle wider. "There was thunder in the church," she says, "and there were streaks of light around the altar windows."

"When did this happen?" we all want to know.

"About 5:40," she says, "at the time of the apparition." Theresa is not alone in her observations. Several people who were also in the church at the same moment observed the same occurrence. It brings to my mind a conversation with a friend from Ohio. She had been present in the church for several apparitions. Each one, she recounted, was preceded by a similar phenomenon.

Dinner concludes and I walk out of the house for a trip to the exchange bank. At the end of the sidewalk, one of our housemates is standing behind a car, staring up at Mt. Križevac. She is oblivious to my presence. I playfully pat her arm. "What are you hallucinating?" I joke. She does not respond. I repeat the question.

She eyes me with hesitation. "Well, should I tell you?"

"Please!"

"Well, I just saw," she relates calmly, as if describing a hockey game, "Four red hearts pass in front of the cross."

I recall yesterday's ordeal. I could have used some hearts. The experience continues to haunt me. My mind seeks reasons. Gradually, theories begin to emerge. I am not as deep a believer as I fancied myself. Despite my disclaimers to the Almighty, I want signs like everyone else. At the same time, I fear supernatural sightings. I would not even make the Stations of the Cross by myself, afraid some of those "Mary on the path" stories might just be true.

I asked a priest friend why we fear seeing an apparition. "Because," he answered, "if you had an apparition, it would mean you are either a big sinner or you have a big job."

More lessons become apparent. One, we were arrogant to assume that our form of worship was more appealing to the Lord than the rest of the "turkeys." Two, God is much more tolerant of "turkeys" than I, even though I am one. Three, I was not called to Medjugorje to escort Kelly to her conversion.

I was called to experience my own. And four, I cannot externalize the message of Medjugorje until I internalize it. "Let there be peace on earth, and let it begin with me."

The morning of our departure, all these answers come together in the reproduction of a painting I discover in the Franciscan bookstore. There is Jesus standing before an untidy crowd, a naked baby crouched in the crook of His right elbow, His left hand extended in a calming outreach. His audience seems in a state of extreme agitation. Children are trying to break free of their mothers' grasps. There is pushing. There is shoving. One can almost hear the Master saying, "Now, if the Germans will sit down over there, the Italians to the left, and the French in the middle."

I gaze a long time at the picture. Theologians say God speaks to us three ways: through Scripture, through people, and through circumstances. I feel he is speaking very pointedly to me through the circumstance of this painting. In reality, the Lord dealt with such disorder, probably frequently. His infinite tolerance for the human condition could not have been proclaimed more loudly if it had been peeling from the bells of St. James. It is a graphic illustration of God's "crazy love."

Ruefully but gratefully, I realized I had come to Medjugorje a Pharisee — a woman utterly satisfied with herself and her stimulating life as a Washington insider, wanting no conversion like the rest of the pilgrims. Hopefully, I will go home like the publican in Jesus' parable, who prayed, "God, be merciful to me a sinner!" (Lk 18:9-14), promising never to judge another human being, knowing every day I will have to pray for the strength to keep that promise. I know, too, that this self-revelation could never have been driven home to me so powerfully anywhere else in the world.

I feel as if I have been divinely "set up." Had we not gone up Mt. Podbrdo on Mary's birthday eve and had we not left prematurely, I would never have been able to see so vividly the contrast between my intolerance and the nonjudgmental, loving attitude of the Blessed Mother, an image I hope will never fade.

There is another and very frightening realization. The devil does indeed exist. He had waged a fierce fight to destroy my growing belief in Medjugorje and ultimately my faith in God, his supreme goal. He came dangerously close to victory. In retrospect, I recognize that it was the Holy Spirit who kept me praying despite my reluctance to do so. And that continuing prayer saved me from the ultimate step of denial. Was the "tear thing" remorse for past sins? What a mother lode I must have had!

Now my prayer is that God will never allow me to be tested that severely again. Certainly, no pilgrim comes without warning. All the reading material on Medjugorje reiterates Mary's caution concerning the presence of the "old apple vendor," as I call the fellow who seduced Adam and Eve with a piece of fruit. One tends to dismiss him as Halloween scare tactics — but that is only at one's peril, as I am now acutely aware.

My mind is struggling with so much new insight that I pass up a sightseeing tour when we overnight en route home in historic Dubrovnik, Croatia — me — the original greedy traveler, ordinarily grasping for every new experience. Instead, I sit alone on the beach, meditating and gazing at the immense red sun hovering over the sea.

It is an extraordinary sight. Other beachcombers point to the sun's size and scarlet color. But after Medjugorje, nothing amazes me anymore — except the fact that I am not the same person I was one week ago; the woman who did not want her life to change has to face the fact that it needs changing: that actions we excused as genes we were born with were, in fact, sins that needed to be and could be remedied.

Despite my regular appearance in the pew, I realize that easy money and the compromises made to make it have resulted in a growing chasm between my Maker and me. Never had I felt further from Him. He is not interested in newspaper stories written by me or about me; or about my success as a writer, artist, entrepreneur, or Washington hostess; or my enumerable posts as program director for this event or president of that political club or that international club.

He is interested in whether I believe in the Beatitudes more than my own press clippings. Headlines by me or about me will not impress Peter when he examines my portfolio at the Pearly Gates.

Even with that realization, I have no idea how radically my life will change, and the amazing adventures that await as a result of that change.

13

NEVER WASTE A
GOLD ROSARY

It was never on my spiritual radar to undertake that exhausting 26-hour journey again. But the story of our strange sojourn and the resulting gold Rosary rouse a surprising curiosity in Washington, revealing a hunger for something more, even among those who seemingly have it all.

It also reveals the child in all of us. People sidle up to me at social events, even embassy parties, and quietly ask, "Is it true you had a Rosary that turned from silver to gold?"

"Would you happen to have it with you?" This happens enough times that it prompts me to slip the gold Rosary into my purse as an evangelistic tool. I am frankly amazed by the awe it inspires, and pleased that its uniqueness lends much more interest in the more serious message that Mary wishes to convey from Medjugorje.

Bill is curious enough to take the Rosary to a jeweler who examines it carefully, quizzing Bill as to the circumstances that brought about the transformation. It has not changed in substance, only in color, now a brilliant gold. The jeweler has no explanation, surprised at the evenness of the color. So when I am questioned, I give the jeweler's analysis.

Ironically, the people most impressed by the changing Rosary are the people hardest to impress: the worldly.

Religious churchgoers are interested, but not awed, not surprised. After all, changing colors is a small feat for a God who walks on water, cures blindness, casts out demons, calls a dead man out of a tomb, and rises from the dead. For me, the most amazing miracles are the lives I witness changing.

But to those dubious about the above, the Rosary is evidence they can see and touch, indicating something unique is going on in this place. The lure of the miraculous and of supernatural sightings is powerful. They are eager to hear my story.

People approach me about going. And will I go with them? Senators, congressmen, a famous football coach and their wives, and even Auntie Mame, who breaks her arm just before her pilgrimage is to depart and thinks she should cancel. "Oh, come on, Pat," I tease her, "I went to Africa with a broken leg."

So she goes, doubtful about the whole enterprise, until one night when she is returning home after dark from St. James Church and loses her way in the fields. Suddenly there is a bright light coming from she knows not where, illuminating the dirt path all the way to her residence.

So many people ask if I will accompany them to Medjugorje that I find myself returning nine times, including four journeys during the brutal Balkan War of 1992-1995. I, who hoped fervently that ABC would never summon me to Vietnam, become a war correspondent and relief worker.

Much as I had hoped after the first Medjugorje pilgrimage that my only job would be to change myself, not the world, it becomes a gnawing thought that the messages Mary delivers to the visionaries once a month *are* for the world and need distribution. Thus begins "The Queen's Digest," which is a simple two-page pamphlet. It contains Mary's monthly message, the latest Medjugorje news, and promotes peace which leads me to action that, only a few years ago, I would have characterized as bizarre.

14

PRAYER AND FASTING
STOPS WAR?

In one of her alleged messages, Mary told the Medjugorje visionaries that prayer and fasting could even stop wars. As the Persian Gulf War looms over the United States, I decide to test that theory.

August 2, 1990

The first major foreign policy crisis since the collapse of the Cold War emerges on the world stage.

Saddam Hussein, president of Iraq, orders the invasion and occupation of Kuwait. He justifies the move by claiming that Western colonialists carved Kuwait out of the Iraqi coasts and Kuwait is therefore an artificial state. In *fact*, Kuwait existed *before* Iraq was created.

Saddam has the fourth-largest army in the world, well stocked with equipment provided by the United States during his eight-year war with Iran. Iraq's invasion sounds alarm bells to neighboring Saudi Arabia and Egypt. They call on the U.S. and other Western nations to intervene.

The U.S. has considerable skin in the game. Kuwait is a major supplier of U.S. oil. Saudi Arabia is also a major source of oil. Were Saddam to capture both countries, he would control one-fifth of the world's oil supply.

August 7, 1990

"This will not stand," President George H.W. Bush declares, "this aggression against Kuwait." Under his leadership, a coalition of interested nations builds as the summer of 1990 wanes. The coalition dubbed Operation Desert Shield includes Britain, France, Germany, Saudi Arabia, and Egypt.

Saddam increases forces in Kuwait to 300,000 and declares a *jihad* — a holy war against the coalition. He thinks fellow Arab states will stand by him. He has miscalculated. Two-thirds of Arab League members condemn Iraq's act of aggression.

November 29, 1990

The UN Security Council authorizes the use of "all necessary means" to remove Iraqi forces from Kuwait if Saddam does not do so by January 15, 1991. Saddam defies the resolution. Coalition forces now number 750,000, 540,000 of whom are Americans.

December 20, 1990

On the eve of the birthday of the Prince of Peace, we are poised on the precipice of war. Saddam Hussein steadfastly refuses to remove his troops from Kuwait before they are forcibly removed by the U.S.-led coalition.

Mindful of the division caused by the Vietnam War, George Bush works to build an American consensus on the Gulf crisis. Americans largely support correcting Iraq's misadventure. A small majority of Congress does, too. But those of us in Washington who have been schooled by the Queen of Peace in Medjugorje believe her admonition that prayer and fasting can end war, and we would like to give that option a try. After all, the *Catechism of the Catholic Church* reminds us that "all citizens and all governments are obliged to work for the avoidance of war" (2308) before any "legitimate defense" can be justified. We need to go that extra mile, and the *Gospa* shows us the way.

Bill Stanton, who collected numerous hero's medals for fighting through the horrors of World War II, suggests an international day of prayer and fasting to alter the path we are treading. Always a great delegator, he leaves it to others to figure out how to implement such a day. Why not the coalition builder, think I? After all, he served in Congress with Bill. And so, boldly, I write Mr. Bush.

Dear Mr. President,

In our house we think of you with great admiration and sympathy. It is an irony that the birthday of the Prince of Peace approaches and you are weighed down with the decision whether or not to go to war as well as a nation increasingly divided as to the answer.

May I make a suggestion that might bring unity?

The world community has applied economic, diplomatic and military pressure on Saddam Hussein. So far nothing has persuaded him to leave Kuwait. Perhaps it is time to apply the ultimate pressure — spiritual pressure.

Mr. Hussein, who is not believed to be a religious man, has invoked God's name on behalf of his cause repeatedly. You, who are a religious man, have refrained from doing so, most probably so as not to appear to be using God.

There is, however, every indication in Scripture that God likes being used. What He does not like is being abused. With this in mind, may I respectfully propose that you consider asking the world community to join America in an International Day of Prayer and Fasting. …

I respectfully propose that you consider broadcasting this request on Christmas Eve, setting a specific date on which the entire world community — Protestants, Catholics, Jews, Muslims — all who believe in God Almighty, would voluntarily fast and pray. Moreover, one specific hour could be designated when all nations and religions agree to pray together on bended knee.

If the World community did indeed respond and I feel sure it would, what a dramatic sight to see the family of man simultaneously on its knees before the Father in Mosques, Temples, Cathedrals, Churches around the world. If enough people were truly sincere, could God fail to hear us?

And could Saddam Hussein, who has called you an "enemy of God" and the West "infidels," withstand the onslaught of a spiritual army such as never before arrayed? It could truly be argued that the world has gone the last mile in pursuit of a peaceful solution.

Is it not possible that God is granting us an extraordinary period of grace — just waiting for us to seek His intervention? Since the greatest gift He has given us is free will, He would surely wait to be asked. What are we waiting for?

Finally, Mr. President, I can think of no greater legacy in history than to be remembered as the man who won the war without ever firing a shot.

Most sincerely,

Peggy Stanton

The president replies two days later with a handwritten note, which reads,

Dear Peggy,

I loved your letter. We just had a day of prayer, which I am told, was widely observed. Thank you for sharing your idea with me.

He did not, however, say he would put it into action.

Bill writes a letter to Secretary of State Jim Baker, suggesting the UN Secretary-General issue the proclamation. Nothing happens. It seems easier to build a coalition for war making than peacemaking.

December 27, 1990

Perhaps the peace initiative should percolate from the bottom up rather than the top down. After more thought, prayer, and consultation, I conclude reluctantly that perhaps the Holy Spirit is nudging *me* to organize a grassroots movement to establish the International Day of Prayer and Fasting.

"Why me?" I ask. Because the harvest is great and the laborers are few. However inadequate, the poor Lord has to take what He can get.

I have been particularly moved by the story of Esther in the Old Testament and her courage in taking a bold step to assist her nation. Esther risked her life. I only have to risk my reputation for sanity.

I say reluctantly because I thought the letter to the president was the sum and substance of my peace effort. At least I was *hoping*. But there is such enthusiasm for prayer and so many people willing to help, just waiting for a signal. I want to be sure this is God's will. I want some very clear sign, but the only clarity seems to be a consistent sense of loss if I don't try.

If we try and there *is* still war, we will know we have made every effort. If we *don't* try and there is war, we will always wonder with sorrow if we could have helped to prevent it. Most important to me is trying to follow God's will, and never turning Him down. I think of so many previous times when I have felt reluctant to make a spiritual move and the good that has resulted if I managed to overcome that reluctance.

What will become of this day of prayer, I do not know, but I feel I must try.

I recall Mordecai's admonition to Esther, which especially hits home: "For if you keep silence at such a time as this, relief and deliverance will rise for the Jews from another quarter, but you and your father's house will perish. And who knows whether you have not come to the kingdom for such a time as this?" (Esth 4:14)

The argument made to me by others is that I know many people who hold influential positions. Do I know them "for such a time as this?"

That thought finally ignites the spark. Only the Lord knows whether the spark becomes a flame or dies a flicker.

I phone two major figures in the Catholic and Protestant worlds, asking them if they will enlist their spiritual networks in a universal day of prayer on January 6. Both agree to do so.

That was much easier than I feared. As I continue, it seems the Grand Designer is opening every door. I am able to reach people who are difficult to reach, able to persuade people who might have scoffed. Busy people commit their time.

Through these intercessors, thousands and thousands of people worldwide can be notified. The plan is simple. Contact one leader in a strategic position in every part of the world; put him or her in total charge of his or her sphere of influence with the easiest of guidelines; and just pass the word to pray on January 6 around the world. Hopefully, God will lead us to a peaceful solution. And we will listen.

Unfortunately, there is another "leader" who is trying to get in the act. The serpent who likes to masquerade as the Savior. The "old apple vendor" is continually trying to pedal his "Granny Smiths" to me in the form of fear, reluctance, laziness, and pride. Sometimes his approach is so clever that I, like Eve, fall for it.

I have asked God to please be the more recognizable voice and to please continue to guide me: to make me speak when I am supposed to speak, to be silent when I'm supposed to listen, and to have the wisdom to know the difference. And I have also asked Him to please let me know when my task is finished, so that I do not wear out my — and most importantly — His welcome.

January 2, 1991

On this date Mother Teresa, future saint and 1979 Nobel Peace Prize winner, appeals to President Bush and President Hussein in a letter:

Dona ora. Grazie!

Dear President George Bush and President Saddam Hussein,

I come to you with tears in my eyes and God's love in my heart to plead to you for the poor and those who will become poor if the war that we all dread and fear happens. I beg you with my whole heart to work for, to labour for God's peace and to be reconciled with one another.

You both have your cases to make and your people to care for but first please listen to the One who came into the world to teach us peace. You have the power and the strength to destroy God's presence and image, His men, His women, and His children. Please listen to the will of God. God has created us to be loved by His love and not to be destroyed by our hatred.

In the short term there may be winners and losers in this war that we all dread, but that never can, nor never will justify the suffering, pain and loss of life which your weapons will cause.

I come to you in the name of God, the God whom we all love and share, to beg for the innocent ones, our poor of the world and those who will become poor because of war. They are the ones who will suffer most because they have no means of escape. ... I beg you to save our brothers and sisters, yours and ours, because they are given to us by God to love and to cherish. It is not for us to destroy what God has given to us. Please, please let your mind and your will become the mind and will of God. You have the power to bring war into the world or to build peace. Please choose the way of peace. ...

I appeal to you — to your love, your love of God and your fellow men. In the name of God and in the name of those you will make poor, do not destroy life and peace. Let love and peace triumph and let your names be remembered for the good you have done, the joy you have spread and the love you have shared. ...

May God bless you now and always.

God Bless you,
M. Teresa, M.C.

Fool though I may be, I am in very good company.

January 8, 1991 ....

January 6, 1991, our great International Day of Prayer and Fasting (IDPF) comes. And goes.

My vivid writer's imagination had envisioned a scene when major leaders around the world would be in cathedrals, temples, and mosques seeking God's guidance.

That's not exactly the way it happened.

I was in Fort Lauderdale on January 6, which also happens to be my birthday. On vacation, Bill and I had been traveling all over the state the previous week, from south to north to west and back to south Florida, visiting friends. In every spare moment, I had phoned and faxed IDPF material throughout the United States. Ironically, I lost my address book before I could call all the people with whom I had intended to touch base.

Nevertheless, the variety of people whom we saw and met just coincidentally in our journey were from Chicago, Houston, Los Angeles, and New York. They may have been the spiritual architecture rendered by the Grand Designer.

There was, however, no visibly grand design on January 6. On my birthday, I was completely alone in an unfamiliar, albeit lovely church, close to our hotel in Fort Lauderdale — St. Sebastian's Parish. As I sat in front of the Blessed Sacrament, one tear descended, then a second down my drooping cheek. "I tried, Lord. I did my best. But I didn't do very well. You should have picked a better leader."

In my despondent state, I asked the question: Didn't our efforts make any difference *at all*?

That night, my good friend Dr. Matt Bulfin reported that a church in Fort Lauderdale had promoted IDPF with flyers and that a special Mass was said.

I learned that 75 people gathered for a special Rosary service in Winnetka, Illinois, and that the news was broadcast there on WGN radio.

One woman made 14,000 flyers about IDPF and passed them out at an interdenominational service. During a dinner party in Maryland, eight people announced they had fasted all day; 150 people had prayed at a church in Kenosha, Wisconsin. On January 5, the Voice of America disseminated word of the day of prayer and fasting to 41 language centers around the world.

International Fellowship Network, based in Washington, D.C., sent appeals around the world from Australia to Argentina.

The Medjugorje network sent postcards to some 900 prayer groups.

Thanks to an Egyptian official at the World Bank, our prayer proclamation was read in every mosque in Egypt, and Middle Eastern newspapers related that the prayer came from America! If it wasn't a tsunami of prayer, then perhaps it was a small tornado.

January 9, 1991

The prayer continues. Secretary of State Jim Baker holds talks with Iraqi negotiator Tariq Aziz.

January 10, 1991

American and Iraqi negotiators remain in session for nearly seven hours. Hopes around the world swell, only to deflate precipitously when Secretary Baker announces the results. The meetings have gone long but not well. The Iraqis remain intransigent.

It is hard to keep our spirits high. Gloom descends on all of us. I remember the feeling that came over me as I left the empty church on Sunday. Perhaps there will be war after all, because so many people are indifferent to the Source of peace. It is the first time I do not feel optimistic about a peaceful settlement. But my feeling this morning is that we must not give up hope. We must keep praying.

January 11, 1991 . . . .

More reports on IDPF surface. Prayers were said in Los Angeles, in Costa Rica, in Peru. Thousands prayed in Dallas. It is heartening to finally realize that one candle lit others. But was it enough? So many people remain eager and ready to go to war.

January 12, 1991 . . . .

Today is an historic and terribly somber day in the nation's capital. After the longest debate in the annals of the Congress, the House and Senate vote to, in effect, give the president the power to go to war.

Those who vote affirmatively do so, they say, because they believe giving the president the authority to use force might convince Saddam to leave Kuwait. Thus, the president will not actually have to take advantage of that authority.

UN Secretary-General Perez de Cuellar is our last human hope for peace, and he is now in Baghdad with a new peace proposal to put before Saddam.

Meanwhile, the prayer crescendo builds. The Basilica of the National Shrine of the Immaculate Conception here in Washington will hold a full day of prayer. All the Masses will be for peace. The Washington Cathedral will hold an ecumenical service on Monday, January 14, and there will be a candlelight procession to the White House. An all-night vigil will be held at an African Methodist Episcopal Church in Washington. We hear of more participation in our January 6 effort; the latest report is from the Knights of Columbus.

I continue to believe that at some point, God will make the difference in the Gulf. In my reading of Scripture, especially the Old Testament, I notice that God seems to play His own kind of brinksmanship, arriving dramatically on the scene when all human endeavor has failed — for the precise purpose of demonstrating that mere human endeavor is not enough.

If God does intervene, I am reminded of what a Muslim said last month: "We forgot to thank God for the end of the Cold War." Let's hope that if we get the opportunity, we don't make that same mistake with the Gulf War.

January 14, 1991 ································

The day before the day before D-Day. All hope for a peaceful settlement of the Gulf crisis appears to have been dashed with the apparent failure of the UN Secretary-General's meeting with the Iraqi president. Among the ideas he was going to share with Saddam were some "religious ideas," de Cuellar claimed. When asked if there would be war or peace, he replied, "If you believe in God, only God knows. If you do not believe, no one knows."

January 15, 1991 ································

A second future saint writes to President Bush. Pope John Paul II joins Mother Teresa's appeal for a peaceful solution to the Gulf conflict:

> To the Honorable George Bush
>
> President of the United States of America
>
> I feel the pressing duty to turn to you as the leader of the nation which is most involved, from the standpoint of personnel and equipment, in the military operation now taking place in the Gulf Region.
>
> In recent days, voicing the thoughts and concerns of millions of people, I have stressed the tragic consequences which a war in that area could have. I wish now to restate my firm belief that war is not likely to bring an adequate solution to international problems and that, even though an unjust situation might be momentarily met, the consequences that would possibly derive from war would be devastating and tragic. We cannot pretend that the use of arms, and especially of today's highly sophisticated weaponry, would not give rise, in addition to suffering and destruction, to new and perhaps worse injustices.

Mr. President, I am certain that, together with your advisers, you too have clearly weighed all these factors, and will not spare further efforts to avoid decisions which would be irreversible and bring suffering to thousands of families among your fellow citizens and to so many peoples in the Middle East. In these last hours before the deadline laid down by the United Nations Security Council, I truly hope, and I appeal with lively faith to the Lord, that peace can still be saved. I hope that, through a last minute effort at dialogue, sovereignty may be restored to the people of Kuwait and that international order which is the basis for a coexistence between peoples truly worthy of mankind may be re-established in the Gulf area and in the entire Middle East.

I invoke upon you God's abundant blessings and, at this moment of grave responsibility before your Country and before history, I especially pray that you be granted the wisdom to make decisions which will truly serve the good of your fellow-citizens and of the entire international community.

From the Vatican, January 15, 1991.

IOANNES PAULUS PP. II

The world is clearly beginning to think about God in this equation, but is it too late and are there too few? I had hoped against hope that it is not, but this morning, quite by accident, just as I had happened on Esther, I turn to the Book of Proverbs, written by King Solomon. A passage from Chapter 1, entitled "A Warning to the Heedless," draws my attention:

Wisdom cries aloud in the street,
in the markets she raises her voice;
on the top of the walls she cried out;
at the entrance of the city gates she speaks:
"How long, O simple ones, will you love being simple?

How long will scoffers delight in their scoffing
And fools hate knowledge?

"Give heed to my reproof;
behold, I will pour out my thoughts to you;
I will make my words known to you.
Because I have called and you refused to listen,
have stretched out my hand and no one has heeded,
and you have ignored all my counsel
and would have none of my reproof,
I also will laugh at your calamity;
I will mock when panic strikes you,
when panic strikes you like a storm,
and your calamity comes like a whirlwind,
when distress and anguish come upon you.

"Then they will call upon me, but I will not answer;
they will seek me diligently but will not find me.
Because they hated knowledge
and did not choose the fear of the LORD,
would have none of my counsel,
and despised all my reproof,
therefore they shall eat the fruit of their way
and be sated with their own devices.

"For the simple are killed by their turning away,
and the complacence of fools destroys them;
but he who listens to me will dwell secure
and will be at ease, without dread of evil."

(Prov 1:20-33)

I can only hope and pray that this does not mean what it appears to mean for the immediate future. Spare us, O Lord.

It is difficult to work after reading the Scripture passage from Solomon. I tell the Blessed Mother that I suddenly feel the need to pray *with* someone, but of course, there is no one to pray with.

I walk over to noon Mass at Georgetown University's Dahlgren Chapel of the Sacred Heart. As I am reaching in my pocket for my Rosary, a strange woman walks up to me. "Want to say the Rosary?" she asks. Then another woman in front of us requests to join us. It's the first time I have ever heard a joint Rosary said before the noon Mass at Dahlgren.

One of the women works for the Government Accounting Office (GAO). When we finish, she says that she, too, had needed to pray with someone. "I felt a sense of relief as we prayed," she commented. I, too, feel it. We all determine not to lose hope.

Right after the Rosary and Mass, a bizarre idea comes to me. An idea that just might move millions to their knees and prevent the war, even at the 11th hour. It is extravagant. It is outrageous. It will at worst be called mad, at best, extraordinarily naïve.

And it just might work.

The idea haunts me all morning. Who should propose it? Should I? I shudder at the thought of being considered a fanatic or a lunatic. And yet, the psychological moment to move a nation already inclined in the direction of prayer is certainly this moment when the whole world is desperately searching for a way out of war.

I pray constantly for discernment and courage. Theologians say God speaks to us in three ways: through Scripture, through circumstance, and through other people. I feel God is using the first way, Scripture, to speak to me, specifically the book of Joshua. In reading Joshua, I am reminded that receiving blessings from God depends on our fidelity to His laws: "Only be strong and very courageous, being careful to do according to all the law which Moses my servant commanded you; turn not from it to the right hand or to the left, that you may have good success wherever you go" (Josh 1:7). The circumstances have already spoken to me. And during Mass, I ask Him to guide me in the third way — through other people.

And the right people just happen to appear on the scene.

I ask both of them their opinion of the idea. Tears cloud their eyes. It becomes clear in my mind that President Bush himself, rather than a third party, should be the one to make the proposal. Saddam Hussein, according to sources, wishes to talk directly with Bush. This proposal was as close as he was going to get to the fulfillment of that wish.

Having discerned, correctly or incorrectly, that this proposal is indeed God's will, I am faced with the problem of how to get it to the president in the short time left before the deadline he has set for Saddam to pull out of Kuwait. There are only a few hours left.

I call my brother Tom, who is a pragmatist, a former CIA agent, and presently the Minority Staff Director of the House Intelligence Committee. He will immediately stomp on his younger sibling's idea if he thinks it is crazy. And I more than half hope he will.

He does not. There is a long silence after I read the proposal to him. To my astonishment, he says, "Give it a shot. It's worth a try." He suggests I share the idea with Iowa Congressman Jim Leach, a close friend of Bush. I do not know of Jim's religious persuasion or if he has any. I know Jim well, but fear grips me as I make the call. Surely he will think Peggy has gone around the bend.

There is the same long silence after I read Jim the proposal. "Profound," he finally says, "and I think you are the one to suggest it. Just take it to the White House and give it to the guard" — which is Jim's way of bowing out of the honor. "It's the kind of thing Jimmy Carter might do, but probably not George Bush," he concludes.

Which is true. Carter was a man who did not mind advertising his faith. George Bush, an Episcopalian, is more inclined to pray in the closet. "And that's the very reason it would be more effective and surprising coming from George Bush," I say.

Jim is right; however, it is my idea and I will have to rise or fall with it. How do I go back to the president with another prayer proposal more radical than my last one, to which he graciously responded but did not accept? Had I known that two pleas from two future saints had preceded this suggestion, I might have had more courage. But the Lord chose not to let me in on that secret.

My next thought is to call the president's personal secretary, Diane Butterfield. She had gotten my first letter to him. The White House line is continuously busy, however, which is very unusual. Obviously, I am not the only citizen with an idea, although most probably the only one with such an outlandish one.

I call Joanne Kemp, wife of Congressman Jack Kemp, a woman of deep faith who is in favor of the proposal. She gives me Diane's private number. After I read the letter to Diane, she, too, wants the president to see it. "Can you fax it to me?" she asks.

Having no fax machine at home, I walk down the block to our neighborhood drug store. At 3:10 p.m. on January 15, the proposal departs from Morgan's Pharmacy to the White House. The clerk who sends it, thank Heaven, never glances at the content, which is entitled, "The Last Initiative." In it, I propose President Bush go on CNN, the network Saddam Hussein allegedly watches, and direct this message to the Iraqi president:

Mr. President,

In the past five months we have found almost nothing upon which we can agree. We have explored every diplomatic initiative and we have failed to find common ground. Until this morning I feared we had none.

In this morning's paper, I saw a picture of you on your knees and I was reminded we do have one thing we share; a belief in a Supreme Being, fount of omniscience and justice.

Mr. President, we have been unable to talk together. Perhaps we can pray together. This afternoon at (name time) I am going to my Church to ask God's guidance. Will you join me by going to your mosque and doing the same?

I invite your people and my people to join us. I invite men and women of goodwill around the world to join us. We know He has a plan greater than our minds can devise. Perhaps it is not too late to ask Him to share it with us.

Article after article has indicated that Saddam Hussein may be looking for a face-saving way to withdraw from Kuwait. To the Arab world, there could be no more honorable exit than to say, "Allah told me to go."

I feel at peace when the ordeal is over. Whether or not Bush ever reacts favorably, I have done my job as a messenger.

January 18, 1991

The messenger fails once again. President Bush does not exercise the spiritual initiative and I do not know if Diane ever got it to him.

According to the newspaper accounts, the president had made up his mind to go to war the afternoon of January 15. Once that mindset was struck, the spiritual initiative probably seemed ludicrous or at the very least, an annoyance. The idea of Saddam (who was considered a devil) praying seemed slightly absurd, I'm sure. The president, no doubt, forgets that to the Iraqi people, he *is* the devil.

At 6:40 p.m., January 16, the attack on Baghdad begins — it is massive, swift, decisive, and very successful. It is the first war televised live in our living rooms. Saddam offers a paltry defense. Where is he? The next night we find out. Iraq lobs between seven and 10 missiles at Israel and one at Saudi Arabia.

I feel numb as the war begins; I am totally without emotion, as if I am watching a bad movie.

It isn't until the next morning as I am saying the Rosary that the tears flow. "Dear Lord, You tried so hard to be heard through church men and women. Nearly every major religious leader as well as the grass roots begged George Bush and Saddam Hussein to stop before they started."

Bush told the nation every diplomatic initiative had failed. He did not tell them about the spiritual initiatives that were never tried.

January 21, 1991

Over the weekend, we are in New York. We attend Mass at St. Patrick's Cathedral and hear John Cardinal O'Connor, quoting extensively from Pope John Paul's Christmas message, give an impassioned homily against the war. One wished the Pope had been quoted so extensively *before* the war began.

January 25, 1991, Washington, D.C.

Just one month after celebrating the birthday of the Prince of Peace, we are engaged in violence. Whose side is God on? Logic would argue the American side. Saddam has been painted alternately as a madman, evil, murderous, and violent; the list of adjectives is degrading and demoralizing. His aggressive move into Kuwait and refusal to leave have caused the conflict.

And yet he is the leader who continuously invokes God's name. All say Saddam's religious references are hypocritical. All but his friend, the Patriarch of the Chaldean Catholics, who claims he is gentlemanly.

America appears to be winning decisively and with only a minimum of American casualties, and yet my own distinct feeling, based on personal and observed evidence and the letters from John Paul II and Mother Teresa, is that God is on neither side — that He did not will this war.

January 30, 1991, Washington, D.C.

The war rages on; people begin to tune out the 24-hour cable news coverage to save their sanity. The president gives his State of the Union address. Having been present in the House chamber for many State of the Union speeches, I know that it is always an electric moment. This night more than most, the Congress is awash in patriotism. President Bush makes a fine case for himself.

I doubt he will ever have such a moment again. His popularity, despite mounting economic problems, is at an historic high. I cannot help but wonder how the Lord looks down on this.

During this period I find myself painting a mysterious picture of the Gulf War. The story begins with two diary entries from a few months earlier:

August 29, 1990

I have begun painting what I thought was the face of Jesus, but somewhere along the route, the title "Abba, Father" keeps coming to mind, and the eyebrows and hair turn white. Now the Father is the subject, not the Son.

Never did I think I would attempt God the Father! But it feels quite natural and not frightening at all. I imagine the father of the Prodigal Son, and the expression is very loving. The human features resemble my Divine Mercy rendition of Jesus. Like Father, like Son.

September 19, 1990

I keep working on the face off and on a few minutes or an hour a day until it is finished, and yet I know it is not finished. Still, I have no idea how to complete it. So I put the picture away for a long time, occasionally taking it out to ponder, but working little on it.

January 1991

After the failed international prayer event, I suddenly know how to proceed with the painting. Under the right eye of the Father, I have superimposed the face of George Bush, under the left eye, Saddam.

I draw the troops on the desert beneath the two leaders. I call it "The Road Not Taken."

I am totally unprepared for the impact of the painting. The publisher of the *Our Sunday Visitor* supplement called *Mary's People* wants to put it on the cover of the newspaper, but the Pentagon says no because Bush and Saddam are side by side.

The founder of the National Museum of Women in the Arts, Wilhelmina Holladay, sends a print of it to *Time* magazine. Then a strange thing occurs. On the left cheek of Saddam, a heart emerges. Not of my doing. I never notice the heart until a viewer points it out to me. Apparently, something similar happens to another artist who is painting a picture of the Madonna of Medjugorje. A heart, not initiated by the artist, appears under Mary's left eye.

Does it signify that the heart is the heart of the problem *or* the solution? Or both?

January 30, 1991

Ivan Dragićević, one of the six Medjugorje visionaries, comes to Washington at this historic and pivotal time. He wants to see the president. There is grave doubt that he will realize that wish. Ivan is coming to our house tomorrow. He says he will have his apparition here.

That the Blessed Mother will appear in my house almost makes me doubt the authenticity of Medjugorje. But then I think about Jesus going to dinner with tax collectors and sitting with sinners (see Mt 9:10; Mk 2:15; Lk 5:29). I also remember the archbishop of Yugoslavia saying that Mary always goes where her children are most in trouble. With that kind of criteria, the *Gospa*'s presence in my living room seems perfectly reasonable.

I am told by Nives Jelich, Ivan's guide and interpreter, that I may invite as many as 30 people for this incomprehensible event. In secular Washington, D.C., capital of the world, whom do you invite to an *apparition*? How do you explain such an invitation? I have tried to ask (with a great deal of prayer) those who are most in need spiritually or physically, or those who might be most beneficial to the *Gospa*'s mission.

It turns out to be the most eclectic group of people ever assembled in my living room, from mega-intellects to the mentally impaired, from multimillionaires to the nearly penniless, senior citizens, junior citizens, and many in between. As they say, Mary is some social secretary! One humble soul brings a dozen pink roses for Our Lady two days ahead of time.

The most surprising people want to come. Some get misty-eyed reflecting on the opportunity. One usually very blasé, rather negative young girl says she is so excited she is afraid she might throw up! God's power is almost frightening to behold.

The night of the apparition finally arrives. Ivan takes a seat in the back of the room at the edge of the crowd. Monsignor John Murphy, former rector of the Basilica of the National Shrine, celebrates Mass on a small table in front of a mirrored wall. My sister, Mary Anne, brain damaged and lately capable of obstreperous behavior, sits next to me.

People are spilling out into the foyer and up the stairwell. As in Medjugorje, crowded and casually arranged as we are, the attendees are deeply involved. You can almost see Our Lord in the raised Host. Mary Anne, who seldom smiles, breaks into a broad grin the moment the Consecration takes place.

When Mass concludes, Ivan leads the Rosary in Croatian, a language that makes the recitation seem doubly reverent. Then, precisely at 5:40 p.m., Ivan suddenly rises, strides rapidly to the front of the room and falls on his knees, his head raised and his eyes fixed upward. His lips move but we can hear nothing, not so much as a whisper.

After a few moments, Ivan's voice returns briefly and then disappears once again. There is more silent conversation for several minutes. Then Ivan lowers his head and stands up.

What a week it has been for this unsophisticated visionary, meeting celebrated members of the Washington community. I never see him lose his way or his confidence. If he has no answer, he quietly says so and does not pretend to knowledge he does not have. If any inquiry treads in the arena of the secrets, he quietly says so and refuses to answer. "A secret is a secret," he responds.

He manages to impress even the skeptical, of whom there are many. At a coffee I hold one morning, the crowd encompasses a former ambassador, former congressman, the wife of the president of the World Bank, the Episcopalian dean of the Washington Cathedral, the former chairman of the Senate Foreign Relations Committee, and congressional wives.

It is anything but an easy audience, and yet one woman who says she is not religious expresses a desire afterward to join a prayer group. "I feel different leaving your house than when I came in," she tells me.

This night of the apparition, Ivan reports to us that the Blessed Mother is joyous and that she has extended her hands over us all, blessing us. In a short Q&A session, one inquisitor demands to know, "How could there be a dawning of a new peace," as Ivan has said, "when war is breaking out all over the globe?"

"Peace is coming," Ivan replies confidently.

We could not fathom how right he was this evening.

January 30, 1991 . . . .

The National Prayer Breakfast is an annual event put on by the House and Senate prayer groups along with an organization known as the Fellowship Foundation. From a small gathering of U.S. government leaders praying together in Washington, it has expanded to an international gathering of thousands that includes Hindus, Jews, Buddhists, and even Communists. The behind-the-scenes leader of the Fellowship Foundation is Doug Coe, a close friend of the Stantons.

Shortly before the day of the breakfast, I discover that Abraham Lincoln called for a "Day of National Humiliation, Fasting, and Prayer." Two days after it was observed, a freak accident occurred that altered the outcome of the Civil War.

Knowing that President Bush will be speaking at the breakfast, I report Lincoln's efforts to Doug Coe.

"Can you get me a copy?" Doug asks.

I can and I do. It reads:

Washington, D.C., March 30, 1863

By the President of the United States of America.

A Proclamation.

Whereas, the Senate of the United States, devoutly recognizing the Supreme Authority and just Government of Almighty God, in all the affairs of men and of nations, has, by a resolution, requested the President to designate and set apart a day for National prayer and humiliation.

And whereas it is the duty of nations as well as of men, to own their dependence upon the overruling power of God, to confess their sins and transgressions, in humble sorrow, yet with assured hope that genuine repentance will lead to mercy and pardon; and to recognize the sublime truth, announced in the Holy Scriptures and proven by all history, that those nations only are blessed whose God is the Lord.

And, insomuch as we know that, by His divine law, nations like individuals are subjected to punishments and chastisements in this world, may we not justly fear that the awful calamity of civil war, which now desolates the land, may be but a punishment, inflicted upon us, for our presumptuous sins, to the needful end of our national reformation as a whole People? We have been the recipients of the choicest bounties of Heaven. We have been preserved, these many years, in peace and prosperity. We have grown in numbers, wealth and power, as no other nation has ever grown. But we have forgotten God. We have forgotten the gracious hand which preserved us in peace, and multiplied and enriched and strengthened us; and we have vainly imagined, in the deceitfulness of our hearts, that all these blessings were produced by some superior wisdom and virtue of our own. Intoxicated with unbroken success, we have become too self-sufficient to feel the necessity of redeeming and preserving grace, too proud to pray to the God that made us!

It behooves us then, to humble ourselves before the offended Power, to confess our national sins, and to pray for clemency and forgiveness.

Now, therefore, in compliance with the request, and fully concurring in the views of the Senate, I do, by this my proclamation, designate and set apart Thursday, the 30th day of April, 1863, as a day of national humiliation, fasting and prayer. And I do hereby request all the People to abstain, on that day, from their ordinary secular pursuits, and to unite, at their several places of public worship and their respective homes, in keeping the day holy to the Lord, and devoted to the humble discharge of the religious duties proper to that solemn occasion.

All this being done, in sincerity and truth, let us then rest humbly in the hope authorized by the Divine teachings, that the united cry of the Nation will be heard on high, and answered with blessings, no less than the pardon of our national sins, and the restoration of our now divided and suffering Country, to its former happy condition of unity and peace.

In witness whereof, I have hereunto set my hand and caused the seal of the United States to be affixed.

Done at the City of Washington, this thirtieth day of March, in the year of our Lord one thousand eight hundred and sixty-three, and of the Independence of the United States the eighty seventh.

By the President: Abraham Lincoln

William H. Seward, Secretary of State.

January 31, 1991, the National Prayer Breakfast, Washington, D.C. ·····························

President George Bush issues Proclamation 6243, which reads, in part:

As one nation under God, we Americans are deeply mindful of both our dependence on the Almighty and our obligations as a people He has richly blessed. From our very beginnings as a Nation, we have relied upon God's strength and guidance in war and peace. ... However confident of our purpose, however determined to prevail, we Americans continue to yearn for peace and for the safety of our service men and women in the Persian Gulf. With these great hopes in mind, I ask all Americans to unite in humble and contrite prayer to Almighty God. ...

NOW, THEREFORE, I, GEORGE BUSH, President of the United States of America, by virtue of the authority vested in me by the Constitution and laws of the United States, do hereby proclaim February 3, 1991, as a National Day of Prayer. ...

Ivan, messenger for the Queen of Peace, is present at the prayer breakfast to hear the proclamation read.

March 3, 1991

Exactly one month after President Bush declared a national day of prayer, Iraq and the allies meet on the battlefield, and Iraq agrees to abide by all UN resolutions.

April 6, 1991

The official ceasefire is signed and accepted. The Gulf War is over, 42 days after it began, one of the shortest wars in American history.

April 7, 1991

It is Divine Mercy Sunday, the feast Our Lord Himself requested to be celebrated on the Sunday after Easter. Appearing in the 1930s, he told a Polish nun, Sr. Faustina, that only through His Divine Mercy would peace come to the world.

Mark Twain is alleged to have said, "Coincidence is God's way of remaining anonymous." The President, an Episcopalian, who as far as I can determine, knows nothing of the Divine

Mercy devotion, has unknowingly chosen Divine Mercy Sunday as another day of prayer. Citing the brevity of the Gulf War and the "miraculously few casualties," President Bush asks America to thank God for His mercy!

The president himself proved to be a dispenser of mercy. Iraqi soldiers, waving the white flag of surrender, were treated with compassion by the conquering American troops, who were ordered not to fire on the Iraqis. Some criticized Bush for not shooting his way into Baghdad and "finishing the job," which undoubtedly meant finishing off Saddam. But Bush did not waver from his stated mission, which was the liberation of Kuwait.

The man who reads the president's proclamation at the Basilica of the National Shrine of the Immaculate Conception during the Divine Mercy service is the man who originally suggested the International Day of Prayer and Fasting last December — Bill Stanton.

When the Madonna of Medjugorje told the visionaries that prayer and fasting could stop wars, she wasn't kidding!

Little do I know that this is not my final involvement in war and peace, nor that I will be moved from the comfort of prayers for peace in my parish pew to the war zones themselves.

15

APPOINTMENT IN ANCONA

May 1992, the Balkan War

From Mostar, just 12 miles from Medjugorje, desperate dispatches arrive from a Franciscan nun, Sr. Janja, informing American nun and frequent pilgrimage guide to Medjugorje, Sr. Isabel Bettye, of the horrors of the brutal Balkan War, the largest European conflict since World War II. Sister Betty faxes them to Medjugorje Marian centers across the U.S.:

> "Mostar is under bomb attack now. Last night, two places were bombed. The only road that could take people out of the city was hit and above that road there is a little Franciscan church. It was completely destroyed yesterday. Two sisters just came from surgery. One sister said, "The hospital smells of nothing but blood. There are so many people wounded, mostly civilians. When you look at those two nuns, you don't recognize them. Their eyes are different. What they are going through! They work 24 hours every second day. Many people are killed and wounded in their basement shelters, which are not really shelters.

> "We are in the 31st day of continuous bombing and shelling. When they start to bomb or shell, it goes on for at least six or seven hours. Grenades are falling around us. ...

> "I think that never in my life have I prayed so much for my enemies, not out of fear, but out of love, that God will change their minds

into something positive ... we need your prayers now. I am sorry to keep asking. But they help us to remain at peace. Sometimes we fight a little with God. Your prayers shorten the fight ... they help us keep only love in our hearts ... with nothing but love for those who would destroy us... ."

May 19, 1992, National Press Club, Washington, D.C.

It is a sight never seen before or since in the Washington National Press Club, home of some of the most sophisticated and secular journalists in America. A brown-robed friar stands before the cameras of CNN, pleading for prayer and fasting to end the Balkan War ravaging his homeland, Bosnia-Herzegovina.

Then Fr. Jozo Zovko delivers an even more astonishing message: "Come to Medjugorje." I look at my companion at the press conference, Mary Garner, wife of the provost of Washington National Cathedral. She and I and the CNN cameraman are practically the only people attending the press conference. Who, us? Go through a war zone, where people are being slaughtered, where women are being raped by Serbian soldiers? Snipers are shooting from rooftops in Sarajevo. Cluster bombs are dropping. Go to an area that is on the U.S. State Department's "no travel list"? Go to Medjugorje, where even the wives and children have fled; where no pilgrims have come for a year; where Mass is being celebrated in a bomb shelter?

Is the man crazy? The husky Franciscan voice continues, however, calling for nine days of prayer and fasting to precede a massive pilgrimage to Medjugorje on June 24, 1992, to liberate the besieged village on the 11th anniversary of Mary's first apparition there. "I am inviting you. Our Lady is inviting you."

That does it. It all makes perfect sense if you believe that the Blessed Mother is actually appearing and proclaiming, *"Only by prayer and fasting can war be stopped."* By the time we leave the press building, we have agreed to be Fr. Jozo's

American news media, to distribute his invitation around the United States via faxes to all the Medjugorje centers across the country.

Of course, if you are going to invite people to risk their limbs, you better be ready to risk your own. One day, I kneel before the Lord in the Blessed Sacrament with a blunt question, "Will I come back alive?" The answer that seems to emanate from the tabernacle is, "That is not for you to know."

How reassuring! "Oh well," I philosophize to myself and friends, "no one gets out of this life alive. You may as well go for a noble purpose."

I ask Susan Finn, a volunteer with The Mary Anne Foundation, an organization I had founded to foster peace — which was named after the mother and grandmother of the Prince of Peace — to organize a prayer service at Holy Trinity Catholic Church in Georgetown for the success of the pilgrimage. She gathers Members of Congress and diplomats together with former Medjugorje pilgrims in a remarkable show of ecumenical entreaty, praying for an end to the war and the safety of the pilgrims making the journey requested by Fr. Jozo.

June 18, 1992

I travel ahead to Europe, accompanying Bill on a business trip. Business concluded, we part at the airport in Madrid, Spain. He heads for the U.S. I head for Medjugorje via Ancona, Italy. Behind a glass enclosure, I can see Bill waiting for his transatlantic flight to the safety of home. He is calmly reading a book, unaware of the terror I am beginning to feel, heading alone to a city I have never been, where I do not speak the language, to meet up with a group of strange men driving ambulances that will deliver emergency supplies to a war zone.

I keep staring at Bill, hoping he will look up, this man who went off to World War II at 18. Tears well up, fogging my vision. If he would just lift his eyes from his book, see me, and signal a thumbs-up sign.

But he never does.

I am on my own. I begin to pray. And suddenly I see a

nun striding through the terminal. Just the sight of the flowing robes sends the message I need.

I am not alone.

June 19, 1992 ·

Six ambulances driven across Europe are attempting to board a ferry for Split, Croatia. Clive, a gray-haired driver with a goatee, tells me the drivers have been reciting the Rosary over walkie-talkies as they motor down the highways, each ambulance taking a turn at leading the Hail Marys.

It is a rainy night on the docks of Ancona. A young Franciscan friar, Br. John, brown robes flying in the wind, walks briskly toward us. "Once you put on a habit, things really get moving. I think we'll get on," he smiles. "I said we can do one of two things," he continues, "we can pray or we can kick and scream. I think a little bit of both works. I think we'll get on."

John is an American Franciscan brother. He is joined by an Irish Franciscan priest, Fr. Raymond Driscoll. Father Raymond is on the pilgrimage, he explains, because "I was visiting my sister and I was asked to go to a prayer meeting and at the prayer meeting I was asked to accompany them to Medjugorje." Laughing, he adds, "I was actually praying that another priest might show up," alluding to the danger of traveling to a war zone. "I'm a man of very weak faith."

Trouble is anticipated in Croatia and war-torn Bosnia. It is not anticipated in Italy — but that is where it begins. The ambulances must vie for space on the ferry with huge lorries already booked for passage. Brother John does the negotiating with the boat owners while pilgrims do the praying and the hymn singing. Father Raymond and Gaelic driver Donnie from Donegal apply the Irish jig to the tension. Four hours, 45 Rosaries, an uncounted number of hymns and Irish jigs later, the trucks and ambulances are all on board our boat, the *Jodrilanga*. A blonde lady says her group of pilgrims kept repeating the Rosary until every ambulance was on board. We are told the *Jodrilanga* will be the last ferry boat to travel to the war zone.

It is a 10-hour sail to Croatia. We soon learn the *Jodril-anga* is not the *QE2*.

There are no berths, and no beds in which to sleep. We stretch out on tabletops and across benches. One man snoozes on the floor. Nuns spend the night in the open air on the upper deck.

June 20, 1992, approaching Split, Croatia ·········

The sea is a deep blue. A sleeping nun rises, still in her habit, and stretches her arms, looking as fresh as if she had spent the night at the Ritz-Carlton. We laywomen, in our rumpled clothes, resemble the cleaning crew. The ambulance drivers happen to be quite musical; they are leaning against the railing, heralding land as they do every situation, with their guitars and their voices. The lyric "Sing hosanna! Sing hosanna! Sing hosanna to the King of Kings" drifts across the Adriatic Sea. The majority of drivers hail from England or Ireland. Their occupations range from engineering to sculpting. They have all volunteered their time to deliver the ambulances and supplies to makeshift hospitals in war-ravaged villages.

In imitation of John Paul II, Fr. Raymond gives the papal salute, sinking to his knees and kissing the ground, as we debark in Split, Croatia. We are greeted by a Croatian Franciscan priest, Fr. Svetozar Kraljević, who salutes Br. John and the Franciscan nuns with a triumphant fist in the air. He and the nuns were made refugees when their convent, where he was chaplain, was bombed while Fr. Svet was saying Mass. The sisters have been in Ancona buying underclothes, since 84 nuns and Fr. Svet escaped with their lives and little else. Father Svet makes his weary volunteers sit down in an outdoor café while he takes ice cream orders, serving us himself. It is amazing how delicious ice cream cones taste for breakfast after a 10-hour boat ride with no food.

"I love to do this," Father says, by way of defining what he dubs his "ice cream project."

Brother John explains what our duties will be when we reach Makarska, where our hotel-turned-refugee-center will be our first stop. I climb into the front seat of a truck driven by Fr. Svet, which leads the ambulance caravan along the coast of the azure-blue Adriatic. We ascend into the mountains, passing picturesque fishing villages en route.

Once in Makarska, we begin unloading the ambulances under Fr. Svet's direction. A tot-size refugee sits in front of banana boxes, happily watching the action. When Clive, our *bon vivant* driver/leader, pulls a medical uniform from one of the boxes, an American nurse wrinkles her nose. "It's pretty pathetic what you do to nurses in England," she says with heavy emphasis, "It's pretty pathetic!" Clive makes no defense of the drab gray garb as the other drivers erupt in laughter.

Refugee priests and nuns now run the Aphrodite Hotel in Makarska, the nuns doling out food from behind the bar counter. The residents are no longer paying guests. They are war victims. A little girl points a toy gun at a visitor as the ambulance drivers again lighten the moment, singing "Buckle down, Jesse James, buckle down" to the strains of an ever-present banjo. Father Svet, sporting a green Notre Dame baseball cap with his brown friar robes, smiles as he listens.

It is not easy for men of the soul to readily discern the needs of the body, I observe, as I listen to the Franciscans try to decide which aid packages should go where. "Medicine and money" are the best donations, Fr. Svet says. They can be applied as the needs manifest themselves, whereas unneeded or unwanted clothes tend to take up room and go to waste.

Hotel balconies are festooned with refugees drying the little apparel they still have. Father Raymond uses one of the balconies to say Mass. We are all tightly crowded onto the balcony. The driver/troubadours provide the music. Below us, refugees gather to attend the service. The presence of the Lord is palpable in this unforgettable celebration amidst so much anguish.

June 21, 1992, Mostar . . . .

We head toward the war zones, the six ambulances remaining in tandem as we travel the mountain highways toward Mostar, our Rosary recitation still linking communications between vehicles. Local residents wave to us, grateful that help is arriving. We make a brief stop in Medjugorje, where we see a cluster bomb that failed to detonate sunk in the ground right across the road from St. James Church. Had it succeeded in its mission, it would have unleashed over 50 smaller bombs. We hear stories of other bombs dropped over Medjugorje failing to accomplish their goal.

The first ambulance is dropped off in Ljubuški, where a gymnasium has been turned into a makeshift hospital. All the medicines, beds, and supplies have been donated by volunteers.

We move on to Mostar, where progress is halted by militia wearing camouflage outfits and Rosary beads around their necks. "You've got to have a very good reason for coming in here," Clive comments tersely. Mostar has been one of the most heavily hit cities in the region. Serbs, hiding in mountain bunkers, rained bombs down on the once picturesque town for months. After examining our credentials carefully, the Croatian militia wave us through. A man in an undershirt rushes from his home with a box of bruised peaches, anxious to share with us the little food he has. As we pull into the heart of Mostar, we are confronted with wrecked cars, destroyed buildings, bullet-riddled schools, and rubble-strewn streets. Saint Paul's Church is in ruins, the sky now its roof, huge stones making mountains out of what was once its floor, its stained-glass windows shattered. Father Raymond kneels and prays atop the rubble, his eyes glazed with saddened disbelief.

Mostar residents, believing they have at last been liberated by Croatian soldiers, emerge from hiding, walking their streets for the first time since the war began, dazed by the devastation they find. An older woman stands weeping in front of St. Paul's Church. She tells Fr. Svet, as the tears fall, that she received her first Holy Communion in St. Paul's in 1943. "My whole life I spent here." She wipes her glistening eyes repeatedly as she tries to absorb the loss.

A young boy clutches a cat in the crook of his arm as he makes his way over the remains of the church. Down the street, above a nest of trees, a bombed department store tilts precariously to the left.

Father Svet tells us St. Paul's Church was built in 1877, "immediately after the Ottomans left, and this was the only church in Mostar for a long time. Later the cathedral was built, and Mostar had only two major churches plus six little mission churches in the whole region; and now Mostar is left with no churches."

The destruction of Mostar is estimated to equal and perhaps surpass that of the much-publicized Sarajevo. Because of the perceived danger, few journalists have traveled to the interior of Bosnia-Herzegovina to witness the devastation here. As we walk, we pass more citizens, many weeping and appearing to be in shock. We can hear gunfire all around us, purportedly Croatian victory salutes, celebrating the fact that they have routed the Serbs from their bunkers.

Father Svet takes us to the edge of the river. He points to the other shore where the Serbs live. Several hotel buildings are no longer habitable; the debris from bombed bridges flows downstream. Father Svet calls the scene "a hint of hell," observing, "This was one city. This was a city of peace where people lived together, and it wasn't necessary to destroy bridges. They destroyed the bridges that connected them to the rest of the world. But over here, Muslims lived, Croatians lived, and Serbians lived."

"Why did they destroy their own property?" I ask. "It's the nature of evil always," Father answers. "He always destroys himself in the process."

As we continue our walking tour of Mostar, we pass a red car with all four doors pulled open, windows smashed, half on the curb and half on the street, food boxes left on the seats. "Two people were killed in this car," Fr. Svet tells us, fired on as they were driving down the road.

If Mostar is a "hint of hell," Medjugorje, just 12 kilometers away, is a hint of Heaven. We are staying at the Jozo Vasilj house (no relation to Shima Vasilj, my first host in Medjugorje) near the base of Mt. Križevac. We do not arrive there till 11 p.m. The village is in blackout, blankets hanging over windows to hide its existence from aerial attackers. Despite the late hour, Jozo, a large man with a large laugh, welcomes strangers as if we were returning relatives, providing us with our own rooms in the handsome house built to accommodate the myriads of pilgrims that flooded the village until the war began. "You are our first visitors in a year," Jozo's pretty teenage daughter informs us.

I am blessed with a room overlooking the valley. I thank God profusely for such a blessing, which I never envisioned for a relief mission. Our first morning in Medjugorje, we awaken to the familiar crow of the roosters sounding across the valley as a red-orange horizon begins to glow behind the mountains.

The Vasilj house rests at the base of Mt. Križevac. Despite warnings not to climb Cross Mountain because of a possible aerial attack or hostage-taking, the drivers are undeterred from making the Stations of the Cross. It is a different mountain from the one we all climbed in prewar days, when trekking up the hill was halted at every level with pilgrims competing for space. This morning the mountains and the cross are ours alone.

"I can't say whether it is better or worse," comments Donnie, the driver from Donegal, Ireland. "It's just completely different. Before, you had the spirit of people being together, sharing together. On the other hand, physically, it's quieter now, so it's easier to find the peace."

Donnie says he never had any intention of returning to Medjugorje after his first trip. But he finds this journey very enlightening, "because what I have seen, especially in Mostar, listening to the various priests preaching about Medjugorje and all that I have read, confirms to me now that Our Lady was appearing here, is appearing here, and [that] the messages are for the world to listen, for people to change their lives, to pray, fast, and do penance.

"When you see the destruction in Mostar, it's terrible what's happening there. It all could have been avoided if people had turned to prayer. The sad thing here is that people are going and buying guns and not listening to the messages of Our Lady. They should arm themselves with Rosary beads instead of revolvers."

And on this day, Vicka Ivanković, the visionary nearly always surrounded by pilgrims before the war came, is also ours alone. Seemingly in good health and slightly heavier than usual, Vicka is her ebullient self, giving advice when asked about the drivers' personal situations. Her mother stands behind her, arm resting on a tree limb, listening to her daughter. "The most beautiful thing we can do," says Vicka, "is give up our sins." Questioned as to whether the *Gospa* is happy about the Peace Pilgrimage, she replies with a wide grin, "Yes!"

Each driver has his own tale as to why he decided to make this risky journey. An Englishman relates his reason to me as he drives: "Back home, I picked up my guitar and started to sing, and another song came out that I wasn't thinking of, and it was the song 'Be Not Afraid, I go before you always,' the very same song that kept playing in my and other pilgrims' heads!"

June 21, 1992, Medjugorje

Saint James Church has only been reopened for two days, the unlocking accomplished by a Franciscan priest and the Eucharistic Lord carried in a monstrance. Today, every pew is empty, however. A lone cleaning lady sweeping the floor is the only occupant. Never before have I seen St. James empty. More often than not, in prewar days, every seat would be taken, people standing in the side aisles, the middle aisle, even at the base of the altar.

Out on the church plaza, there is just a trickle of pilgrims. A young American woman walks toward us and says she came because she felt "called" to be present. The danger was a "reality," she says smiling, "but I just felt that Mary would take care of us." The most poignant site on the plaza is the bruised statue of Mary, her beautiful marble façade scarred with black marks, as if she absorbed all the strikes meant for the village.

One of Jozo Vasilj's daughters says she thinks this pilgrimage will have special significance. "I think there will be a miracle," she grins. She isn't referring to events such as the spinning sun, she makes clear. "You will see a miracle with the people. Because a miracle is when … all the people come from somewhere else; you feel happy and that's a miracle! Everybody will smile. It will be beautiful. It will be special. Really special I think."

June 24, 1992, Ljubuški . . . .

The day of the Peace March has arrived. It is 10 miles from the monastery in Ljubuški to Medjugorje. Anywhere along the road, the Serbs can launch an aerial attack on the marchers. Men in militia outfits are all around us, but Br. John, in his brown friar's robe, says they will not travel with us as protection. They are citizen militia. "They live in that dirt mound. That's their bunker." Does that mean we are going with only Rosaries as our weapons, as Fr. Jozo says?

"Yes," Br. John nods.

The pilgrims seem not to be concerned. A group of young people are seated on the lawn, singing lustily. An Indian woman from Wimbledon, England, admits she thought about the danger, but she, too, feels "Our Lady would protect us."

A redheaded man with a goatee says that last October people had been warned, "Be prepared to die. Medjugorje had been targeted. But nothing has happened." An older Indian woman wearing a white baseball cap thinks an attack would provide a nice photo op. "It would help in a way," she laughs, "if we got killed. The whole world would know about Medjugorje." There must be an easier publicity route, I am thinking. Her younger companion, under a straw hat, tied with a blue ribbon, thinks more reassuringly. "Our Lady is for love and peace," she says serenely, "not death and war."

The last man to enter the monastery is Fr. Jozo Zovko, the man who called for this international pilgrimage to send the message, "Love is stronger than hate." He is surrounded by admiring pilgrims. He is smiling broadly. As he steps on the altar, he is embraced by Fr. Slavko Barbarić, the psychiatrist-author of the book, *Pray With the Heart: Medjugorje Manual of Prayer.*

It is announced that 30 different countries are assembled here to show their solidarity with the suffering of the Bosnian people. And on this day, June 24, the marching pilgrims are the only representatives from the Western world bringing supplies and concern to the besieged people. Many pilgrims have lugged extra suitcases filled with humanitarian aid. Germany and the U.S. have loaded lorries with food, clothing, and medical supplies. Italy has been active. And at the same moment, the Red Cross and the United Nations (UN) have fled in fear of their lives.

"We go together to Medjugorje that we may pray for peace in our homeland and peace in the whole world," a deep male voice intones over a microphone. The room is packed with pilgrims. The air is electric with soul-stirring music, singing, and clapping. It feels surreal, like a scene from a war movie. The Franciscans have baked large circles of bread. A circle of bread is given to every region of the world, and every region of the world is represented. The first to receive a circle is Archbishop Frane Franić of Sarajevo, a vocal believer in the Medjugorje apparitions.

The ceremonies conclude and the March begins. The 10-mile journey will take about two-and-one-half hours. Father Jozo stands outside the monastery door, blessing the pilgrims as they depart. Father declines to join the excitement. Instead, he spends the whole afternoon sitting outside St. James Church hearing confessions.

Local residents stand outside their homes and on the street waving and cheering the marchers on, some with tears in their eyes. A life-size figure of Christ, borne on a large truck, leads the march. There are flags from different countries. There are flags with crosses. A small boy runs out to meet the crowd with a Croatian flag larger than he is. There are horse-back riders. The ambulance drivers are bringing up the rear with horns blaring, and all along the way, Franciscan priests are marching, their brown robes afloat in the wind. There is a feeling of triumph and joy in the air.

When the parade passes visionary Ivanka Ivanković's house, she joins the marchers. Visionary Maria Pavlović reads prayers over a loudspeaker.

Ten miles later, the pilgrims round the turn that takes them into the heart of Medjugorje. St. James Church is in view. An Italian woman takes a small bow as she claims first entry into the village. I am up in the St. James choir loft with my videocam, which presents me with a thrilling view of the town swelling from empty to full in a matter of minutes. It is a sight never to be forgotten, like watching a liberation army.

On the plaza in front of St. James, Fr. Slavko leads the throng in the signature Medjugorje hymn before the pilgrims enter the church. And on this day, it has an impassioned, victorious ring. Watching pilgrims pour into the pews until there is not a single seat left recalls the glory days of Medjugorje. Outside the church, the overflow crowds sit on benches on the grass or kneel on the pavement, listening to the Mass over a loudspeaker. Standing in the back of the church and observing this surreal scene is Archbishop Franić, still marveling at the sight unfolding before him. Later, he celebrates the Mass. In his homily, the archbishop loudly proclaims his belief in the apparitions. Close to 50 priests from all parts of the world celebrate the Liturgy with the archbishop.

At the conclusion of the service, the church roof is nearly raised with the congregation's triumphal rendition of "Ave Maria." The pilgrims have made history and they know it.

June 25, 1992, Medjugorje ....

The first young woman to witness the apparition in June 1981, Ivanka Ivanković, is visited by the Virgin. For this apparition, which now occurs for Ivanka just once a year, some visitors and some villagers are allowed to be present. I am fortunate to be one of them. I stand inches from Ivanka, but I am dismayed that I will be unable to share such a privileged view. Though I have been given permission to video Ivanka during the apparition, my camera battery needs charging. It is completely dead. It resides in my pocket next to the Rosary that turned gold during my first trip to Medjugorje.

"Lord," I pray for help, reminding Him, "It's your story. Not mine." Immediately a thought comes into my head: "*Put the dead battery into the camera.*" *Well, that makes no sense*, I think in response. But the thought is persistent. "*Put the dead battery in the camera.*" All right, what have I got to lose? I reach in my pocket, pull out the battery, and am amazed to feel how warm it is. What is going on? I insert the battery into the camera and *voilà*! The camera lights up. I turn the camera on Ivanka and it films the entire apparition. Later on, a TV engineer tests the battery and says it is fully charged!

Ivanka prays out loud with the pilgrims before Mary arrives. Then suddenly she drops to her knees with almost a gasp. Her eyes fixate on one spot. They scarcely blink. Her voice disappears. The visionary is oblivious to all the activity around her: flashbulbs lighting up her face, camera steadily clicking pictures, pilgrims with eyes fixed on her every move.

At various moments her voice returns briefly. This occurs when she is praying with Mary for those present. The Lady is very, very serious on this visit, Ivanka tells us later. She pleads with the world to root out the evil one's influence. The Blessed Mother has said repeatedly that war can be stopped only with prayer and fasting.

When Ivanka's voice disappears, there is much animation in her face. She nods her head often. Her lips move with no sound emerging. She lifts her hands and smiles as she continues to look upward. After more nodding, her head tilts back; she is still looking up, then her head drops to her vaulted fingertips. She crosses herself. Her voice returns and she begins to pray. We onlookers join her.

When the praying concludes, Ivanka, speaking through translator Helen Sarcevic, relates to us Mary's message: "Satan wants to destroy everything within us, so this is the only way to conquer the evil, with prayer and fasting. And we have to be serious about this. Our Lady was pleading with us. She was very serious." Helen tells us that when Ivanka stretches out her hands during the apparition, "It is to touch Our Lady's hands." Ivanka begins to cry. Helen hugs her as Ivanka wipes her cheeks.

Five of the six visionaries are present in Medjugorje for the Peace March. Ivan Dragićević, now 26, meets with pilgrims in the church rectory. Helen Sarcevic again serves as translator. Ivan relates Our Lady's words: "*Dear children, I am bringing you peace and I desire that this peace be brought to others, and I am inviting you that you be my missionaries of peace.*"

Visionary Marija Pavlović, speaking to a small group of pilgrims outside her home, stresses the importance of young people: "Our Lady has chosen young people in a special way. … You can make a difference." To a young man who asks what he can do, Marija responds, "She knew what was going to happen in this situation in the war. She knew that you would come, and she wants all of you to be the witnesses to the truth, to the truthful message she is giving. It is important to witness to others with our life."

It is to Marija that Mary gives her monthly message for the world on the 25th day of each month, and on this day, June 25, 1992, Marija says Mary gave her this message:

Dear children,

> *Today I am happy, despite there being some sadness in my heart for all those who took this path and then abandoned it. My presence here is to take you on a new path, the path to salvation. This is why I call you, day after day to conversion. But if you do not pray, you cannot say that you are on the way to being converted. I pray for you and I intercede to God for peace; first peace in your hearts and also peace around you, so that God may be your peace.*

> *Thank you for having responded to my call.*

The estimated 7,000-10,000 pilgrims who responded to the *Gospa*'s call in June 1992 turned out to be the "liberation forces" for Medjugorje. Once more, pilgrimages resumed until eventually they reached prewar size. Every year since that first Peace Pilgrimage, there has been a commemorative march. Helen Sarcevic estimated that perhaps 250,000 pilgrims were in Medjugorje for the 26th anniversary of the Blessed Mother's first apparition and the 11th anniversary Peace March.

16

MISSION IN MOSTAR

The plight of the Croatian people who had so gener-
ously housed millions of pilgrims in their homes before
the war moves some of us pilgrims to organize relief
missions to Medjugorje and its environs, leading to the
second of my four trips to the war zone. On this jour-
ney, a strange sense begins to haunt me: that there is
an unknown mission for me in Mostar, where the war
now rages between the Croatians and the Muslims.

It is early morning in Medjugorje, this world-famous oasis of
peace encircled by war. The guns of evening are stilled as the
soft rays of sunlight mix with the constant crow of roosters
greeting the dawn. A young man is walking up Apparition Hill
as I am walking down. We are the only two people on this
mountain once overpopulated with pilgrims praying at the site
where the Blessed Virgin Mary first appeared to six Croatian
young people purveying urgent prescriptions for peace to the
people of Bosnia-Herzegovina and the world.

I do not know why we begin to speak. It is the nature of
this village where the Virgin resides. Strangers speak. There
is an edge to the young man's words, as if they are being
unleashed from a tautly strung bow. His name is Petar and
he is from Mostar, the once magnificent town of mosques
and minarets and bridges, now flattened and full of rubble.
Petar is a refugee living in Medjugorje, where there is no war.
But every day, he returns to his hometown to fight on the
front lines. His wife of seven months is also from Mostar. She
witnessed a massacre in Mostar; her brother lost half his leg in
the massacre. She is, he says, "too shook" to return to Mostar.

I tell Petar that I am from the United States, and that I
am in Medjugorje with a trauma relief corps for the specific

purpose of helping people emotionally cope with ordeals such as the one his wife has just gone through. The corps, trained in Washington by the National Organization for Victim Assistance (NOVA), will work one month in western Herzegovina, directly counseling refugees and teaching local caregivers the skills of trauma counseling.

Studies have shown that when victims can ventilate and validate their horrific experiences to a sensitive listener, they have taken a very important step toward exercising negative emotions that may surface in a very harmful way much later if never dealt with at the time of crisis.

The NOVA pilot project is being funded by monies raised through "Coffees of Concern" given by women around the U.S. Women United Against Violence (WUAV) is a special project of The Mary Anne Foundation, an organization inspired by the Queen of Peace. As president and founder of the foundation, I am here to observe rather than participate in the trauma counseling, though I have taken the training and even "graduated" with the team.

Petar is at first suspicious of the team, thinking we might be a psychiatric unit. "My wife is not crazy," he says heatedly. "When she sees such things, what she is feeling is normal."

"It certainly is normal," I tell him, "and part of our work is to reassure victims that it *is* normal and they are not crazy for responding deeply to atrocities."

I ask Petar about the severity of the fighting between the Croats and the Muslims in Mostar. He echoes the summation given us yesterday by the Danish UN commander. The situation in Mostar, the commander had warned us, is "very dangerous, too dangerous for your team at this time. … There will be plenty of work for you later."

"You don't have a good enough reason to risk it now," he said, making it clear the UN would not provide a chauffeur.

"I would like to go to Mostar," I tell Petar.

"I can get you in," he responds. "*Nema problema.*" My new soldier friend assures me he knows the back roads. He is confident he can get me there. He shows me his Croatian

Defense Council ID. He suggests we meet right after breakfast in front of Vicka Ivanković's house. Everyone knows Vicka's house, since she is one of the six visionaries who see the *Gospa*.

Trauma Relief Team leader Constance Noblet, a motherly woman with cropped gray hair, looks quietly concerned but resigned when I announce my intentions. She has been aware all week that I have had a strange inner sense that there is a mission in Mostar waiting for me. And she, like the UN commander, feels my "mission statement" is weak. Intuition is not a compelling enough reason to ride into a war zone. Unless you are the person with the intuition.

"I'm not being reckless. I've given this a lot of thought. And prayer," I assure Connie.

"I know you have," she responds softly.

We arrange that Petar and I will follow the team bus to Široki Brijeg to observe the corps work with the refugee children in the center there, and then Petar and I will drive into Mostar. When we arrive in Široki Brijeg, the center is not yet ready for the briefing. But Fr. Jozo Zovko is there.

Father Jozo was the pastor of Saint James church when the apparitions began. Initially skeptical, when convinced, he endured torture and imprisonment on behalf of the apparitions' authenticity. He initiated the historic pilgrimage in 1992 that liberated Medjugorje. If this holy man tells me not to go to Mostar I will listen. I will know that I am being foolish; that I can ignore the premonition. It is not from God. There is no mission for me in Mostar.

But he looks at me solemnly. " It *is* possible for you to go to Mostar," he says quietly. He is the only person to give this assurance. But the word of this prophetic man is enough.

Petar suggests we drive into town to get an up-to-date reading on the war in Mostar from some of his Široki Brijeg friends.

We drive to the office of a local official who is dressed in a white T-shirt and blue jeans and who immediately asks what I would like to drink. When I say, "Coke," he sends for a large economy-size bottle. He pours Petar a shot of bourbon, a somewhat disconcerting move as Petar is not only driving but toting his rifle, which is sometimes pointed at my toe as we walk. The postage-stamp-size office soon fills up: another soldier and a former official from Sarajevo arrive.

The news from Mostar is not good. The Muslims have launched a new offensive and are doing very well with it. Sounds of the offensive can be heard frequently in Široki Brijeg. The official complains that his son was just months from achieving his college degree when he was forced by the government to go to war. The official opens his desk drawer and brandishes a hand grenade. He is ready if the war comes to his office.

The entire group agrees that today marks a very serious chapter in the war. They do not recommend a visit to Mostar. The possibility that the "*musimas*" — as Petar amusingly calls *muslimas* (Muslims) — may take me prisoner is raised.

Our Trauma Relief Team is taking no sides in the war, but the argument would be hard to prove to a Muslim who encounters me riding in his enemy's car. Recent Muslim atrocity stories circulating in western Herzegovina have been chilling. Even Petar is wavering now.

What do you think?" he asks me. I am beginning to think I am crazy, but the idea that there is a mission for me in Mostar does not depart. I have decided, however, to leave the decision to Petar. He is a young newlywed with a child on the way. If he backs out, I will not push him. And I am half hoping he *will* back out.

"Well, let's try," he says. "But let's go now." Clearly, the other option is "never."

As we begin the drive to Mostar, an increasing number of sonic booms thunder around us. "They are grenades," Petar explains. "We are lucky. They could land right in front of us." As we draw closer to the ruined city, which first endured shelling from the Serbs and now from the Croatians and the Muslims, Petar starts down a road thick with army checkpoints.

Petar warns me to remove my NOVA ID and to have my passport ready. He hopes the police will not ask for it. He hopes the Croat soldiers, seeing his uniform, will not ask who his passenger might be. It works for several checkpoints. About the fourth checkpoint, I must surrender the passport. But the soldier apparently likes "Peggy Marie" as a name, because he smiles when he repeats it and returns the passport.

A turn on a new road brings a signal from a man on a high ridge warning of danger, and Petar is forced to travel a stone-riddled road to the left. The hilly avenue proves a challenge to Petar's frail vehicle. In the mountains, we again hear artillery fire. "Maybe when you return," Petar laughs, "people will applaud. You are alive."

"Petar, if that's my mission, we may not make it back. I'm praying for God's protection. I doubt He would feel compelled to protect bravado and egotism."

Petar nods agreement.

"I don't know why, Petar, but I feel God wants me to go to Mostar." Inwardly, I am guessing the mission is to obtain fresh video footage of the ravaged city I first filmed a year ago when the Croats liberated the town from the Serbs. Then the Croats and the Muslims were allies. Now they are fighting one another.

"War is stupidity," Petar comments, "madness. These people are crazy."

"Why do you participate?"

"Look!" Petar begins most sentences with "look" or "listen, me," as if I am not getting the point. "I have no choice. I am small people. And the big people make the wars."

"But the big people couldn't have a war if the small people refuse to fight it."

"That would mean revolution," Petar says.

"A revolution of the spirit," I agree. "They say there's a good chance of a peace treaty coming out of the peace talks in Sarajevo. The leaders may come to an agreement."

"There will be no agreement," Petar says with a snorting sound. "They are not peacemakers. They are war makers."

Years ago, Petar says when he saw a movie about Vietnam, he told his fiancée, "I would never do that. And now I shoot. Now I shoot."

"Why?"

Petar shakes his head. "I don't know. Maybe because if I don't shoot, my enemy will shoot me. Only God can stop this war. He is the only one."

"But God works through men and women."

"Maybe this is … " Petar stops, searching for the right English word. He has learned the language through movie subtitles. "Maybe this is … " He makes a horizontal line with his left forefinger, then a vertical line atop it with his right forefinger.

"Cross?" I guess, assuming that's what the gesture indicates.

"Yes," he says. "A cross for Croatian people." He goes on, "I say all the time to God, 'I know I must have cross, but please don't make it my dying in this war.'"

"If only God can stop this war, why do you think He doesn't stop it?"

Petar keeps his eyes on the rocky terrain he is trying to navigate. "Maybe we need more prayer. More sacrifices." If unbelievers won't pray, believers have to pray for them, he thinks.

As we descend the hill, the city of Mostar spreads out beneath us. Petar points to the hospital where we are headed. Winding the back roads, I am aware of the casualness with which the women and children walk the side streets. At times children point us in a safer direction. Some signal the V-sign.

"Life must go on," Petar explains.

When we pull into the hospital driveway, it is filled with soldiers and medical staff. Petar seems to know a number of the soldiers and some of the medical people. A man in light green surgical pants and white jacket takes Petar's arm and talks to him rapidly in Croatian for several minutes. Petar's eyes widen with shock and disbelief. When the conversation concludes, Petar tells me five of his friends have been killed in this morning's fighting. Eight other friends have been wounded. Petar's large brown eyes grow dark with stunned rage. My gaze travels to the rifle he is carrying.

An ambulance pulls up and we watch silently as a bare-chested, bandaged soldier is removed and carried into the hospital. Minutes later, a very weathered station wagon drives into the same space. A soldier on a crude litter is unloaded by his peers. Petar rushes over to help carry the litter into the hospital.

I stand there alone for a while surrounded by Croatian soldiers. If they wonder who the woman in the plaid shirt, blue jeans, and slouch hat might be, they do not ask. My videocam is in a bag at my waist, and the artist/journalist in me is struggling mightily to obey Petar's admonition not to do any filming.

To convey such scenes; to help raise the consciousness of the American people; to graphically present the horrors of the Balkan war — this was the reason I had supposed I was to come to Mostar. I am beginning to become aware that such a supposition is wrong and that I have come to Mostar for a reason I never could have foreseen. Or was it all a figment of my imagination?

Petar returns for me and tells me to follow him and "say nothing. You are not supposed to be here." He walks me through the wounded soldiers' ward and as their eyes search mine. I am glad I am not filming, not trespassing on their misery. The world has seen enough blood and gore from this war. The problem has been well exposed. What is ignored is the solution.

The soldiers lay huddled together, beds practically touching. Some are still in uniform. One is in a jogging suit, his head back, eyes closed, mouth agape. Another young man's chest is wrapped in a gauze covering, the blood in a puddle from his back on the bed sheet. No one speaks. One soldier is propped on a pillow reading a magazine. I see a few nurses. I long to extend a comforting hand, but respect Petar's command to "say nothing."

We walk through several rooms quite quickly. Petar is obviously anxious to exit. Artillery fire from the surrounding hills is frequent. Soon we are back on the dirt road, Petar keeping a wary eye on the thermometer gauge. Suddenly he stops in the middle of the road. "Something is wrong with the car," he says. We both get out of the car. He lifts the lid of the trunk to reveal the radiator tank spewing water down its side. Will we be forced to walk our way out of this war zone?

I can think of nothing to say but the Rosary. Petar thinks it is a good idea. We pray and wait. When the tank seems sufficiently cool, Petar pulls a bottle of water from the back seat of his car where his rifle is resting. He pours the water into the troubled tank and within a surprisingly short time, pronounces the car operable. A certain symbolism seems apparent. The road to Mostar, where a sign reads "Welcome to Hell," has been relatively easy. The road from Mostar to Medjugorje, where the message is peace, forgiveness, and reconciliation, is much more difficult.

As we resume our escape up and down the stony dirt pass, we begin to incorporate language instruction into our Rosary. One Hail Mary is said in English, the next in Croatian. Each leader says two words, each follower repeats those two words. Petar easily repeats "Hail Mary." I fumble with "*Drago Maria.*"

"English is easy," Petar comforts graciously, "Croatian is very difficult."

"Let's say this Rosary for the friends you have just lost," I suggest.

"And for me," Petar says in a low voice, "that I can forgive my enemies." When we pray the Our Father and come to the line, "forgive us our trespasses as we forgive those who trespass against us," I wonder if Petar will be able to repeat it, and I am frankly surprised when he does not hesitate. What can it be like to have just lost five friends in one morning? I can only imagine the ensuing immense emotion. But the Rosary is visibly cooling the cauldron of his white-hot anger.

Suddenly, we are off the dirt road, back on a main thoroughfare, twisting our way through small villages into the center of Široki Brijeg. I feel an overwhelming sense of gratitude to Divine Providence. We drive back to the refugee center where the Trauma Relief Corps has just completed a

debriefing session with children. The children have been drawing pictures, and all the pictures are of war, houses on fire, and
rockets flying. One little girl has drawn a picture of a man with
a machine gun pointed at her head.

At the moment we enter, local caregivers are treating the
American crisis interveners to a coffee break; the Balkans being
the Balkans, a dash of liquor is in the brew. Someone pours me
a jigger of clear alcohol and I, a light drinker, raise it in Petar's
direction and swallow it whole. As does Petar.

A cab driver had quoted me a $50 fare to Mostar. "War
zone," was the explanation. When I hand Petar a $50 bill,
he almost slaps it out of my hand. "That is too much! Too
much!" I try a $20. Nevertheless, this agricultural engineer
with no job does not want to take it.

"Well, how about my buying you and your wife a cappuccino tonight?" His eyes light up, "Good! Good!"

With this promise, Petar departs the refugee center for
Medjugorje. I stay on with the Trauma Relief Corps for more
time with the children. It is late in the day when we return
to Medjugorje, and I feel much too tired for a cappuccino,
but the cardinal rule in trauma counseling is "Never break a
promise."

Searching for Petar and his wife, Melanie, I find a small,
white hotel converted to a refugee center. Children are everywhere. Young mothers balancing babies stand in the courtyard
and converse. They are very friendly. They know Petar and
Melanie, and immediately a chorus of "Melanie, Melanie!"
rises to the fifth-floor balcony.

Several minutes later, a slim, pale-faced woman with
salmon-colored hair emerges from the hotel lobby, greets me
with a shy smile, and invites me up to the room she shares with
Petar. We walk up the five floors. There is no elevator. The
room is just large enough to house two beds pushed together.

Petar has changed from army fatigues to a T-shirt and
lively Bermuda shorts. His friend and fellow soldier Victor is
there with his black-haired wife and three-year-old daughter.
Out on the tiny balcony stands Petar's mother, a resident of

Mostar, who has fled to Medjugorje just today because of the heavy fighting in Mostar.

"Please sit down," Melanie urges me to a windowsill. She offers me grapes that are resting in a bowl on the pink bedspread. "I want to take you all for a cappuccino," I say.

"Is it all right," they ask, "if we go first to the Croatian Mass at St. James Church?"

The pews in St. James are filled as they are every evening. No other church I have attended anywhere in the world has a full house for a weekday Mass. Except for the high-vaulted ceiling over the altar, the church is dimly lit, which adds to the feeling of solidarity among the congregation as they sing their beautiful Croatian hymns with full throats. Petar beckons the women to seats, indicating that he and Victor will stand in the back. The sense of community and solidarity that faith brings to a war is extraordinarily moving.

It is twilight when we emerge from St. James to walk across the street to the café. The two young families pause to look at the white marble statue of Mary, the statue that graced the cover of *Life* magazine just two years ago. I photograph the five of them there beneath Mary's maternal gaze.

The contrast to St. James on the other side of the street at the cappuccino bar could not be sharper. The atmosphere reverberates with American rock music. The restaurant is crowded with soldiers and friends of soldiers. We sit on chairs so small that one move to the left or right will put us on the floor.

I huddle around a tiny round table with Petar, Melanie, Victor, and his wife and their beautiful baby with limpid brown eyes. I am reminded of Rick's bar in the classic war movie "Casablanca." Petar announces that he and Victor will pay. I protest that I thought we had a deal.

"This will be my treat," Petar insists, "I break deal. Like Serbs." In this country, he explains that men always pay. Never women.

"Good custom," I laugh.

I ask their ages. Petar is 29. Melanie is 27. Victor is 30,

his wife 28. They are so young, but the men look much older. Melanie says she is frightened every morning Petar goes off to war. They waited seven years to marry due to family illness and finances. They have been married just seven months. She speaks about the brother who lost half a leg in the massacre she witnessed.

Talk turns to the "why" of this war.

"Maybe God wants the war because we didn't pray," Petar says.

"God *never* wants war," I counter. "He wants peace. He *is* peace. It is man who makes war. God sent the *Gospa* to tell you how to prevent war."

Four pair of eyes fix on mine. Victor's seem especially large and sad. It is commonly believed in Medjugorje that the messages given by the *Gospa* would have averted the tragedy had the messages been heeded. When she called for conversion to God, forgiveness, and reconciliation, "she was talking about inner peace," a village teenager said, adding, "*a man who is at peace on the inside does not make war on the outside.*"

Petar knows all about the *Gospa*'s messages. He has talked about them frequently this day. He knows she has said that only prayer and fasting can stop war. For the fifth or sixth time he repeats, "Only God can stop this war."

And I repeat, "God works through men," and once again suggest they lay down their guns. I tell the story of the two teenage Croatian soldiers who came to Medjugorje from the front lines in Mostar and were invited to witness Vicka during an apparition. Afterward, both quit the army. One with a badly wounded eye was flown to America, where his eye was repaired thanks to donated surgery and medical care.

Four young adults are staring even more earnestly now, and for once Petar does not say the reason he shoots at his enemy is to prevent his enemy from shooting him. "We need a revolution," he declares.

"Yes, why not?" I ask, borrowing a favorite Croatian expression. "Maybe the Croatian 'small people' should lead all the Muslim 'small people' and all the Serbian 'small people' who feel like you do. Lead them against the 'big people,' the war makers. Be not afraid."

Petar laughs. It would be easier, he says, "to move to Zimbabwe. There is no hope for this country."

"Never lose hope. This war will end. You will begin again."

Victor says, someday, if the war ever does end, he wants to come and see me in Washington. It is one of the few things he has said this evening.

I must return to Marinko's house where the Trauma Relief Corps and I are staying, I tell them. I embrace the young wives, and their husbands drive me back to the house at the base of Apparition Hill where my day with Petar began. I bid goodbye to Victor and pat his very large hand. He nods and smiles a little, one of the rare smiles he has displayed.

Outside the car, I hug Petar, this boy who is just a few years older than my new son-in-law, and who must face the front lines in the morning — the front lines he would not let me see. He gives me the European kiss on both cheeks.

"I will not forget you, Petar. I will pray for you every day till this awful war is over."

"I will never forget you," Petar replies.

I feel my eyelids smarting. Inwardly, I thank God for today's journey; that He placed me where a young man needed a brake on his actions when he received the terrible news that five friends were killed in battle; news — had he not felt responsible for his female passenger — that might have sent him in a rage to the front to avenge those friends. And a young, expectant mother might be a widow tonight.

Sometimes your job is just to show up. Rosary in hand.

Only now do I realize my mission in Mostar was Petar.

I never saw him again.

PART THREE

Alack, thou knowest not
How little worthy of any love thou art!
Whom wilt thou find to love ignoble thee,
Save Me, save only Me?
All which I took from thee I did but take,
Not for thy harms,
But just that thou might'st seek it in My arms.
All which thy child's mistake
Fancies as lost, I have stored for thee at home:
Rise, clasp My hand, and come!. . .

    — Francis Thompson, "The Hound of Heaven" (1909)

17

A VOICE CRYING IN
THE WILDERNESS

*In the early 1990s, apostolic work was dominating my
life in ways I could never have anticipated or predicted.
The Balkan War led The Mary Anne Foundation into
fundraising, trauma relief missions, peace programs,
art exhibits, religious cards, and, ultimately, our
biggest project, Kids for Peace Week.*

It is just one small voice crying in the wilderness and confusion of the brutal Balkan War, but it is a voice that launches an international children's movement. On June 24, 1994, as 100,000 pilgrims gather for peace in Medjugorje, kids on three continents do the same. In Washington, D.C., a black children's choir rocks the renowned Basilica of the National Shrine of the Immaculate Conception, America's largest Catholic church. In Windsor, Ohio, little feet process through the fields to the world's tallest statue of Our Lady of Guadalupe.

In Lourdes, France, teenagers march through town to pray for peace at the grotto where the Blessed Mother appeared to another teenager, Bernadette Soubirous. In French West Africa, village girls pray for peace with a Peace Corps volunteer.

When Slavica Ramjlak writes a desperate letter to The Mary Anne Foundation in the winter of 1993, she has no way of knowing her words will touch so many hearts around the world. "Only to you," the letter says, "am I making my voice heard."

The previous fall, The Mary Anne Foundation, through a special fundraising effort, had financed a pilot trauma-counseling project in Medjugorje. Father Slavko Barbaric provided rooms in St. James rectory where professionally trained crisis intervention counselors schooled local care-givers (including Franciscan nuns) in the art of healing the psychologically wounded.

As part of the month-long program, the counselors, all volunteers from the U.S., working under the direction of the National Organization for Victim Assistance, or NOVA, visited nearly 1,000 refugees. As previously discussed, I spent a week with the crisis counselors of The Mary Anne Foundation, observing the effectiveness of their efforts.

At a refugee center in Široki Brijeg, the crisis counselors concentrated on a large group of children, asking them to draw pictures of their lives, a method of excising the trauma within. The portraits were heart-searing: pictures of neighbors firing guns at one another, bombs falling on houses, and roofs in flames. My videocam and still camera attempted to record as much of this activity as possible.

The children were so anxious for love that they swarmed around all of us, strangers though we were, looking for hugs with longing gazes. My photography captured some poignant studies.

So many little faces stared into the camera that I can-not recall to which child I handed a Mary Anne Foundation business card as we departed Široki Brijeg; I wrote a quick note on the card, "Write to me." And that little child took my invitation seriously.

Several months later, much to my astonishment, a letter arrives in The Mary Anne Foundation post office box from a ref-ugee camp in Bosnia-Herzegovina. Thinking that Mary Anne is a person, Slavica Ramljak addresses me as her godmother, Mary Anne. Mark Twain is quoted as saying "Coincidence is God's way of remaining anonymous." For me, this was truly a "Mark Twain moment."

For months, my efforts to attain a godchild through a program started by Fr. Jozo, International God-Parenthood for the Herzeg-Bosnian Child, have been frustrated by checks disappearing en route from Washington, D.C., to Wichita, Kansas, where Nives Jelich directed the program's American office. Both Nives and I have been puzzled by the disappearing checks until Slavica's letter arrives. Obviously, Someone other than Nives has chosen my godchild for me. Immediately, Nives fits Slavica into the International God-Parenthood program, which essentially pairs a war orphan with an adult who will write, visit, and send financial support. Slavica is not a total orphan. Her father was killed in the war. Her mother survived but had lost her job and now lived in a refugee camp with her several daughters.

In her letter, Slavica pours out the misery of being a child of war. She asks for, among other things, letters. Using the photographs of refugee children I had taken in the Široki Brijeg camp, The Mary Anne Foundation launches the "Letters to Slavica" project through *Life* magazine. In the article, the foundation asks American children to write to refugee children, promising to see that the letters are personally delivered to Bosnia.

Life runs the pictures and Slavica's request for mail toward the end of the issue on page 117. "You may get some extra mail," the editor warns me. "You may need to bring in extra help." How much mail is he talking about, I ask. "Cover stories usually get about 50 letters," he answers.

Slavica's appearance on page 117 brings in over 3,000 letters from all across America and Canada, more mail than the magazine had ever received since becoming a monthly edition, one *Life* staffer estimated. A year-and-a-half after the article appeared, The Mary Anne Foundation still receives letters from children wishing to console war victims in Bosnia.

It soon becomes obvious that such a huge volume of mail needs more than the United States Postal Service. The Mary Anne Foundation appeals to the Medjugorje network for help and it literally delivers. Helen Sarcevic of Clarks Summit, Pennsylvania; Sandy Tobin of Clearwater, Florida; and Nives Jelich of Wichita, Kansas, all take bundle after bundle of letters as they make their regular pilgrimage/relief journeys throughout the war.

Mail pouches even go through such unlikely couriers as banker John Figge of Washington; Jesuit hospital chaplain Fr.

Dan Gatti; Georgetown University student volunteer Tom Shakow; and Croatian ambassador Petar Šarčević.

Rita Falsetto, one of the original volunteers with our Trauma Counseling Program and a partial Mary Anne Foundation Scholar who is working with Fr. Slavko Barbaric in Medjugorje, receives many of the letters and sees to their translation and delivery to children. Rita and a friend and fellow volunteer invite Slavica and her family to Medjugorje and wind up becoming godmothers to Slavica's sisters.

It is not merely the quantity of mail that astounds us; it is the quality. "If adults cannot handle peace," writes one 8-year-old, "perhaps it is time for you and I to pick up the banner and show them the folly of their ways."

Soon letters and pictures of the Balkan children receiving their mail begin returning to the U.S. Peace links are being forged across the ocean. It is not long before we realize that Project SLAVICA (Sending Letters And Voices In a Children's Alliance of Love) needs more avenues of expression. Thus is born the Kids For Peace Pilgrimage.

Inspired by the great peace pilgrimages that have been held on June 24 in Medjugorje, we choose the Feast of St. John the Baptist as equally appropriate for the Kids for Peace Pilgrimages, since it is literally a small voice crying in the wilderness that awakened all of us. June 24 is also John the Baptist's birthday.

The first pilgrimage is held, just two months after the *Life* magazine article appears, at the Basilica of the National Shrine of the Immaculate Conception. Next door, the Catholic University of America puts together an impressive art exhibit of the children's letters and pictures. The university publicity department works overtime alerting Washington to the event, which is to start at 3 p.m.

At 2:59 p.m., there are adults everywhere; the Croatian ambassador and his wife are seated in the front row. *Life* magazine has sent a special photographer. Musicians are in place. A prominent clergyman is waiting to say Mass. Not a child is in sight. As the clock ticks toward the hour of Divine Mercy, I kneel in front of the tabernacle and beg for a massive dose of mercy in the form of petite people.

When I stand up and turn around, one of the most politically correct little group of pixies on the planet come strolling down the middle aisle. Every hue of the human rainbow — Americans, Asians, Africans, and Europeans — greets our eyes. Even a non-pious observer, the *Life* magazine photographer, doesn't miss the point. "They walked in just as you finished praying," he notes. He is elated with the diversity they provide his lens.

Tiny as they are, the children sit perfectly still throughout the Mass, listening attentively to Fr. Peter Daly talk about the meaning of peace. A young Croatian girl, who has been away from the war just one month, reads Scripture in English. A blind teenager plays the music and sings for the Mass. The pilgrimage continues with a candlelight procession around the chapels flanking the Queen of Peace Chapel, where the Mass has been said. It concludes in Our Lady of Hope Chapel, which has been donated by Dolores and Bob Hope.

This very humble beginning starts the parable of the Mustard Seed replaying in my head. Our Lord compared the Kingdom of Heaven to the tiniest seed, the mustard seed, which ultimately becomes the tallest tree (Mk 4:30-32). I wonder, I thought to myself, what a mustard seed looks like. Just days later, a new batch of SLAVICA letters provides the answer. Speaking about their small efforts for peace, the children write, "We feel like we are like the mustard seeds." In a carefully folded piece of notebook paper, the children had enclosed a batch of mustard seeds!

And just like the mustard seed, the Kids for Peace Pilgrimage has grown. Three years after it began, the pilgrimage has spread to six countries and three continents. The third annual pilgrimage receives encouragement from Bishop Anthony Pilla, president of the National Conference of Catholic Bishops; the Archbishop of Washington, Cardinal James Hickey; and from the Holy Father himself.

From the Vatican comes a letter stating that His Holiness, Pope John Paul II, "invokes God's blessings of joy and peace upon all taking part in the pilgrimage."

When Our Lady first appeared in Medjugorje, she said, "I have come to tell the world that God exists. He alone is the fullness of life. To enjoy this fullness and obtain peace, you must return to God."

As each pilgrimage unfolds, I feel something is sorely missing. What Project SLAVICA, the Children's Alliance of Love, really needs is a *child*, not an adult, as its principal spokesman, a young person with a deep spiritual sense who would be comfortable talking to the media. In my mind I can see such a child.

One day in 1996, imagination becomes reality in the form of Tommy Tighe from Fountain Valley, California. Tommy, who is now 14, has been working for peace since he was 4 years old. At that age, watching a television news program showing scenes of people clubbing a woman with a baby, a horrified Tommy ran to his room and closed the door.

After a long period of time, his mother, Katie Tighe, went in to see if Tommy was all right. She found him writing on strips of paper in his 4-year-old scrawl, "*Peace, please! Do it for us kids.*" The strips were signed simply, "Tommy."

One morning, Tommy awoke, his face all aglow. He had had a dream that his house was bombed. Then he heard a voice telling him this was only a dream, but that it could really happen and that he, Tommy, had to do something to stop it.

"You know what?" Tommy told his startled parents. "God told me I could cause peace in the world." Furthermore, he said, God had told him, "I don't have to fight the people. I just have to tell the people not to fight."

The best way to accomplish his mission, Tommy reasoned, was to put his peace message on a bumper sticker. "Almost everyone has a car or at least sees one every day," he said. To pay for printing the bumper stickers, Tommy, who was now 5, went to the Children's Bank and took out a $454 loan and produced 1,000 bumper stickers.

Tommy then sent free bumper stickers to heads of state, including Ronald Reagan and Mikhail Gorbachev. A youth group traveling in Russia claims they see Tommy's bumper sticker gracing Mikhail Gorbachev's limousine.

The man whose Children's Bank tendered the loan to Tommy is Mark Victor Hansen, coauthor of the bestselling book *Chicken Soup for the Soul,* which started the extremely successful book series of the same name.

Tommy becomes a chapter in the book. Once the news media learns of the young peacemaker/entrepreneur, Tommy's business is off and running. Tommy meets with his mayor and U.S. senator, his governor, and a host of reporters and talk show luminaries.

People are charmed by Tommy's sincerity and innocence. When comedian Joan Rivers asks Tommy if he really thinks his bumper sticker could cause peace in the world, he responds, "So far, I've had it out for two years and got the Berlin Wall down. I'm doing pretty good, don't you think?" Indeed. Mrs. Tighe estimates that Tommy has sold over 10,000 bumper stickers to some eight countries, including Iran and China. American soldiers working in Bosnia have bought them for their tanks.

After we meet in Los Angeles it becomes apparent to both Tommy and The Mary Anne Foundation that we share the same vision. God loves to use children in His efforts to bring peace to the world.

Tommy Tighe agrees to become the first national chairman of the Kids for Peace Pilgrimage.

From that tiny beginning, Kids for Peace is moved from June 24 up to December, in order to involve schools. It is the birthday month of the Prince of Peace.

Originally planned for only one day, the pilgrimage grows to a full week of activities centered on avenues to peace. Monday is "Peace in the Heart," which leads to Tuesday, "Peace in the Home," which leads to Wednesday, "Peace in the Community," which leads to Thursday, "Peace in the Country," which leads to Friday, "Peace in the World."

An internet website is set up with a giant peace chain. Every school that joins the pilgrimage becomes a link in the chain. The Mary Anne Foundation furnishes brochures to the schools free of charge with suggested activities for each day of the week.

From 40 children in Washington, D.C., the program spreads across America, eventually involving around 40,000 children — all because a child of great faith in a refugee camp dared to become a "voice crying in the wilderness."

18

MOTHER OF ALL PEOPLE

Medjugorje also transformed my burgeoning art career. No longer was there a desire to paint portraits or presidential eyes. The Madonna and her village took over my canvases, leading to an exhibit at the Marian Home of Prayer in Washington, D.C., called "A Pilgrim Paints Medjugorje." Sometimes it seemed Someone else was in control of the picture.

Nothing is more alarming than to be told we are not in control. And yet only One is in control. Artists realize they are not really in command of their brush or their chisel. Michelangelo is alleged to have said he just picked away at stone until the figure within emerged.

The painting "Mother of all People" was that kind of accident. Its life began as a commissioned portrait of U.S. Senator Chuck Percy's grandchildren. It is a painting on paper, and when the children's mother requested a lighter shade of paper than the dark paper I had chosen, I put it aside and began a new picture that became the finished portrait.

But the dark paper had been "sized" and mounted on a 40" x 40" board and so I thought I must do something with it. A friend told me she was writing a book titled "Mother of All People." The theme intrigued me and thus became my inspiration. The book eventually was published with a different name, so I adopted it for my painting.

Another friend, Charlotte Conable, wife of former World Bank president Barber Conable, traveled with her husband to Third World countries often and photographed many of the women and children there. One of her pictures of an African woman in native costume became Mary's dress.

The picture almost painted itself. Mary's face is that of a Croatian woman, Shima, our first hostess on our first trip to Medjugorje. The children's faces are also faces of actual children, pictures collected from newspapers and magazines. Now as I look at these faces chosen so many years ago, I ask myself why there are so many with Third World countenances, some looking so sad, some clinging to one another or to the Blessed Mother?

Was there a message being conveyed of which I was unaware?

The intended message, like the painting, just evolved. At the very top of the painting, barely visible, is Calvary and the Crucified One. Beneath the Cross two figures, Mary and the apostle John, symbolizing Jesus' final gift to the world, His Mother. The multitudes in front of the Cross represent the refugees of the world, which at the time of the painting numbered about 50 million. A tsunami added a million more. The next grouping are then world leaders. The most prominent group stand in front of the Madonna. They are the future of the world — the children.

Mary is portrayed as very strong. Her hands are deliberately large and protective. She does not piously cast her eyes to the ground. She stares directly out at the viewer, just as she did in the final scene of "The Passion of the Christ." She challenges us. She is indeed the New Eve, the mother of all people, just as God, Father and Creator, loves all His children, even those who do not yet know Him under the Name of Jesus. Hopefully, some are beginning to recognize this, while there is still time.

Time. How much time do we have before Jesus returns as the Just Judge? One week? One year? One century? One millennium? No one knows but the Father. Jesus made that clear: "Watch therefore, for you know neither the day nor the hour" (Mt 25:13). We do know He is coming back. He made that equally clear: "You will see the Son of Man coming on the clouds."

One prayer group in Florida, fancifully speculating on the Second Coming, raised this question: How would the whole world see Jesus return at the same time, with all the different time zones? The answer they hit upon was that for some, He would come in the daylight; for others it would be at night. They ultimately concluded that the Creator of the universe will have no trouble being seen when He chooses to be seen.

Would we be frightened at witnessing a giant figure in the sky, no doubt surrounded by myriads of angels? The terror of a tsunami might pale by comparison — except for the very pure of heart, who no doubt will be thrilled.

The general consensus among clergy and laypeople in the Catholic faith seems to be that this is an event in the far-distant future. And there is a great deal of evidence to back that theory. After all, 2,000 years have already gone by without the Lord's reappearance. What is another 2,000?

Perhaps 2,000 too many. In speculating on the end times, it's important to remember this: Whether or not it's end times for the world is insignificant. What's important are *our* end times. And those end times could come with little warning, as they have for so many afflicted with COVID-19, a disease unheard of until 2020.

None of us is going to get out of this life alive. And just as we cannot predict when the Second Coming will occur, "we know not the day nor the hour" of our departure. Where we wind up will depends on how close we have stayed to the One Whose coming we still anxiously anticipate.

19

DIVINE MERCY AND ME

A prayer I almost threw away becomes a dominant force in my life.

For five years in an upper room of the Basilica of the National Shrine of the Immaculate Conception, a $7\frac{1}{2}$-foot painting of the Divine Mercy image stood shrouded in a carton. How it got there and why it remained there for such a long time is another intriguing chapter in the history of that devotion, which has experienced a roller coaster ride since Jesus revealed His messages to a Polish nun, now St. Faustina, in the 1930s.

The story of this image begins in the unlikely setting of the ladies' lounge in the elegant Connaught Hotel in London, England, where the artist (yours truly) who painted the above-mentioned painting, encounters an Irish maid reading Fr. Slavko Barbarić's *Medjugorje Manual of Prayer*. This leads to a long discussion between artist and attendant, comparing notes on Medjugorje. Before the conversation concludes, the attendant presses a newsletter about a "wonderful new devotion" into my hand.

Later, in my hotel room, I retrieve the newsletter from my purse, ready to throw it out. I am, I think to myself, in devotion overload. Before the paper makes the wastebasket, however, curiosity conquers. And I read for the first time the history of the Divine Mercy devotion. I am intrigued by the extravagant promises attached to the recitation of Divine Mercy prayers and cannot resist testing their validity.

I discover that answers to Divine Mercy prayers are quite remarkable and consistent. I am hooked. I soon find myself experimenting with a portrait of Divine Mercy. Nothing satisfies. Every face seems trite.

One day I lunch with a senior management analyst from

the Commerce Department in Washington, D.C., who wishes to share with me her extraordinary experiences in Medjugorje, including, she claims, several visions of Our Lord. I am frankly skeptical. The woman is either an authentic loon or an authentic mystic.

I joke to the analyst, "Why doesn't Christ appear to poor artists who are struggling to paint His face?" Her response is, "Ah, but he does! On their canvas." Thinking of my recent futile attempts to paint Divine Mercy, I counter, "Not on mine."

Shortly after the luncheon, I am awakened from a sound sleep at 3 a.m. with the sense I am being *commanded* to go to my studio, where I will see the Lord! The idea leaves me paralyzed with so much fright that one would have thought I was contemplating an encounter with the serpent rather than the Savior.

The command seems so insistent, however, that I finally rise, creep down the hall, and with trembling fingers switch on the light in my studio. There is no one there. Never have I felt such a sense of relief! But now I am wide awake. I might as well do a little work. Slightly bleary eyed, I begin yet another study of Divine Mercy.

By 4 a.m., a penetrating pair of eyes are staring back at me from a piece of paper. The next night, I am awakened again at precisely 3 a.m. This time I do not struggle. A third night I am awakened at 3 a.m. I am literally "getting the picture." But not without reluctance. "If you don't mind, Lord, I prefer working in prime time," I complain. An instant reply fires into my brain: "So, could you not watch with me one hour?" (Mt 26:40).

Oh. OK.

And amazingly it *is* only one hour. For nine consecutive nights, I awake at the same time, work until 4 a.m., and am remarkably able to return to a deep sleep until my usual rising time — 7 a.m. Even more remarkably, I never disturb my husband's sleep in the process.

At the end of nine nights, the picture is concluded, and at last, I have a face that I am happy with. And it required a novena. But I put the picture away and show it to no one, not even my husband, until my friend Dorothy Shula is in George-town University Hospital for cancer surgery.

Every day I go to the hospital to pray with Dorothy. One day, after experiencing what seems a strong interior urging, but feeling rather foolish, I spirit the painting into Dorothy's room in a black plastic bag. When I unveil it to Dorothy, the emotion she expresses makes me realize I must do something more with the painting.

I know, however, that I can never repeat the face. I also know that the portrait of Divine Mercy needs a body drawn to the proportions of the head, which is 8 inches by 11½ inches in size, requiring a much larger body than I have ever contem-plated, much less attempted. And since the head is on paper, the body must be also.

How does one control an 8-foot piece of paper? One day, I discover, quite by accident, in my attic, a huge piece of plywood, just exactly the size I need! But how do I carry this massive piece of wood down the stairs to my studio? I walk out my front door into my courtyard, and there I see several construction workers rehabbing a neighbor's home.

An interior nudge moves me to approach perfect strang-ers to come into my house and carry an 8-foot piece of wood down a delicate drop-down ladder! I sheepishly explain my need. The construction workers would be delighted to help, they say, as if they get this kind of strange request every day. Within minutes the men have carried the plywood down the rickety stairs and installed it in my studio. What do I owe them? I ask, more than happy to pay whatever they stipulate. Absolutely nothing, they insist. And they mean it.

I stretch just the right amount of paper, matching the exact color used for the head, over the plywood, and in only two weeks the body is completed. When the head is attached to the body, in the right lighting the match appears seamless.

I share the story with Br. Leonard Konopka, MIC, of the Marian Fathers of the Immaculate Conception, who is chairing the committee organizing the first celebration of Divine Mercy

Sunday at the Basilica of the National Shrine in Washington, D.C. I am serving on the committee.

Just days before the celebration, it is discovered that they do not have the large image of Divine Mercy we had expected to exhibit in front of this enormous basilica. A major emergency. Brother Leonard remembers my story. Could they use mine? But it's not even framed, I protest. It's an emergency. They do not care.

All through the celebration, I gaze at the image, with a sense of wonder at the Lord's humility that He allowed a portrait of Him drawn by an unknown artist to be displayed before an audience of thousands. When the service is over, the presiding bishop helps me carry the picture to the van.

Several days after the service, I receive a phone call. The voice on the other end belongs to a Spanish lady who asks if I am the artist who drew the portrait of the Divine Mercy image used at the National Shrine celebration. I admit same. The lady says she had to talk to me and tell me that *before* the celebration she had had an incredible dream of Jesus. And the face in her dream was the same as the face in the painting.

Years later, a former ambassador and director of the Peace Corps, Loret Ruppe, who was dying of cancer, tells me that during a very difficult moment, she sees herself walking down a beach with Jesus, who is holding her hand. "You know me," she says, "I'm not the type to have visions." Indeed, she is not. A highly intelligent woman, she is religious but more pragmatic than mystical. "What did He look like?" I ask.

"Like the face in your painting," she responds.

That face remains hidden in the Basilica of the National Shrine for five years until the fall of 2000 when I am asked to do an exhibit for the Marian Research Museum at the University of Dayton, Ohio, which has the largest collection of Marian material in the world and is under the aegis of the Vatican. The exhibit is to be all about Mary. I agree to the exhibit on one condition: Mary can bring her Son with her. He comes and of course, just as His Mother wishes, He dominates the event.

And that is where He remains until this very day, awaiting His next appearance, which is right here, thanks to photographer Visko Hatfield, who volunteered his considerable skills to travel from Connecticut to the Marian Library Museum in Dayton, Ohio, and photograph the painting for reproduction in this book.

20

A POPE FOR ALL PEOPLE

We are in Rome, seated in St. Peter's Square, bathed in brilliant sunshine, just 20 feet from the Holy Father's beige velvet, gilt-edged chair. The square is filled with pilgrims and tourists from around the globe. A group from Argentina is waving blue and white flags and chanting for John Paul II to bless Argentina.

We are here because we received a special invitation from the Vatican at our hotel. The invitation indicates a specific entrance where a Swiss guard greets us and escorts us to the front row. Several rows behind us is singer Diana Ross and a black male companion in a morning suit.

A cheer goes up from green- and black-hatted schoolchildren as the Popemobile enters the square. One can just see the top of the papal white beanie as John Paul circles the crowd, seemingly unprotected. On the far-right side, girls are dressed in Asian costumes. Band music is playing, sounding like a high school football game. We are all on our feet. The Holy Father glides like a white dove through the square, blessing the various groups.

Those of us in the front row are in black, except my spouse, Bill Stanton, who is in his sport coat — perhaps his effort to ensure an audience. In a tier of seats behind us is a group hardly concerned about dress protocol. There are jogging suits, red sweaters over blue shirts, and even a lady in blue jeans.

Now John Paul comes down the center aisle toward the baldachin and, beneath, his canopied chair. He shakes hands with all the nuns in the front row. The Argentinians chant, "Juan Pablo! Juan Pablo!" The red, white, and green flag of Italy is prominently displayed in the front row. The little nuns all cheer. John Paul returns with a bright smile to bless a baby. The nuns alternate between squealing and taking pictures, while thrusting their hands forward for a papal grip.

The Holy Father stops en route up his steps to greet little Asian children, who run forward. With a wide grin, he hugs them. Bill snaps a picture. The Pope waves, seemingly at Bill.

Priests read from the Book of Wisdom in Dutch, English and Italian as John Paul listens and then nods to each lector. A child squeals. The Holy Father looks at his watch. He is handed his speech. He reads with expression but does not lift his eyes from the page, while a child in the front row plays under a chair with another child as his mother squirms nervously.

When the Pope finishes his talk, a monsignor gives a greeting to the different nationalities in the square: now the Germans, now the French, now the Polish. The Holy Father waves to each group. He then blesses all the Rosaries present.

John Paul now delivers another message, this time in French, similar to the first theme, which warns against materialism and Marxism. Behind and above the Pope, the majestic statues of the apostles and Jesus rim the top of St. Peter's Basilica; several of the apostles obscured from view by scaffolding where restoration is taking place. Christ's powerful hand rises above the green netting.

The Holy Father speaks again, this time in English: "God is the source of all that is good," he tells the crowd, then talks about developments in the Third World. A little Indian boy trundles around the square just in front of the Pope, greeting all of us, to the amusement of the seated cardinals.

The universality of the Catholic Church is clearly evident by the variety of countries present: Taiwan, Germany, Australia, Austria, Latin America, the U.S., Denmark. The Pope smiles and waves to each nationality gathering, apparently mouthing a greeting as his lips move. He is kindness personified.

The sun grows hotter. A sudden breeze relieves us. The bells of St. Peter's peal the noon hour, and the Holy Father speaks in German. A blind man up front claps vigorously at a papal remark.

A black-haired monsignor takes over the microphone and gives greetings in Spanish and Portuguese. The Argentinians rise and sing a response. The monsignor's lips just barely curve upward, a contrast to John Paul's broad smile.

Suddenly we hear the loud, sing-song squeals of a police car as it drives by. Heads turn. The moment passes. The Pope continues to speak, his voice echoing across the vast square. He finishes. The crowd claps. The Poles begin to sing. John Paul holds his hand to his eyes, then glances at his watch and waves at the conclusion.

A nun with a straw bonnet resting on her black-habited head stands up to wave as her country is introduced. Schoolchildren make themselves heard; the males are especially boisterous. The pontiff is amused. The Swiss Guards, in their orange- and purple-striped pants and "Don Quixote" red-plumed hats, stand on either side of the baldachin, leaning on their spears, their pink-cheeked baby faces belying the serious security they provide.

Finally, the Holy Father rises, the cardinals join him, and they all sing the Benediction. It is now time for the big moment when we will be presented individually to the Pope.

Yesterday, at lunch, I conducted a quiz as to what each person had in mind to tell the leader of 1.1 billion people. According to this correspondent's observations at the White House, the president of the United States would linger longer with a person who proffered a provocative statement in greeting. Everyone, I intoned, therefore, ought to have a specific and significant thing to say to John Paul. All nodded in solemn agreement, and everyone follows the speaker's advice, except, of course, the speaker.

Susannah Botafogo, normally reserved, speaks up to announce that she is from Brazil, and the Holy Father responds warmly how much he likes Brazil. José Botafogo says he is from the World Bank and that his institution is helping the poor in the developing countries. " Good! Good!" nods the pontiff. Bill Stanton informs John Paul that he, too, is from the World Bank and that the bank is going to try to help the

Holy Father's charitable foundation. "Bless you! Bless you!" exults the Pope and gives Bill's hand an extra firm shake.

Then he arrives at me, Miss "Please Be Sure You Have Something Momentous to Say." And he stands and waits. And waits. I actually do have my sentence as well as a little gift at the ready. But as the supreme pontiff looks at me with his kind eyes and smile, my own unimportance rises up to cover my mouth and I say *nothing*.

John Paul continues to wait for another instant and then he volunteers, "God bless you and your family." It is probably the first time in my life that words fail my too voluble tongue. "Well," my loving husband says later, with a note of envy for such power, "it took the Holy Father to finally silence you."

> *As one reflects back on that and four other moments with John Paul II, the question is raised, "What was his charisma?" Webster's first definition of charisma as "a rare quality or power attributed to those persons who have demonstrated an exceptional ability for leadership and for securing the devotion of large numbers of people" certainly fits John Paul II, as the amazing outpouring of respect at his funeral demonstrated.*
>
> *But why? He was not particularly imposing in appearance, albeit athletically nice looking in his younger days. The most striking quality evident in the Polish Pope one-on-one was his humility. You might have been talking to a peasant. There was nothing in his demeanor that suggested he was a brilliant philosopher, theologian, poet, actor, and playwright. He was that unassuming. Perhaps the answer lies in Webster's second definition of charisma: "A divinely inspired gift or power such as the ability to perform miracles."*
>
> *The most memorable moments for me with John Paul II were not the private visits (including a half-hour with just four other people), but his appearance on the mall in Washington, D.C., before at least*

250,000 people, all of whom had walked to hear him from a far-distant parking lot.

Watching the throng assemble under a mystical sky rolling with dark clouds, listening to the Pope's then-magnificent voice speak into a microphone that echoed the Gospel from the Washington Monument to the base of the U.S. Capitol, his liturgical robes swirling in the wind, one's imagination traveled back in time 2,000 years to the Sermon on the Mount.

It was then that I realized we had not come to see Karol Wojtyła, who after all, was merely a man; we were seeking a vision of the One for Whom he was the vicar on earth, Who was not merely a man. In his humility, John Paul emptied himself of self. As a result, Jesus could take him over completely. And the Christ that shone through him was the charisma to which we and millions more around the globe were so drawn.

It is a charisma of which we are all capable if we can similarly divest ourselves of ourselves and give Jesus room to let God be God in us.

21

A TINY LADY SCORES A BIG HIT

In a town replete with presidents and prime minis-
ters, a person without title finds it almost impossible
to be noticed. Not so with Mother Teresa. She came to
Washington to deliver a speech that shook the nation's
capital and that continues to resonate to this day. And
a Catholic cardinal almost stopped her from delivering
that speech until Bill Stanton helped change his mind.

There she stands, in the international ballroom of the Washington Hilton Hotel, all 4-feet-3-inches of her 83-year-old frame barely visible above the podium, two big black microphones unfortunately positioned directly in front of her eyes.

In the audience of 3,000 people are the president of the United States, five heads of state, the diplomatic corps, representatives from 150 countries and all 50 states of the Union, Catholic Church hierarchy, members of the U.S. Congress, and a legendary football coach. In a heavily accented voice, she reads her speech, seldom glancing up while struggling with pages that sometimes stick together.

And she delivers what columnist Cal Thomas describes as "the most startling and bold proclamation of truth ... I have heard in my more than 30 professional years in Washington."

As previously mentioned, the National Prayer Breakfast is an annual event designed and run by the Fellowship Foundation, a largely Protestant organization. It began humbly during World War II when the vice president, some members of the Senate, and a Supreme Court justice met to discuss the war and pray. Under the leadership of the Fellowship Foundation, the breakfast has grown to its present size, encompassing representatives from every faith and every political stripe.

The president and vice president of the United States are always present and always speak. This day, however, they are taking a back seat to the keynote speaker, and they know it. The speaker's identity is usually kept secret till the breakfast begins.

That is not so this morning, February 3, 1994, due to the controversy surrounding her appearance. The speaker is Mother Teresa of Calcutta, and she will be on the same program with President Bill Clinton and First Lady Hillary Clinton, whose advocacy of abortion is directly opposed to the saintly nun and her Church's advocacy of life.

It is because of that juxtaposition that Catholic Church hierarchy have opposed her speaking at the National Prayer Breakfast. The Archbishop of Washington, D.C., Cardinal James Hickey, a kindly, reserved man, knows nothing about the National Prayer Breakfast, having never been invited to it. He fears her presence might be politically exploited.

Mother tells Doug Coe, the spiritual father of the breakfast, that she thinks Jesus wants her to make the appearance, but she will not disobey her Church hierarchy.

Doug, who is a close Stanton family friend, appeals to us to intercede with the cardinal. My husband Bill and Cardinal Hickey know one another. Bill's former congressional district abuts the city of Cleveland, where Cardinal Hickey had once presided as Bishop.

Many letters on the fellowship's behalf descend on the cardinal's desk, one allegedly from Senator Ted Kennedy. But as Cardinal Hickey tells me at the prayer breakfast (to which he is finally invited), it is Bill's intervention that begins to change the conversation.

Mother Teresa's appearance is finally approved, but not without restrictions; Mother is not to be seated on the dais before her speech. She will only make her appearance when she is called to speak.

Vice President Al Gore precedes Mother Teresa, and he reflects on what it feels like to talk about the power of God in *his* life on the same podium with such a holy woman, "who epitomizes selfless dedication to God's work." He likens the moment to a basketball game where Michael Jordan scored 68 points. After the game, a rookie on the team who had scored one point was interviewed and asked what he thought of such an extraordinary game. The rookie answered, "I will always remember this as the occasion when Michael Jordan and I combined for 69 points."

President Clinton follows Mother Teresa and joins in Vice President Gore's humor of humility. "I feel like the guy who comes in with five seconds left to go, where the team's gotten a 40-point lead and all I have to do is hold the ball until the buzzer rings."

The president and vice president are not merely acknowledging greatness. They are in awe of sanctity. All of us who are blessed to be present realize we are witnessing a morning we will never forget.

It turns into one of the most dramatic moments in the history of the nation's capital, where electric events are the staple of society. Though I have observed Mother Teresa in person on many occasions, only once have I met her. When she took my hand and held it with both of her large, soft, warm hands, looking directly in my eyes with intense focus, I sensed the Presence of Christ in this woman, more than in any other person I had ever met.

Mother Teresa begins by calling her listeners to attention, much like she might have done when she taught slum children under a plum tree in Calcutta. She has requested that the peace prayer of St. Francis of Assisi be put at every place setting and so she asks everyone to recite it with her.

When she hears little reaction, she peers to the side of the microphones obscuring her, eyeing us all with a little nudge. "You have the prayer with you? Will we say it together?" *Yes, Sister.* Voices began to swell from the floor, "Make me a channel of your peace."

The theme is love. Tough love. No hearts and flowers kind of love. It is "spinach love" — love that energizes and empowers, the kind of love that sent her into the streets to pick up the forgotten, diseased, dying dregs of society, housing them and giving them a dignity in death they never had in life.

This 20th-century legend was born Agnes Gonxha Bojaxhiu in Skopje, present-day North Macedonia, in 1910. She was just 12 years old when the desire to belong wholly to Christ first entered her mind. At 18, after a six-year process of discernment, she departed Skopje to become a missionary Sister of Loreto in Calcutta, India. For 20 years, she taught mostly middle-class girls behind the convent walls of Loreto, where in her words, "I was the happiest nun in the world."

On September 10, 1946, riding a train from Calcutta to Darjeeling for a retreat, she heard her Master's call to follow Him into the slums. "It was a command." A command she did not hesitate to follow. But it was not easy. "To leave Loreto was my greatest sacrifice," Mother Teresa admitted, "the most difficult thing I have ever done."

Nevertheless, after a two-year process, gaining permission from the Vatican, she shed her impressive robes and the title of headmistress as well as the security of the convent community to don a $1 sari, edged in blue for the Blessed Mother.

To serve the poor, she became poor. All alone, she knocked on the doors of huts in a Calcutta slum, asking residents if they wished to educate their children. Sitting under a plum tree, with her first four or five students and no money for chalk or a blackboard, Sr. Teresa scratched images in the dirt with a stick. It was fine, she said, "until the monsoons."

Soon there were 40 children. Within 10 years, there were 15 Missionary of Charity schools throughout Calcutta, each school having at least 100 pupils.

As she worked with the slum children, Mother Teresa could not ignore those dying on the streets she crossed. The first forgotten soul she rescued from the gutter was a woman riddled with rat and ant bites. She carried the near corpse to a hospital and refused to leave until the hospital accepted the woman as a patient.

The indomitable nun later told clergy in West Beirut, "If I hadn't picked up that first person, perhaps I never would have picked up the next 42,000." She transported them in rickshaws, even wheelbarrows. When a man was rejected by all possible shelters, Mother Teresa rented a room and personally tended him.

Soon there was a second patient delivered to her door. That was the beginning of the home for the dying, later to be known as Kalighat.

Mother Teresa's former students from the Loreto Convent, many from upper social castes, were her first followers. Eventually, her network would encompass brothers, priests and lay "coworkers."

Her labors would become world famous, and she would receive the highest honors from many countries, including India and America, which gave her a title shared by only three other persons: "Honorary Citizen of the United States." In Norway, she received the Nobel Peace Prize.

It is this background, unmatched in the modern world, which has 3,000 international breakfasters listening in awed silence.

No political correctness on this podium. Mother Teresa does not hesitate to tell her audience of Buddhists, Hindus, and even Communists threaded among the mostly Protestant Christians, just Who inspired such an incredible biography.

"We are reminded," she begins, "that Jesus came to bring the Good News to the poor. He told us what is that good news when He said, 'My peace, I leave with you. My peace I give unto you.' He came not to give the peace of the world, which is only that we don't bother each other; He came to give the peace of heart, which comes from loving, from doing good to others."

She points out that God Himself had so much love for the world that He gave His only Son to the Virgin Mary. "And what did she do with Him? ... she went in haste to give that good news" to her cousin Elizabeth, and as Scripture relates, the son in Elizabeth's womb, "leaps with joy. ... The unborn was the first one to proclaim the coming of Christ."

That unique thought is a hint of the bombshells Mother Teresa is about to drop. But first, she continues to warm her listeners with love. "It is not enough for us to say, 'I love God.' But I also have to love my neighbor. St. John said that you are a liar if you say you love God and you don't love your neighbor. How can you love God, whom you do not see, if you do not love your neighbor, whom you see, whom you touch, with whom you live? And so it is very important for us to realize that love, to be true, has to hurt."

"Loving until it hurts" will become a constant and uncomfortable reiteration as Mother Teresa speaks, not of the poverty in Calcutta, but the poverty she witnesses in America. "I can never forget the experience I had in visiting a home where they kept all these old parents of sons and daughters who had just put them into an institution and forgotten them, maybe.

"I saw that in that home, these old people had everything: good food, comfortable place, television, everything, but everyone was looking toward the door. And I did not see a single one with a smile on the face. I turned to the sister and I asked: 'Why do those people who have every comfort here, why are they all looking toward the door? Why are they not smiling?'

"I am so used to seeing the smiles on our people; even the dying ones smile. And Sister said: 'This is the way it is nearly every day. They are expecting, they are hoping that a son or daughter will come to visit them. They are hurt because they are forgotten.'

"And see this neglect to love brings spiritual poverty. Maybe in our own family we have somebody who is feeling lonely, who is feeling sick, who is feeling worried. Are we there? Are we willing to give until it hurts in order to be with our families, or do we put our own interests first?"

In an audience well stocked with professional people, whose time is consumed with climbing the corporate or governmental ladder, it is a prickly moment.

She does not stop with the lonely old. She moves on to the neglect of the young. "I was surprised in the West to see so many young boys and girls given to drugs. And I tried to find out why. Why is it like that, when those in the West have so many more things than those in the East? And the answer was: Because there is no one in the family to receive them.

"Our children depend on us for everything, their health, their nutrition, their security, their coming to know and love God. For all of this, they look to us with trust, hope, and expectation. But often father and mother are so busy they have no time for their children, or perhaps they are not even married or have given up on their marriage. So the children go to the streets and get involved in drugs or other things. We are talking of love, of the child, which is where love and peace must begin, there in our own family."

And then Mother Teresa fires off the quotes that will be heard around the world because they are said before advocates of the very thing she is condemning, seated immediately to her right and to her left — the president and first lady of the United States, Bill and Hillary Clinton.

"I feel that the greatest destroyer of peace today is abortion, because Jesus said, 'If you receive a little child, you receive Me.' So every abortion is the denial of receiving Jesus, is the neglect of receiving Jesus."

The audience erupts in sustained applause which turns into a continuous, standing ovation in which, it is widely noted, the Clintons do not join. Mother Teresa waits for the noise to subside and coolly continues.

"It is really a war against the child, a direct killing of the innocent child, murder by the mother herself. And if we accept that a mother can kill even her own child, how can we tell other people not to kill one another? How do we persuade a woman not to have an abortion? As always, we must persuade her with love, and we remind ourselves that love means to be willing to give until it hurts.

"By abortion, the mother does not learn to love, but kills even her own child to solve her problems. And by abortion, the father is told that he does not have to take any responsibility at all for the child he has brought into the world, so that father is likely to put other women into the same trouble. So abortion just leads to more abortion."

And then she offers the prophetic summation of the consequences that abortion brings to America into the 21st century. "Any country that accepts abortion is not teaching its people to love one another, but to use any violence to get what they want. This is why the greatest destroyer of love and peace is abortion."

She says God has given her congregation, the Missionaries of Charity, the "gift" to "fight abortion with adoption. ... by care of the mother and adoption of her baby... ."

"Please don't kill the child," she continues. "If you don't want the child, I want the child. Please give me the child. I am willing to accept any child who would be aborted and to give that child to a married couple who will love the child and will be loved by the child."

This declaration brings forth more thunderous applause. And then Mother Teresa dares to tread on an area that divides even Christians, and there is silence.

"I know that couples have to plan their family and for that there is natural family planning. The way to plan the family is natural family planning, not contraception. In destroying the power of giving life, of loving, through contraception, a husband or wife is doing something to self. This turns the attention to self, and so it destroys the gift of love in him or her.

"In loving, the husband and wife must turn the attention to each other as happens in natural family planning, and not to self as happens in contraception. Once that living love is destroyed by contraception, abortion follows very easily. That's why I never give a child to a family that has used contraception. Because if the mother has destroyed the power of loving, how will she love my child?

"I also know that there are great problems in the world that many spouses do not love each other enough to practice [natural family planning]. We cannot solve [all] the problems in the world, but let us never bring in the worst problem of all — to destroy love, to destroy life."

Wall Street Journal columnist Peggy Noonan captures this startling moment in an article she writes about Mother Teresa's speech. "Perhaps she didn't know that we don't talk about birth control in speeches in America. Perhaps she didn't know, or care, that her words were as they say, not 'healing' but 'divisive', dividing not only Protestant from Catholic but Catholic from Catholic. It was all so unhappily unadorned, explicit, impolitic. And it was wonderful, like a big fresh drink of water, bracing in its directness and its uncompromising tone," Noonan wrote, declaring the speech, "a great success ... she softened nothing, did not deflect division but defined it. She came with a sword."

To bring peace.

It was generally agreed among breakfast attendees that only a future saint, a woman who had given so unstintingly of herself to the poorest of the poor could wield such a "sword" in front of such an audience — only a woman who had met supreme challenges herself.

"I find sometimes it very difficult to smile at my spouse, Jesus, because He can be very demanding sometimes," Mother says. "This is really something true. And that is where love comes — when it is demanding and yet we can give it with joy."

She brings laughter to the moment when she tells how she tried to console a patient in pain by telling her that her suffering was "the kiss of Jesus." Mother told her she was "so close to Jesus on the Cross that He can kiss you." The patient responded, "Mother, would you please tell Jesus to stop kissing me?"

She closed with a vision of what America could be if it responded to God's demand that we love till it hurts: "If we remember that God loves us and that we can love others as He loves us, then America can become a sign of peace for the whole world, a sign of joy. From here, a sign of care for the weakest of the weak — the unborn child — must go out to the world. If you become a burning light of justice and peace in the world, then really you will be true to what the Founders of this country stood for."

22

A TALE OF TWO 9-11s

September 11, 2001 . . . .

"Dad, do you have the television on?" Our daughter's voice sounds urgent in Bill's ear.

"No," Bill answers. He is in his favorite easy chair next to the large living room window, in our Washington apartment at The Westchester, getting his news from the *Washington Post*, the secular Bible of the nation's capital.

"Turn it on," our daughter, Kelly commands from Grosse Pointe, Michigan. "The Pentagon has been attacked."

I am hurrying out the door, late for a National First Ladies' Library board meeting in Congressman Ralph Regula's office on Capitol Hill.

"Peggy you better listen to this," Bill says after turning on the television. "The Pentagon has just been hit by a plane."

I barely slow down. This is the nation's capital after all. Somebody's always attacking something. Just a short time ago a small plane landed on the White House lawn. Get used to it.

Well," Bill sighs, "at *least* keep the radio on."

I hurry to the parking lot, angry with myself for not getting an earlier start. Rush-hour traffic will be terrible.

It is one of those perfect autumn mornings. The oppressive 92-degree heat of Washington summers has cooled to the mid-70s. The sky is an endless stretch of azure blue unmarred by a single cloud. Nothing can trouble such a day.

I am so looking forward to this reunion with congressional friends at the board meeting. Last night, the First Ladies' Library hosted a gala dinner where we had given awards to outstanding American women, including Barbara Walters, Coretta Scott King, and Elizabeth Dole, who plans to announce a run for the presidency today.

As I speed down Massachusetts Avenue, I reluctantly heed Bill's admonition and turn on the radio.

I do not want to hear any bad news on this spectacular day — as if by sheer willpower I can alter reality. From the dashboard comes the voice of my former colleague at ABC, Peter Jennings. Always the calm, cool anchorman, Peter is anything but calm; he is almost hysterical. "It's collapsing! It's collapsing!" he gasps. He is talking about the demise of the two World Trade Center towers, which have been struck by airplanes.

This cannot be true. America can't be under attack. My brain refuses to absorb such news. Just keep on driving to the Capitol. If you ignore reality, it will surely change. I am a willing victim of the merry-go-round called denial.

Now the announcer is saying that Capitol buildings are closing down; occupants are being evacuated. That would include Congressman Regula's office.

Clearly I am heading in the wrong direction. Face it. There is not going to be a First Ladies' Library board meeting on September 11. So I will go visit my sister, whom I had planned to see after the board meeting instead. I reach for my cellphone to call Bill and inform him of the new agenda. The cellphone does not work. I hear the radio announcer say that cellular networks have deliberately been silenced, in case the terrorists are keeping in touch with one another by cellphone and spreading their attacks across America.

It is chilling to comprehend that we can no longer reach our loved ones with the ease of communication to which we have become so accustomed. Realizing Bill will be worried not knowing what has happened to me, I decide to turn around and return home. This is not a time for husbands and wives to be apart if they can help it.

Bill is still in the same chair in which he was sitting when I left an hour ago, staring at the television screen, his handsome face wreathed in solemn sadness. A veteran of the Greatest Generation, he has experienced war in its grimmest circumstances. And he has medals that bear witness to his witness.

"We will never be the same," he prophesies quietly, "we will never be the same." The words carry extra weight coming from a man who usually sees the glass half full. He is exaggerating, I think, but I do not say it. This great country cannot be cowed. Then I look at the television screen for the first time.

The news says another hijacked plane was headed toward Washington, either aiming for the White House or the Capitol until the courageous passengers on Flight 93 brought the plane down in Shanksville, Pennsylvania.

It's surreal to realize the terrorists and I had been headed in the same direction at the same time. Sobering to absorb the fact that we are in one of the terrorist's chief target cities and to speculate on what other ugly surprises they may have planned for us.

The sights of my beloved New York in smoke and ashes are so horrifying, I flee to the grocery store in the basement of our apartment building to stock up on necessities, in case we are grounded.

In the grocery store, I meet an elderly resident of our building. She has a German accent. She confirms my assumption. She is from Berlin, she says. "This must bring back very unpleasant memories for you?" I ask her.

"Ya! Ya!" She nods. Especially because she lives alone. I give her my phone number. "Call us, if you need anything at all." But she never does.

After I put away the groceries, I feel the need for some air; the journalistic juices flowing through my veins, I want to see what is happening on the street. The normally noisy skies are eerily silent. All planes have been grounded.

I walk to the corner where Wisconsin Avenue and Massachusetts Avenue converge. An astonishing sight greets me. Up Massachusetts Avenue, a main artery from Capitol Hill to Northwest Washington, comes a procession of refugees — government workers with their portable goods strapped to their backs, trudging their way home on foot, having been denied access to their mobile transportation. They are four and five rows deep, heads bent, tongues silent, just walking.

By evening, Bill, who has scarcely moved from monitoring the horror unfolding on our television screens, has had enough. "Let's go eat." I head for the kitchen and my newly acquired groceries. "No." Bill wants to go to a restaurant, his favorite way to unwind. Just up the street is a northwest neighborhood hangout, Chef Geoff's. I complain we will be the only people there. Who else would want to go out to dinner on a night we are at war?

Lots of people. Chef Geoff's is jammed. Predominantly with young people. Apparently, I am not the only person dallying with denial. Comfort comes with camaraderie of shared experience, particularly when the experience is cosmic.

September 12, 2001 . . . .

The Republican Congressional Wives, a club for spouses of Members of Congress, has scheduled a luncheon for cabinet wives at the Library of Congress, which is located on the vulnerable and now closed-down Capitol grounds. As a former president of the club, I speculate as to whether I would cancel the luncheon. I conclude that if allowed, I would not cancel. And that, I find out through several phone calls, is what the current president has decided. The luncheon will carry on.

The question is how to get onto the Capitol grounds; will the Capitol police believe me when I claim to be a former congressional wife?

My only credential is a jeweled, nontransferable, and numbered pin designed by a forward-thinking congressional wife, meant to be worn as an immediate symbol of recognition by Capitol police. I had never before used it and, in fact, balked at buying it.

As I near the Capitol, I view a mile-wide perimeter of security surrounding all the buildings. Not a soul, other than police, to be seen in an area usually swarming with Members of Congress, staffers, and tourists.

A policeman stops me. I explain my destination and show the pin. To my astonishment, he waves me to the Library of Congress. No further checking of credentials. No further questions. I clasp the pin I almost did not purchase as if it's a glass of water in a dry desert.

I pull into the Library of Congress parking area, and I have my choice of spaces. When I enter the building, there is still no one visible but police, who see my pin and move me on to the dining room.

To my surprise, just as in the restaurant last night, all the cabinet wives have shown up, as have many congressional wives.

We take our places at large round tables, where I launch what would become my favorite parlor game: "Where were you yesterday when you got the news and what did you do?" Joyce Rumsfeld, the wife of the Secretary of Defense, was at a military base outside of Washington when she received news that the Pentagon had been struck by a plane.

She learned of her husband's activities through television news reports that showed Don Rumsfeld helping to carry injured employees on stretchers to ambulances.

As each woman relates her own circumstances, it is apparent that we are enveloped in our own form of trauma counseling, unloading emotions sustained during shared, totally unexpected, and horrific events. But the very fact that we are all at the luncheon shows the American determination to follow the Gospel admonition "Do not fear" (Lk 12:4), lest the terrorists think they have won.

What is so evident is the resilience of the human spirit — the will to soldier on, even when no one knows on this day what lies ahead for our country or our world.

September 11, 2002

What so many remember about the weather on September 11, 2001, is the brilliant blue sky. The weather factor many may remember about September 11, 2002, is the wind.

There are two big differences between September 11, 2001, and September 11, 2002. The first is personal. This September 11, there is no one waiting for me at The Westchester. The man who predicted America "will never be the same" did not live to see the accuracy of his prophecy. Seven months to the day of the terrorist attack, he succumbs to an attack of severe pneumonia. On this September 11, I am alone again.

The second difference is readiness: not the readiness of the missile launchers that surround Washington, and not the readiness of a code orange terrorism alert signaling high threat-level status. America's lifesaving readiness this September 11 consists of hands folded in prayer and feet marching to church.

The Washington Post contains two full pages of memorial services for September 11. Most of them are in churches and those that are at the Pentagon or Ground Zero are suffused with prayer.

It is 7 a.m. in the nation's capital; the streets are strangely empty of speeding bureaucrats clutching Starbucks coffee cups on their way to work or joggers exercising before 10 hours in the office. There is a small-town atmosphere as people emerge from their homes and their apartment buildings, some in their Sunday best, walking slowly to the Washington National Cathedral for an ecumenical prayer service led by South African archbishop Desmond Tutu.

An orange sun is rising along the right side of the mag-nificent Gothic structure, 100 years in the building, throwing a golden glow over the towering trees whose limbs and leaves are nearly still.

This is the nondenominational cathedral where the Madonna of Medjugorje appeared to visionary Ivan Dragićević before a crowd of some 800 onlookers in the early 1990s.

It is a mixed crowd of worshipers: suited State Depart-ment diplomats adjacent to a blue-jeaned journalist types, catching a glimpse of the morning paper before the service starts. Down the center aisle come ministers, priests, rabbis, Muslim imams, and Jesse Jackson on crutches. Behind them, cathedral school students solemnly carry flags from countries that had lost nationals one year ago — a heartbreakingly long, colorful procession.

The cathedral resounds with the first hymn, "Oh, God, Our Help in Ages Past." Then, prayers from the Hindu, Jewish, Buddhist, Muslim, and Christian traditions. Imam Mohammed

Nur Abdullah's invocation is particularly pertinent: "If any do seek for glory and power, to God belongs all glory and power. To Him mount up all words of purity. He exalts all righteous deeds. But those that lay the plots of evil, for them is a terrible penalty; and the plotting of such He will not abide."

As Archbishop Tutu is delivering his homily, the cathedral's great Bourdon bell begins tolling. It is 8:46 a.m. and the bell is commemorating the first airplane to strike the World Trade Center. The Archbishop falls silent as the tolling continues for several minutes. Throughout the church, sophisticated Washingtonians can be seen reaching for handkerchiefs, wiping eyes, hugging shoulders. Throughout the morning, the bell will sound again and again to commemorate the moment of each succeeding terrorist blow.

The final blessing admonishes us to "Go forth into the world in peace; be of good courage." The cover of the program we clutch reads, "Courage is fear that has said its prayers." As we step into the warm September air, a rushing wind suddenly sweeps through the trees, bending limbs and flapping flags. It feels symbolic of something I cannot name.

At noon across town, at the great Catholic Basilica of the National Shrine of the Immaculate Conception, whose height rivals that of the National Cathedral and where the Madonna of Medjugorje also appeared to Ivan in the 1990s, a huge American flag hanging from the bell tower is being tossed and swirled by that same strong wind.

Inside, the church that seats 4,000 is jammed beyond capacity with adults, children, and students from Catholic University of America and other schools attending the national Catholic bishops' commemorative Mass. At Communion time, a lilting soprano leads the congregation in a favorite Medjugorje hymn, "Ubi Caritas."

In contrast to the formal services are the quiet Holy Hours held throughout the day at churches such as Annunciation Parish, just blocks from the grand Washington National Cathedral.

At Holy Trinity Church, where John Kennedy went to pray on his inauguration day, schoolchildren hold an outdoor peace ceremony as cars and passersby pause to watch. And up the street at Georgetown University, the third Washington site where Mary once appeared to Ivan, students hold a series of commemorative events, beginning with a new ecumenical service on campus attended by an estimated 1,000 worshipers.

At sunset, the Archbishop of Washington closes the day with yet another Mass in the heart of downtown Washington, where hungry homeless, overfed lobbyists, and judges mingle side by side. Inside St. Patrick's Church, a blue-coated police-man play "Taps" from the choir loft as the Archbishop holds his hand over his heart. After Mass, one congregant tells a *Catholic Standard* news reporter that prayer is the best thing she could do for 9-11 victims. She is also praying to forgive the perpetrators of the terrible deed. "Why not try to forgive and get all this hatred gone?" she adds.

Throughout the day, as President George W. Bush makes his way from Washington to New York to Shanksville, that mysterious wind carries him, sometimes so strong as to be noted by TV commentators. Says a CNN correspondent, it is almost as if "Heaven drew in a breath and exhaled all over us."

All day, my mind searches for the reason the wind seems so significant, and only in the late evening hours does the rea-son for *déjà vu* reveal itself. In 1792, Bishop John Carroll, the first Catholic bishop of the United States, placed this young frontier country under the Blessed Mother's patronage. How often during the early years of Medjugorje, did we hear the *Gospa* quoted as saying, "*The wind is my sign. When you feel the wind, you will know that I am near.*"

And on that first Pentecost Sunday, Scripture recounts, "And suddenly a sound came from heaven like the rush of a mighty wind, and it filled all the house where they were sitting ... And they were all filled with the Holy Spirit" (Acts 2:2,4).

23

SUFFERING SERVANTS

Mother Teresa — now St. Teresa of Calcutta — claimed that the person who is suffering is receiving kisses from Jesus. If that is true, it explains why my sister and my husband are such extraordinary and enduring presences in my life.

The first thing you noticed were the eyes: honey-colored when she was young; deep brown as she grew older; always huge, questioning, observing, often challenging. "God needs on this earth empty vessels in whom He can pour Himself completely" was the way a nun once explained the mentally handicapped to me.

My sister Mary Anne was such a vessel. At the time of her birth, the umbilical cord caught around her neck, choking off oxygen just long enough to severely damage her brain, leaving Mary Anne an innocent child her entire life. Never knowing what sin was, she never knew sin.

Named after Jesus' mother and grandmother, Mary Anne was a kind of link between Our Lady of Medjugorje and Our Lady of Lourdes. She made the acquaintance of the Croatian Madonna during a particularly stressful period in her life. Dependent on medications to keep her mentally stabilized, Mary Anne was experiencing the difficulties and misbehavior associated with wrong treatment. Her caregivers had almost reached the limit of their imaginations attempting to find methods to prevent sudden bouts of self-mutilation and screaming.

At this same time, as I have described before, I was asked to host a Mass and provide a place where Medjugorje visionary Ivan Dragicevic, in Washington to give a speech, might have his apparition. Despite Mary Anne's sometimes obstreperous behavior, I was determined she would not miss the opportunity to be in the presence of the Mother of God and whatever blessings she might bestow.

I considered asking Our Lady to intercede for a complete healing for her namesake, but I thought better of it after contemplating the difficulty someone who had lived a life of dependence would have adapting to independence at the age of 54. Instead, I prayed that God would bring Mary Anne real "peace."

The afternoon of Ivan's apparition, our living room was crowded with friends, relatives, and former Medjugorje pilgrims. To my delighted surprise, I need not have worried about Mary Anne's behavior. It was near beatific during the entire event.

When Ivan knelt for his apparition, every pair of eyes was on the visionary, except Mary Anne's. She, alone, looked precisely where Ivan was gazing, and a broad smile broke over a face that was almost always solemn.

Just one day after the apparition, Mary Anne's doctors prescribed a new medication for her, and with it came a dramatic transformation in behavior. Gone were the tantrums, the self-abuse. Present at last was the peace Mary Anne's caregivers had been seeking and for which I had prayed.

Mary Anne remained so docile that, a few years later, I dared to take her as a *malade* (sick person) on a chartered Order of Malta pilgrimage to Lourdes. Mary Anne had been baptized but never received the Holy Eucharist, as my parents did not think a child with such limited mental capacity would be permitted the privilege.

At one of the liturgies, I observed another mentally handicapped woman receiving Communion. And I felt I was being prompted to ask Order of Malta chaplain Edward Egan, then bishop of Bridgeport, Connecticut, later Cardinal Egan, leader of the New York Archdiocese and a canon lawyer, whether it was possible for Mary Anne to make her first Holy Communion.

Bishop Egan said it would be possible if Mary Anne could be brought to some understanding of Jesus' Real Presence in the Eucharist. I took on the challenge, although doubtful I could fulfill the mission.

One day, Mary Anne was wheeled into a chapel where there happened to be Eucharistic Adoration. Not expecting to see the Lord exposed, I had given Mary Anne no previous instruction. Thus, it made no sense to ask her a question many Catholics of normal intelligence could not answer. But for some reason I did.

"Who is that, Mary Anne?"

To my astonishment, without a moment's hesitation, my brain-injured sister answered, "Jesus."

At a special Mass in the Poor Clares' chapel, Bishop Egan announced to the Knights and Dames of Malta that Mary Anne Smeeton would receive her First Communion. The most famous First Communion to ever take place in Lourdes was that of Bernadette Soubirous at the time of her apparitions from Our Lady.

A question plagued me, however. Did Mary Anne truly realize Who was residing in that Host Bishop Egan placed on her tongue? I attempted to assuage my curiosity.

"Mary Anne, what did you say to Jesus?" Again, I really did not expect an answer. Mary Anne, who usually only spoke in half sentences, never using the personal pronoun, responded, "I said, 'Hi, Jesus.'"

I was so startled, I pursued the questioning further. "And what did He say?"

Mary Anne replied, again using a full sentence. "He said, 'Thank you.'"

Why, I puzzled, would Our Lord say, "Thank you"? Perhaps because she *actually recognized* His Presence when so many communicants do not. Or perhaps because, she, like Him, had endured so much suffering? She was a victim soul.

Or could the answer be both?

At the end of her life, Mary Anne's body came under assault from a curious cocktail of diseases: rheumatoid arthritis, osteoporosis, and osteomyelitis complicated by recurring infections. Despite numerous hospital visits and treatments, her ravaged infrastructure continued to disintegrate, her bones literally turning to dust.

Mary Anne lay completely helpless in Carroll Manor, a nursing and rehabilitation center run by the Sisters of Charity in Washington, D.C. She was in need of the strongest medications to relieve her pain.

Food, once her greatest pleasure, no longer appealed. But the One who first fed her in Lourdes continued to sustain her with the Bread of Life. When Eucharistic Ministers initially asked Mary Anne if she would like Holy Communion, she replied, "No." When they reported this to me, I told them they were asking the wrong question.

"Ask her if she would like to receive Jesus."

Her answer to that question was always "Yes."

When Mary Anne died, I was consoled by an image of her Savior welcoming His suffering servant to paradise won. Perhaps, I thought, He once again said to her simply, "Thank you."

Life is in the journey

Bill Stanton never made it to Medjugorje. A man who enjoyed his comforts, the former congressman used to joke he would wait until Conrad Hilton got there. When hotels did spring up in that little mountain town, he had a new excuse: "I've never been invited," he said, alluding to the popular phrase, "One is called to Medjugorje." To which his family would reply, "Mary's been calling you, but she keeps getting a busy signal."

But *his* Medjugorje was not in the hills of Bosnia-Herzegovina. His Medjugorje lay nestled in the hills of Kentucky. When he returned from World War II at age 21, the youngest captain in the Pacific with multiple decorations, he discovered Gethsemane, the Trappist home of the famed monk and author Thomas Merton. And for some 50 years he never missed a pilgrimage to the monastery for a portion of Holy Week. Over the years, a platoon of friends and sons of friends began joining that pilgrimage.

He had every gift but health. God gave him faith, looks, charm, intelligence, great professional success, and initially good physical condition, which began to erode with World War ll. He emerged from that conflict with lungs scarred by a stress-acquired smoking habit, lungs which would eventually trigger his death.

Perhaps Medjugorje's greatest insight for pilgrims is a new understanding of death, a partial vision of the eternal home. My first journey to that mystical village eliminated fear of my own demise and greatly helped me accept the departure of dearly loved ones.

So it was that when my best friend, who also happened to be my husband Bill, crossed over to the "other side," as my father described dying, I was able to accept the pain with peace. Much of that peace came from God working through wonderful family and friends who helped engineer what I consider a "Purgatory bypass."

"Bypass" was a familiar word in Bill's vocabulary. He underwent two coronary surgeries in 16 years. Despite the illnesses he battled and defeated — a ruptured appendix, a strangulated hernia, a ruptured aneurysm, and heart attacks — he enjoyed his existence more than anyone I have ever known.

"Life is in the journey" was his favorite mantra. His life was a series of peaks and valleys. When he was in the valley of illness, his eyes were fixed on the peak of health and the Man on the Cross. "This too shall pass," he consoled me. He considered suffering redemptive. There were no sad songs, no complaints, just great joy when he conquered one more challenge.

He overcame so many trials, including the loss of four siblings and the wounds of a world conflagration, that many people, myself among them, expected him to "go on forever." And he gave his final illness a gallant struggle, but virulent pneumonia in his damaged lungs led to heart attacks and heart failure in rapid succession.

When he realized he was being attacked on too many fronts at once, he was as brave in surrender as he had been in victory. "God's will always," he said. "There is a time to come and a time to go," he told the doctor in refusing the artificial aid of a ventilator. "Quality of life is everything."

And quality he had, right to the end of the journey. His illness came at the close of a month that had seen him in Washington, D.C., to attend a Bread for the World board meeting; in Ohio for a speech that would turn out to be his farewell to his former congressional district; in Kentucky for his Holy Week retreat at his beloved Gethsemane; and in Florida for a family Easter reunion that he had designed with our daughter, Kelly.

He watched his grandchildren romping in the marsh, searched with them for Easter eggs during the day, and hosted an Easter family dinner in the evening. Easter Monday morning, suffering severe chills during Mass, he went into the hospital. I was certain he would leap this health hurdle just as he had so many others, especially in the season of the Resurrection.

But Bill's health was rapidly deteriorating as the Feast of Mercy was approaching. The juxtaposition was amazing. In rendering my own version of the Divine Mercy painting, I used some of my husband's physical characteristics as models, particularly the shape of the eyes and the hands.

In 1991, in Washington, D.C., at the first Divine Mercy celebration in the Basilica of the National Shrine of the Immaculate Conception, Bill had read President Bush's thank you to God for His mercy in bringing the Gulf War to a swift conclusion.

Jesus told St. Faustina that whomever made a good Confession on or just before the feast of Divine Mercy Sunday (thus being in a state of grace) and received Holy Communion on that feast day would receive **"complete forgiveness of sins and punishment"** (*Diary of Saint Faustina Kowalska*, 699). An amazing promise, and I wanted to be sure Bill could be a beneficiary of such grace. If I had to lose my husband, the least I could do was try and book a nonstop flight to paradise for him. But the Mayo Clinic hospital in Jacksonville, Florida, where we were, was not a Catholic hospital and priests were hard to come by.

At 6 a.m. on Divine Mercy Sunday, I relayed the Divine Mercy promise to Dr. Matt Bulfin in Fort Lauderdale, begging for a priest. He called Dr. Tom Carney in Delray Beach, who called former baseball commissioner Bowie Kuhn in Jacksonville, all of whom were Knights of Malta, as was Bill. By mid-morning, three priests arrived in the intensive care unit, providing Bill with the Sacraments of Reconciliation and the Sick, just in time for the man who had spent a lifetime on airplanes to make his direct flight to Heaven.

The beautiful gift of God working through all these people was extraordinarily consoling to both Bill and myself. If Our Lord had promised a plenary indulgence, surely He could be trusted to give it. The bishop who presided at Bill's funeral Mass told this Divine Mercy story in his homily, finishing with the assurance, "Jesus keeps His promises."

And at the final hour, there was dramatic evidence of a promise fulfilled. A daily communicant, Bill's deep faith was in his walk, not his words. Which is why his last sentence was so meaningful. His eyes looking up, he said, "I am seeing God."

At the end, it was just the two of us, just the way we had started. I held his hand, read him Scripture, and softly sang him a hymn as his soul slipped slowly into eternity. I was at peace, because he was at peace.

"It's been a great journey," he said.

Yes, indeed it has.

He has "ridden on ahead," as the Irish say.

And I have miles to go, before I sleep.

ACKNOWLEDGMENTS

It takes a village to birth a book, and I owe a debt of gratitude to a number of "villagers." First to Fr. Chris Alar, MIC, who directed me to Marian Press. My deep thanks to my friends; Marcia McBrien, who made skillful editing suggestions that brought pace to the narrative. Lorrie Peck was a treasure of enthusiasm, energy and spiritual insights. Her prayers and suggestions over early morning post-Mass coffee chats, were absolutely invaluable.

Chris Sparks was a patient editor who managed to drag necessary revelations out of a reluctant author. Mary Sue Eck, indefatigable editor of *Medjugorje* magazine, was my first religious publisher, giving space to my column, "The Queen's Digest," which ultimately became chapters in this book.

A huge thank you to Dr. Joe McAleer, my final editor, for his belief in the project, his encouragement, his sense of humor, his drive and determination to "move the train down the track" to its final destination.

All of the photographs herein are from my personal collection. Special thanks to Visko Hatfield for photographing my Divine Mercy painting especially for this book.

ABOUT THE AUTHOR

Peggy Stanton was ABC Television network's first female news correspondent in Washington, D.C., in 1966. In 2022, she uses the reportorial skills acquired reporting the bad news on secular networks, to report the good news on Catholic networks, including Ave Maria Radio, where she has hosted several shows, including the "Order of Malta Minutes with the *Catechism*."

Her columns and articles have appeared in numerous newspapers and magazines, including *The Washington Post, The Washington Times, The Saturday Evening Post, The News Leader,* and *Medjugorje* magazine. Her paintings have been exhibited in museums, churches, and art galleries.

Peggy is the author of *The Daniel Dilemma,* a book about the moral man in the public arena, and co-author and illustrator of *How to Help Your Child Eat Right,* one of the earliest guides to better nutrition for children. She was founder and president of a Washington, D.C.-based special events firm, Creative Solutions, which specialized in seminars on Capitol Hill.

She was founder and president of The Mary Anne Foundation, named after the mother and grandmother of the Prince of Peace, whose motto was "Peace Through Love." The organization sponsored peace activities for grade school and high school children, which involved schools across the nation and participated in refugee missions during the Balkan war.

Peggy served as president of the Republican Congressional Wives Club, the International Neighbors Club, and the Nassau Republican Women's Club. She has been a board member of the Order of Malta American Association, Pregnancy Aid, and the Ivy Foundation, and currently serves on the Order of Malta Dental-Medical Clinic board.

She is the widow of deceased former Congressman Bill Stanton, the mother of Kelly Fordon, and the grandmother of Jack, Charlie, Megan and Peter Fordon.

Join the

Association of Marian Helpers,

headquartered at the National Shrine of The Divine Mercy, and share in special blessings!

An invitation from
Fr. Joseph, MIC, director

**Marian Helpers is an Association of
Christian faithful of the Congregation of
Marian Fathers of the Immaculate Conception.**
By becoming a member, you share in the
spiritual benefits of the daily Masses,
prayers, and good works of the Marian
priests and brothers.

This is a special offer of grace given to you
by the Church through the Marian Fathers. Please consider this opportunity
to share in these blessings, along with others whom you would wish to
join into this spiritual communion.

1-800-462-7426 • Marian.org/join

Spiritual Enrollments & Masses

Enroll your loved ones in the Association of
Marian Helpers, and they will participate in
the graces from the daily Masses, prayers,
good works, and merits of the Marian
priests and brothers around the world.

Request a Mass to be
offered by the Marian Fathers
for your loved ones

Individual Masses
(for the living or deceased)

Gregorian Masses
(30 days of consecutive Masses
for the deceased)

1-800-462-7426 • Marian.org/enrollments • Marian.org/mass

Essential Divine Mercy Resource

Diary of Saint Maria Faustina Kowalska:
Divine Mercy in My Soul

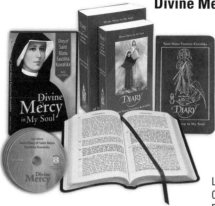

The *Diary* chronicles the message that Jesus, the Divine Mercy, gave to the world through this humble nun. In it, we are reminded to trust in His forgiveness — and as Christ is merciful, so, too, are we instructed to be merciful to others. Written in the 1930s, the *Diary* exemplifies God's love toward mankind and, to this day, remains a source of hope and renewal.

Large Paperback: Y102-NBFD
Compact Paperback: Y102-DNBF
Deluxe Leather-Bound Edition: Y102-DDBURG
Audio Diary MP3 Edition: Y102-ADMP3
e Also available as an ebook – Visit ShopMercy.org

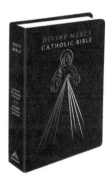

Divine Mercy Catholic Bible

Many Catholics ask what version of the Bible is best to read. In the Revised Standard Version Catholic Edition (RSV-CE) you have the answer.

The *Divine Mercy Catholic Bible* clearly shows the astounding revelation of Divine Mercy amidst the timeless truths of Sacred Scripture. This Bible includes 175 Mercy Moments and 19 articles that explain how God encounters us with mercy through His Word and Sacraments. Y102-BIDM

Explaining the Faith Series
Understanding Divine Mercy
by Fr. Chris Alar, MIC

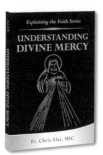

Finally, the entire Divine Mercy message and devotion is summarized in one, easy-to-read book! Explaining the teaching of Jesus Christ as given to St. Faustina, *Understanding Divine Mercy* by Fr. Chris Alar, MIC, has it all. Written in his highly conversational and energetic style, this first book in his *Explaining the Faith* series will deepen your love for God and help you understand why Jesus called Divine Mercy "mankind's last hope of salvation." Paperback. 184 pages.

Y102-EFBK

For our complete line of books, prayer cards, pamphlets, Rosaries, and chaplets, visit ShopMercy.org or call 1-800-462-7426 to have our latest catalog sent to you.